# Extracting Home in the Oil Sands



The Canadian oil sands are one of the world's most important energy sources and the subject of global attention in relation to climate change and pollution. This volume engages ethnographically with key issues concerning the oil sands by working from anthropological literature and beyond to explore how people struggle to make and hold on to diverse senses of home in the region. The contributors draw on diverse fieldwork experiences with communities in Alberta that are affected by the oil sands industry. Through a series of case studies, they illuminate the complexities inherent in the entanglements of race, class, Indigeneity, gender, and ontological concerns in a regional context characterized by extreme extraction. The chapters are unified in a common concern for ethnographically theorizing settler colonialism, sentient landscapes, and multispecies relations within a critical political ecology framework and by the prominent role that extractive industries play in shaping new relations between Indigenous Peoples, the state, newcomers, corporations, plants, animals, and the land.

**Clinton N. Westman** is an environmental anthropologist and Associate Professor in the Department of Archaeology and Anthropology at the University of Saskatchewan, Canada.

**Tara L. Joly** is Research Director at Willow Springs Strategic Solutions, Inc. in Cochrane, Alberta, Canada. She recently received her PhD in social anthropology from the University of Aberdeen, UK.

**Lena Gross** recently completed her PhD in social anthropology at the University of Oslo, Norway.

## Arctic Worlds

*Communities, Political Ecology and Ways of Knowing*

Series Editors: David Anderson and Robert J. Losey

This series aims to integrate research from across the circumpolar Arctic from across the humanities, social sciences, and history of science. This region—once exotised as a remote and unknown "blank spot"—is now acknowledged to be the homeland of a variety of indigenous nations, many of whom have won or are seeking home rule.

The Arctic was the central axis of frozen confrontation during the Cold War. At the start of the twenty-first century it is a resource hinterland offering supplies of petroleum and minerals for aggressively new markets with great cost and risk to the environment. The indigenous nations of the region are unique for their "ways of knowing" which approach animals and landscape as alive, sentient entities. Many share cultural commonalities across the Arctic Ocean, sketching out a human community that unites disparate continents.

This series takes history seriously by bringing together archaeological work on ancient Arctic societies with ethnohistorical studies of the alternate idioms by which time and meaning are understood by circumpolar peoples, as well as science and technology studies of how the region is perceived by various scientific communities.

Titles in series:

**Dogs in the North**
An Educational Approach
*Edited by Robert J. Losey, Robert P. Wishart, and Jan Peter Laurens Loovers*

**Reading Life with Gwich'in**
Stories of Cooperation and Co-Domestication
*Jan Peter Laurens Loovers*

**Extracting Home in the Oil Sands**
Settler Colonialism and Environmental Change in Subarctic Canada
*Edited by Clinton N. Westman, Tara L. Joly, and Lena Gross*

For more information about this series, please visit: www.routledge.com/Arctic-Worlds/book-series/ARCTICW

# Extracting Home in the Oil Sands

## Settler Colonialism and Environmental Change in Subarctic Canada

**Edited by Clinton N. Westman, Tara L. Joly, and Lena Gross**

Routledge
Taylor & Francis Group
LONDON AND NEW YORK

First published 2020
by Routledge
2 Park Square, Milton Park, Abingdon, Oxon OX14 4RN

and by Routledge
605 Third Avenue, New York, NY 10017

First issued in paperback 2021

*Routledge is an imprint of the Taylor & Francis Group, an informa business*



Publisher's Note
The publisher has gone to great lengths to ensure the quality of this reprint but points out that some imperfections in the original copies may be apparent.

*British Library Cataloguing-in-Publication Data*
A catalogue record for this book is available from the British Library

*Library of Congress Cataloging-in-Publication Data*
A catalog record has been requested for this book

ISBN 13: 978-1-03-208306-3 (pbk)
ISBN 13: 978-0-8153-5665-3 (hbk)

Typeset in Times New Roman
by SPi Technologies India Private Limited

# Contents

# Illustrations

**Figures**



**Tables**

# Foreword

In 1948 my settler maternal great-grandfather purchased land on the western shore of Baptiste Lake, a few kilometres west of the town of Athabasca, to build a hunting cabin alongside his friends from Edmonton, the Littles. This cabin has stood on sandy banks of this small lake for seventy years, weathering erosion, algal blooms, storms, ice heaves, and all manner of environmental change over the last seven decades. It is where my settler mom and my Métis dad introduced me to so many of the non-human kin I grew up with—perch, spot-tailed minnows, jackfish, walleye, suckers, horsetails, misaskwatomina, high-bush cranberries, wild strawberries, blueberries, spruce, aspen, leeches, red squirrels, moose, black bears, and all manner of critters and creatures who populate my mind and my thinking as a Métis woman from central Alberta. This lake, and this cabin, are a node through which I strive to understand the complex relations between my settler family, my Indigenous family, the land, waters, and the other non-human beings who make up the world I grew up in. It is a site through which I not only theorize, but also practice, my responsibilities to my family and to the beings that comprise the territories that make up what is currently known as Alberta.

Baptiste Lake is a small body of water in north central Alberta that has existed as a productive lake for at least 4,600 years (Atlas of Alberta Lakes, n.d.). It has a creek on its northeast corner that flows into the Athabasca River, tying this small unprepossessing watershed into the broader water flows of the Athabasca River, and by extension, via the Peace-Athabasca Delta and Great Slave Lake, the mighty Mackenzie River watershed, and the Arctic Ocean. In the 1880s, Métis from Saskatchewan took narrow lots along the lake, before the lake was shifted to settler agricultural use circa 1904 (Atlas of Alberta Lakes, n.d.). There are conflicting identifications of the man the lake is named for: Baptiste Majeau. Sources identify him variously as a Métis man who lived on the lake in the nineteenth century (Summer Village of South Baptiste 2018) or as an "early settler" of the lake (Maturié [1972] 2013, 232). In either case, the Métis history of the lake is rich and dynamic, and ties into broader Métis relations across this part of Alberta.

In the summer of 2018 I flew back to Alberta for my first extended visit in three years. My last visit to the lake was in the summer of 2014, just before global oil prices fell and Alberta fell into a deep recession (Gibson 2016). On that trip, my mom and I stood in muted sadness as we watched fish jump for hours in a pea-soup green algae bloom on the lake and we toured the large McMansions being built up around the lake for folks using the small boreal lake as a permanent, year-round residence and, I suspect, as a commuting village for working in the oil sands (Todd 2015). In 2018 I was lucky to spend time with my maternal (settler) family, taking in the small upgrades to the cabin (a composting toilet, an outdoor rain-fed shower), and bearing witness to still more environmental degradation. As we sat in the hot July sun, our conversation turned to the intense real estate market that surrounds the lake—something unfathomable to me as I looked at the simple, small cabin my settler great-grandfather built just after the Second World War. The lake is now serviced by high-speed cellphone service, so we pulled out our smartphones and googled local real estate and found many of those same McMansions that were being built in 2014 up for sale. I suspect one reason for the sudden return of these massive houses to the real estate market is that the economics of living within a reasonable (three-hour) commuting distance of the oil sands are no longer as favourable as they were four short years ago. I was born in the infamous Alberta oil bust of the 1980s, so it is hard for me to fathom humble Baptiste Lake as a "hot" commodity. I was shocked to discover some of these massive houses—better suited to a suburb in Calgary or Fort McMurray and utterly ill-matched to the small, sensitive ecosystem of the lake—going for hundreds of thousands of dollars (with one down the road listed at over a million dollars). However, as the chapters in this volume demonstrate, the ebbs and flows of settler colonial resource economies stretch so much farther than the actual site of extraction. The entire province I grew up in is enmeshed in complex dynamics and reactions to the bitumen drawn from lands in northern Alberta. Even small unassuming prairie lakes are caught up in the impacts of global resource economic entanglements.

The most heartbreaking part of my visit in 2018, however, was the water. The water was rust coloured—washing up on the shore in waves that crashed with each passing powerboat, sea-doo, and the ubiquitous pontoon boats that seem to be the current status markers on Baptiste Lake. As a self-styled "fish philosopher," I pride myself on being able to find the fish in most places, whether it's the highly polluted Rideau Canal next to my employer in Ottawa (Todd, forthcoming), or the nibbling river fish of the River Cam on a visit to Cambridge in 2016, or sunfish and crappies in lakes I've camped alongside in Quebec. Even on our visit to Baptiste Lake in 2014, my mom and I saw evidence of myriad lively fish jumping in the blue-green algae outbreak. But what struck me about this visit in 2018 was the lack of fish. As a little girl, my family and I spent our summers on the lake. My mom, my Métis dad, my sisters, and I would load up the powder-blue family K-car and drive up for our stays on the lake as soon as school was out. Some summers, my dad would pack up his lumbering 1970s Ford pick-up truck, replete with the box he had converted into a plywood and canvas caravan, and my sisters and

I would camp out in the back of the truck on hot summer days. We spent our days collecting leaves and seeds, seeking out the delicious nectar in the red clover that dotted the land around the cabin, and playing amongst the minnows who flashed silver in the shallows below the cabin. We fished, we ventured out into the water on the wooden boats my dad built by hand, and we immersed ourselves in the lake in every way possible for those hazy and all-too-brief Alberta summer days. This was the 1980s, long before the explosion of oil sands investment and building north of us in Fort McMurray and the Peace River region that would flourish in the late 1990s. It was a brief interlude between intensive oil booms and their concomitant exploitation of bitumen and other petro-products in every corner of the province. In the late 1980s and early 1990s, people were discussing the spectre of the proposed Al-Pac pulp and paper mill not far to the northeast near Boyle, Alberta, and the clear-cutting of the forestry sector (Burton et al. 2003, 20; Novek 1993). Oil was a present but relatively less pressing issue.

On any given visit to a lake in Canada, it is the flash and wriggle of minnows and small fry in the shallows that always give me hope. If they are swimming in those waters, they are an indicator that life can flourish, in spite of all that the settler capitalist state has done to lands across the country. And this summer, to my great horror, the minnows were nowhere to be seen in the rust-coloured water of Baptiste Lake.

In 2012 I spent time in the Western Arctic, working with local Inuvialuit fishermen to learn more about how they assert their laws through land- and water-based engagements within their territories (Todd 2014). There, I experienced a landscape where water is incredibly abundant and still healthy. The contrast between crystal clear water in Paulatuuq, into which local community members dip their water bottles and teapots to drink directly while fishing on the land, and the polluted waters of Alberta are stark and upsetting. This is not to say that arctic waters are untouched by global pollution streams by any means, but rather to point out that the heavy resource exploitation of my home province has altered waterways in lasting and deleterious ways.

As I stared out at the altered water of the lake I spent my childhood summers on, I was struck by the cost that the local landscapes across the boreal forest in Alberta have paid for the settler colonial imaginaries imposed upon them. Or, to think more directly with the chapters of this volume, it is evident that Baptiste Lake, already documented to be under stress from cumulative agricultural, residential, and industrial impacts in the 1970s (Atlas of Alberta Lakes, n.d.), has continued to undergo troubling "watery transformations" as settler industrial projects continue unabated in Alberta's boreal forest (Wheatley and Westman, this volume). This is arguably the result of efforts to "improve" the lands of northern Alberta for settler benefit (Spady, this volume). As Sam Spady writes, "Improving the productivity of the Athabasca region is a goal with deep roots in the colonial project. Once the frontier has been settled, the mission then turns to improving the land, or uplifting it to a 'higher purpose' (Veracini 2010, 20). As part of the national myth, the

Canadian National earns his right on the land through labour, which supposedly makes our settlement a peaceful and hard-working one (Ignatieff 2000)."

This brings me to the works presented here in this volume: each chapter sweeps the reader into a different facet of human-environmental and socio-political relations in the Alberta petro-state economy, elucidating different aspects of the complex entanglements between humans, capital, and environment that shape the province today. Questions of toxicity (Lee-Jones), deferral (Wanvik), "improvement" (Spady), interconnection (Baker), accidents (both environmental and social) (Gross), spectacle (Joly), watery transformations (Wheatley and Westman), and the "multiple and deeply entangled" ontologies that inform life in the oil sands (Westman, Joly, and Gross) animate the contributions to this collection.

What each chapter really comes back to are matters of relationality, reciprocity, and relationship. Each author demonstrates, in different ways, how relations between humans and the environment are thrown out of balance in the social, economic, and political entanglements that foster the Alberta oil sands. But the chapters also offer hope and insight, weaving together stories of the lived experiences of Indigenous and non-Indigenous people dwelling in and around the major oil sands projects in northern Alberta. Each author exposes a different complex knot of relations in the oil sands, providing further nuanced insight into the dense structures and relationships that shape life in the bitumen economy. For example, Indigenous interlocutors that Gross interviewed discuss the ways they are navigating the impossible paradoxes of working in an industry premised on the long and visceral "accidents" through which settler colonization and capitalism deploy their worst human and environmental violations. Wanvik demonstrates how Métis and First Nations communities come together to refuse the settler colonial "deferral" of help and support for Métis community members, after Métis communities mobilized their own resources to help settlers displaced by the 2016 Fort McMurray wildfire. Spady demonstrates how the notion of "improvement" of lands and people by settler colonial actors is premised on the stripping of reciprocal relations between humans and non-human kins in order to re-order the world around individualist white settler imaginaries of personal achievement. Lee-Jones demonstrates the lengths to which state and corporate actors will go to, quite literally, gaslight and stymie landowners who are intimately aware of the visceral poisoning of themselves, their livestock, lands, and communities through the long and pervasive leaks, haze, clouds, plumes, and spills of the petro-state economy.

These out-of-balance settler capitalist relations to lands, waters, and other non-human beings in the carbonscape (Wanvik, this volume) of the oil sands are shaped by the legal imperatives the state set out in its land grabs of the region in 1899 (Longley, this volume). These legal frameworks, manifested through distorted settler understandings of Treaty negotiations, lay the groundwork for contemporary violations of kin relations and reciprocal obligations between humans and non-humans. As Joly demonstrates, settler legal frameworks evacuate Indigenous legal orders from dominant understandings of appropriate ways to engage with the land, water, and other non-human beings. As a result, bison as non-human persons are co-opted into the spectacles of land reclamation and environmental harm mitigation in oil sands management. These same frameworks disrupt the watery environs of Baptiste Lake, evacuating the minnows and small fry, leaving the rusty waters washing up against eroding lakeshore with an eerie emptiness.

So what can we do to refuse (Simpson 2014) the settler state's imaginaries of its carbonscapes and petro-economies? And how do we disrupt dominant settler capitalist narratives of improvement (Spady), deferral (Wanvik), and surveillance (Lee-Jones) that drive the current petro-state? We must turn to the possibilities opened up to us by the imperative of relationships and reciprocity, as Baker and Joly demonstrate in this volume. We must tend to one another and to the landscapes around us with greater care, honour the relationships that sustain not only human life but the entirety of existence in northern Alberta. This requires tending and attention. As Janelle Marie Baker illustrates in this volume, "tending means collecting, hunting, trapping, and, in the past, it also meant starting fires under the right conditions. When people do not tend to their responsibilities and cycles of respect, imbalances occur, and massive uncontrollable fires ignite, or bears attack. (Gross 2016). Sometimes those imbalances are more subtle: bears eat garbage instead of berries because it is simply easy and pleasant to find, or the bears change their habits and spend more time during the summer in inland berry patches rather than along the river. Living creatures, humans included, adjust and adapt, but when do imbalances become chaos, and a threat to food security and sovereignty?"

In my own work (Todd 2016), I gesture to the notion of tenderness as a state of being in constant awareness of, and/or relation towards, those around us. As Baker demonstrates, in this state of shared awareness, we are better equipped to respond collectively to our shared entanglements with humans and non-humans alike. It is our responsibility to enact these acts of attention. As anthropologist Anna Tsing argues, "I have suggested we watch patches of livelihood come into being as assemblages" (2015, 132), or as Donna Haraway (2016) argues, it is necessary for us to "stay with the trouble" in these chaotic times. Through these "arts of noticing" (Tsing 2015) and through tending and interconnection (Baker, this volume), or as Haraway (2007) argues, the labour of "becoming with," we are better equipped to observe the relationships necessary to respond to and engage with the rapidly shifting realities of the environments we inhabit. And, just maybe, we will be better equipped to console and care for one another through the changes ahead. This volume helps to move us towards these crucial conversations and re-orientations and opens space for us to ask difficult questions with earnest attentiveness. Indeed, these are the only things we can count on as systems, structures, landscapes, and whole orders of being shift tectonically before us.

**Zoe Todd**

## References

Atlas of Alberta Lakes. n.d. "Baptiste Lake." Accessed September 9, 2018. http://albertalakes.ualberta.ca/?page=lake&region=1&lake=29.

Burton, P. J. Messier, C. Weetman, G.F. Prepas, E.E., Adamowicz, W. L. and Tittler, R.. 2003. "The Current State of Boreal Forestry and the Drive for Change." In *Towards Sustainable Management of the Boreal Forest*, edited by Philip Burton, Christian Messier, Daniel W. Smith, and Wiktor L. Adamowicz, 1–41. Ottawa: NRC Research Press, 2003.

Gibson, John. 2016. "Alberta Recession One of the Most Severe Ever, TD Economics Report Finds." *CBC News*, July 18, 2016. https://www.cbc.ca/news/canada/calgary/td-economics-report-alberta-recession-gdp-forecast-1.3684056.

Gross, Lena. 2016. "(Uncomfortable) Solidarities: Doubtable Belongings and Human and Non-Human Relations in Alberta's Tar/Oil Sands Region." Paper presented at *the SOLIDARIT(I)ÉS, Canadian Anthropology Association Conference*, Halifax, June 2016.

Haraway, Donna. 2007. *When Species Meet*. Minneapolis: University of Minnesota Press.

———. 2016. *Staying with the Trouble: Making Kin in the Chthulucene*. Durham, NC: Duke University Press.

Ignatieff, Michael. 2000. *The Rights Revolution*. Toronto: House of Anansi Press.

Maturié, Pierre. (2013) [1972]. *Man Proposes, God Disposes: Recollections of a French Pioneer*. Edmonton, AB: Athabasca University Press.

Novek, Joel. 1993. "Environmental Impact Assessment in Practice: Exploring the Contradictions." *Great Plains Research 3* (August): 337–57.

Simpson, Audra. 2014. *Mohawk Interruptus: Political Life across the Borders of Settler States*. Durham, NC: Duke University Press.

Summer Village of South Baptiste. 2018. "Summer Village of South Baptiste." Last modified August 17, 2018. http://www.southbaptiste.com/.

Todd, Zoe. 2014. "Fish Pluralities: Human–Animal Relations and Sites of Engagement in Paulatuuq, Arctic Canada." *Études/Inuit/Studies 38* (1–2): 217–38.

———. 2015. "Decolonial Dreams: Unsettling the Academy through Namewak." In *The New (New) Corpse*, edited by Caroline Picard, 104–17. Chicago: Green Lantern Press.

———. 2016. "Tending Tenderness." *Urbane Adventurer: Amiskwacî* (blog), September 18, 2016. https://zoestodd.com/2016/09/18/tending-tenderness/.

Todd, Zoe. Forthcoming. "The Rideau Canal in Fall: Understanding Ontology and Epistemology through Fish and Canals in the Heart of the Canadian Empire." In *Seasonal Sociology*, edited by Tonya Davidson and Ondine Park. Toronto: University of Toronto Press.

Tsing, Anna Lowenhaupt. 2015. *The Mushroom at the End of the World: On the Possibility of Life in Capitalist Ruins*. Princeton, NJ: Princeton University Press.

Veracini, Lorenzo. 2010. *Settler Colonialism: A Theoretical Overview*. Basingstoke, UK: Palgrave Macmillan, 2010.

# Preface

Our book is the product of multiple scholarly networks, including social media–based groups such as the Social Scientists in Alberta's Oil Sands research collective. Nevertheless, one possible founding moment for part of this relational nexus came when Janelle Baker and Clint Westman each enrolled in a graduate-level oral history methods class taught by Professor Andie Diane Palmer at the University of Alberta in 2003. Both of us interviewed a member of our own family: Westman interviewed his grandmother, a respected founder in her northern Alberta pioneer community, and Baker interviewed her Métis great-grandmother, who had come from a farming settlement in Saskatchewan to Alberta to find work as a single mother. As we shared our results with the seminar, a striking point of commonality in our family and community histories emerged: the importance of oil and forestry, as well as agriculture, in providing an economic base for rural people in Alberta, including women, during the second half of the twentieth century, though not without ups and downs. Many Indigenous and non-Indigenous individuals and communities have had similar experiences, grappling with both the risks and rewards of fossil fuel extraction (see Gross; Lee-Jones; Wanvik, this volume).

While several of us knew one another previously (as the above example demonstrates), it was conferences that brought us together as a group. Many of us came together to meet through panels and meetings funded by the Cultural Politics of Energy in Northern Alberta research partnership, supported by the Social Sciences and Humanities Research Council of Canada and directed by Westman. For some of us, mutual conversations also occurred through our participation in other research groups led by David Anderson, Robert Crépeau, Ståle Knudsen, and Colin Scott. When a few contributors to this book presented (mainly in different panels) at the American Anthropological Association annual meeting in Denver 2015, those of us who met or spoke there soon realized that we needed to collaborate more closely as a group. Among other work, this collaboration led to two panels, one at the joint conference of the Canadian Anthropology Society and the Society for the Anthropology of North America in Halifax 2016, and one at the American Anthropological Association meeting the same year in Minneapolis. These panels—the first-ever sessions on oil sands at major anthropology meetings—provided an opportunity to discuss and work through much of the data presented in this book. Some of us also participated in a panel on related themes at the Canadian Anthropology Society conference in Santiago de Cuba in 2018. We are grateful to our discussants and interlocutors at each of these panels. Through sustained international meetings and more informal conversations, we laid the groundwork for this book.

Profoundly, this collection relies on collaborations with Indigenous and other northern communities. Many of the collaborators describe their research partnerships in detail herein. As an example, the Cultural Politics of Energy research partnership, which has involved many of our contributors, draws on members' engagement with multiple Indigenous communities and environmental organizations. This partnership includes a steering committee composed of Indigenous representatives and senior scholars, who provided direction on the research program and funding priorities, including the conference panels that were the basis for this book and some of the research behind it. This book would not have been possible without these and other collaborations. We especially honour the Elders who guided our meetings.

Together with our research participants, we and other colleagues have been building momentum towards a new line of investigation in this extreme extraction zone. We have developed our international partnerships and our community-engaged research strategies through a combination of fieldwork, professional consulting, contributions to grey literature (including overviews of the field), partnership meetings and steering committee sessions with community representatives, conference panels and presentations, invited lectures, and peer-reviewed publications.

Crucially, one of the two 2016 panels (organized by Whitney Larratt-Smith and Westman) focused on human/non-human relations in the oil sands, while the other (organized by Lee-Jones and Joly) focused more on themes of political economy and settler colonialism. Each of the chapters in the book stakes out ground within one of these theoretical frameworks, often while simultaneously making interventions in others. As editors, it is the productive intersections between these questions of ontology, materiality, identity, ecology, economy, politics, and history that interest us most.

Since our panels, we have continued talking, exchanging our work, and discussing our ethnographic material. Some of us have started a reading group, while others have collaborated on co-authored articles. Several contributors initially met in Fort McMurray through consulting work. Still others met regularly in their shared research groups. We also acknowledge the long-term contributions that Patricia McCormack has made to this project (including providing detailed comments on several of the chapters for this book and at our Cuba panel) and to ethnological research in northern Alberta. As well, we honour the ongoing connections and inspirational dialogue that many of us enjoy with Zoe Todd.

Our episodic conversations soon led to the conviction that we needed to write something together. We all were aware of the surprising gap in anthropological or ethnographic literature on oil sands extraction and its impacts on the inhabitants of the region, albeit some of the participants in this volume have already taken strides to fill this gap by advancing and defining the state of inquiry through our scholarly studies and contributions to grey literature.

While our research intertwines, we were struck by differences in our approaches and variations by case and region. However, broadly speaking, our findings and conclusions concurred with one another. Also, our regional foci are complementary, covering nearly the whole region of oil sands extraction (an area larger than many European countries), within all three oil sands zones, partly overlapping with one another while mostly breaking our own ground through our engagements with specific individuals and communities. One outcome of these conversations, collaborations, and friendships—our book—lies in front of you.

The editors would like to thank the communities and people with whom we work, who have made significant contributions to each of our learnings as both scholars and individuals. We also thank each of the contributors to this volume for their hard work and dedication over the past few years in bringing this volume together, and for helping to build a network of researchers. Thank you to Joanne Muzak, who provided profoundly helpful copy edits to the entire volume. Additionally, Alessandro Pasquini created the maps for our volume. Two anonymous reviewers provided feedback that has been helpful to us in developing the ideas in this book. Finally, we are grateful to our editors and peers David Anderson and Robert Losey for creating a dynamic book series with which our volume is in conversation. This book is dedicated to those who call northern Alberta home.

# Contributors

**Janelle Marie Baker** is Assistant Professor of Anthropology in the Centre for Social Sciences at Athabasca University.

**Lena Gross** recently completed a PhD in Social Anthropology at the University of Oslo and currently maintains a research affiliation there.

**Tara L. Joly** holds a PhD in Social Anthropology from the University of Aberdeen. She is Research Director with Willow Springs Strategic Solutions, Inc.

**Tristan Lee-Jones** recently completed a PhD in Anthropology at Rutgers University.

**Hereward Longley** is a PhD candidate in History at the University of Alberta.

**Patricia A. McCormack** is Professor Emerita in the College of Native Studies at the University of Alberta and Principal of Native Roots Consulting.

**Sam Spady** is a PhD candidate in Social Justice Education at the Ontario Institute for Studies in Education, University of Toronto.

**Zoe Todd** is Associate Professor of Anthropology in the Department of Sociology and Anthropology at Carleton University.

**Tarje I. Wanvik** is a Postdoctoral Fellow in the Department of Geography at the University of Bergen.

**Clinton N. Westman** is Associate Professor of Anthropology in the Department of Archaeology and Anthropology at the University of Saskatchewan.

**Katherine Wheatley** is Project Lead for Reconciliation and Responsible Investment with the Shareholder Association for Research and Education.

# Introduction

## At Home in the Oil Sands

*Clinton N. Westman, Tara L. Joly, and Lena Gross*

What does it mean to make a home in the middle of one of the world's largest extraction sites? This question has driven us for years, and each contributor to this volume has grappled with it in their own way. We all work in northern Alberta, and collectively we show how industrial activity there creates and disrupts homes and livelihoods in uneven and contradictory ways (Figure I.1). Our book is the only one to provide detailed ethnographic accounts of production processes and lived experience in all three oil sands zones.[1] It includes reference to both mining and in situ extraction processes. Most of us work primarily with Indigenous communities and topics. Boreal forest Indigenous Peoples, including those in both urban areas and small, isolated communities where most people eat bush foods and speak Cree and/or Dene languages on a daily basis, are on the front lines of globally significant expansions in the energy sector's investments. Yet, as we show, northern Alberta and the oil sands have historically been understudied by social scientists (see McCormack, this volume). This region, although often described as frontier, wilderness, or hinterland by both national and international media, has a history of trade, cultural exchange, and habitation that dates back millennia. Within western Canada, Alberta connects the prairies and parklands with the boreal forest to the north and mountainous environments to the west. Linked by different watersheds to the Arctic Ocean and Hudson Bay, the province's northern boreal forest region lies in the Canadian subarctic, which links moderate climate zones to Arctic ones, contrasting forest with agriculture on its fringes and in parts of the Peace River region. We contend that northern Alberta merits study as a homeland rather than a hinterland—and as a paramount site of capitalist extraction. We add that the region's importance also lies beyond a sole focus on bitumen itself, but also with the people and other beings who relate to it in varied ways (see Todd and others, this volume).

Canada's oil sands industry is in the global public eye as both a major source of fossil fuel revenues and a key contributor to climate change and pollution. Alberta's oil sands reserve is one of the world's most important energy sources, as it is the third largest proven crude oil deposit after those of Saudi Arabia and Venezuela; oil sands production is expected to increase from 2.8 million barrels per day in 2017 to 3.9 million barrels per day by 2027

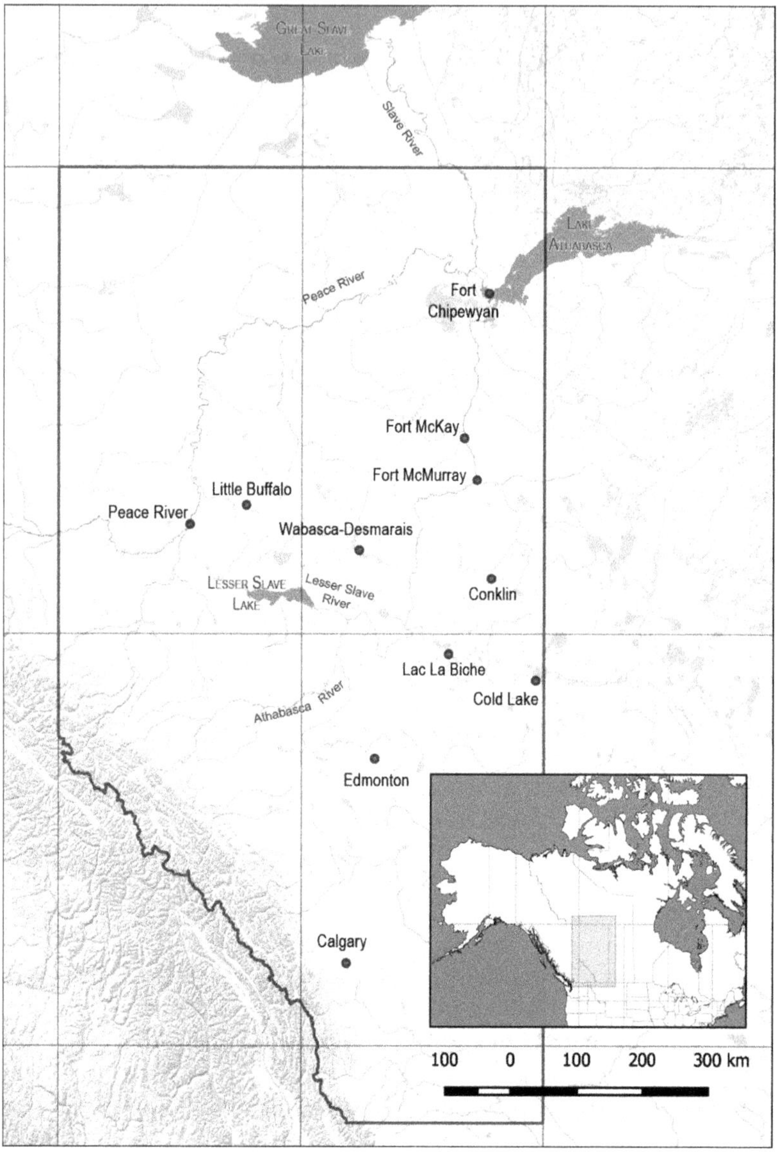


*Figure I.1* Map of Alberta showing selected communities and geographical features. Map by Alessandro Pasquini.

(Alberta Energy 2018b). Alberta's proven oil sands reserves equal approximately 165.4 billion barrels. As such, capital investment in Alberta's upstream energy sector (including oil sands, conventional oil and gas, mining, and quarrying) was about CAD$28.3 billion in 2016, estimated around $26.5 billion in 2017, and forecast at $23.7 billion in 2018; correspondingly, bitumen royalties are the largest single source of revenue for the provincial government: $1.48 billion in 2016–17 alone (Alberta Energy 2018a). Alberta's oil sands underlie some 142,200 square kilometres of land in the Athabasca, Cold Lake, and Peace River areas in northern Alberta.[2] The Athabasca deposits are the most extensive. Reserves shallow enough to mine (up to 75 metres) are found only within the Athabasca oil sands area (Alberta Energy 2018a), to the north of Fort McMurray. In addition to mining, various in situ techniques (the fastest-growing extraction method in the past decade) are used to extract non-mineable deposits in all three regions. Because the oil is mixed with sand and water, and sometimes other fossil fuels, extraction techniques are relatively energy- and water-intensive, with high production costs. Ongoing developments include the deployment of new technologies to access bitumen and heavy oil deposits and to revitalize (often through fracking) dwindling reserves of conventional oil and lower-value natural gas or by-products (for historically oriented discussions of oil sands extraction, see Longley, McCormack, this volume). This same region produces considerable quantities of timber and pulp, as well as sand, gravel, and other minerals. These other industries (some of which are ancillary or symbiotic with fossil fuel industries) also have complex synergistic and cumulative environmental and socioeconomic impacts (in tandem with impacts of fossil fuel extraction) that are not well understood. In spite of the scale of change currently underway in the oil sands region, scholarly investigation of this phenomenon has, until recently, been sparse. Indeed, as prominent water ecologist David Schindler (2010) pointed out in *Nature*, the "tar sands need solid science" to document the impacts of the industry and to support land management decisions. We are also convinced that the "tar sands" (and all energy extraction projects in Alberta and beyond) *need solid social science* to improve understanding and support ecological justice (Ageyman et al. 2009; Joly and Westman 2017). This conviction is what brought us together.

Our volume's goal is to examine oil's cultural impacts, ecological consequences, and political processes in a particular period and region of the circumpolar north. We collectively make a significant contribution to knowledge of Indigenous and energy issues in the context of rapid environmental change, allowing for theoretical advances in settler colonial studies, multispecies ethnography, and the anthropology of oil (Rogers 2015). It is our conviction that social science research on the Canadian oil sands is of interest beyond regional (subarctic/Canada) and topical (resource extraction) boundaries. Extractive industry on Indigenous lands magnifies issues of inequality, Indigeneity, land rights, colliding cosmologies, neoliberal markets, and rapid environmental changes.

## "Perhaps the Most Interesting Region in all the North"

Alexander Mackenzie, one of the first Europeans to view the oil sands, during the 1770s, referred to the oozing surface deposits along the Athabasca River as "bituminous fountains" (quoted in Nikiforuk 2010, 8). Over one hundred years later, accompanying the Treaty 8 Commission and the Half-Breed (i.e., Métis) Scrip Commission parties in 1899 (see Longley, this volume), Canadian government official Charles Mair referred to the oil sands region as "perhaps the most interesting region in all the North" due to its evident petroleum wealth:

> In the neighbourhood of McMurray there are several tar-wells, so called, and there, if a hole is scraped in the bank, it slowly fills with tar mingled with sand. This is separated by boiling, and is used, in its native state, for gumming canoes and boats. Further up are immense towering banks, the tar oozing at every pore...and anon, past giant clay escarpments... everywhere streaked with oozing tar, and smelling like an old ship.
>
> Mair (1999, 212)

The most interesting region in all the North? Perhaps indeed.

Notwithstanding such early accolades, in academic terms, northern Alberta has been somewhat neglected until quite recently. Indeed, within circumpolar scholarly circles, the subarctic or boreal region in general often plays second fiddle to the Arctic tundra. Perhaps the Subarctic seems socially and geographically less remote and pristine than its polar counterpart. In some ways, northern Alberta, which includes mid-sized, rapidly growing cites and substantial regions of arable land with agricultural communities, exemplifies this ethnological lacuna. Within Canada, the middle or provincial North has been described as a forgotten North (Coates and Morrison 1992), being less visible and less frequently the site of policy innovations and advances in self-determination seen largely in the federally administered northern territories—though not forgotten by provincial governments, who pursue extractivist policies there. Indeed, the provincial norths have largely been administered as internal colonies. For example, in Alberta, a very substantial portion of total government revenue is derived from extractive activities in the province's relatively lightly populated northern regions. There is thus an inequitable distribution of risks and benefits best characterized by the dynamics of colonialism and environmental racism. Indigenous people remain the most prominent "visible minority" group throughout the region. In some districts, Indigenous people comprise the great majority of the population.

Northern Alberta is inhabited by Athapaskan-speaking Dene (primarily Chipewyan, Beaver, and Slavey [Dene Tha]) and Algonquian-speaking Western Woods Cree (*nehiyawak* or *sakâwiyiniwak*) First Nations Peoples, bands of foragers who learned to live well in the northern landscape. Beginning in the late eighteenth century, European fur traders entered the region, following a century of indirect access to trade goods on the part of local people. Additionally, another Indigenous People, the Métis (descendants of First Nations people and European fur traders), became established in northern Alberta and elsewhere in western Canada. Finally, in a related process, First Nations people from eastern Canada also came west to work in the fur trade. The extent to which each of these groups maintained a separate social and ethnic identity was variable, depending on location. Many First Nations include people with a mix of Cree, Iroquois, Ojibwe, Dene, Métis, and/or Euro-Canadian heritage. During and following the Treaty 8 and Half-Breed Scrip commissions in 1899, perceived racial and ethnic categories were fluid for a time as individuals were allowed to select Indian or Métis status. At other periods, these boundaries became solidified, and gaining or losing Indian or Métis status has been the subject of litigation, legislation, or regulation.

Notwithstanding their agricultural and extractive potential, northern and boreal forest regions of Alberta in many cases remained a "delayed frontier" (Leonard 1995) until well into the twentieth century. Incremental changes included the negotiation of Treaty 6 (1876, in central Alberta and Saskatchewan, including much of the Cold Lake oil sands deposit), Treaty 8 (1899, covering the majority of oil sands in Alberta and Saskatchewan–bearing lands, including most of the Athabasca deposit and all of the Peace River deposit), and Treaty 10 (covering portions of the Cold Lake and Athabasca deposits in Alberta and Saskatchewan, although no Alberta First Nations signed Treaty 10); the subsequent arrival of agricultural settlers in some places; and the creation of Indian Reserves and Métis settlements. Furthermore, many Indigenous people were forcibly sent to residential schools and other institutions during the twentieth century. Nevertheless, in important respects, social relations of the fur trade era persisted well into the post–Second World War period throughout much of northern Alberta, as elsewhere in northern Canada. For many groups, addressing land rights and title only became more pressing with the resource booms of the mid- and late twentieth century. Indeed, some communities (particularly Métis and non-status Indian communities, but also until recently including the Lubicon Lake Band at Little Buffalo Lake [Ominayak and Thomas 2009]) are still engaged in negotiations, litigation, and advocacy over reserve land, band recognition, and/or federal services for their communities. First Nations and Métis communities are also pressing on broader issues, generally seeking more input and control in resource management decisions.

In ethnological terms, the Canadian subarctic in general (along with some adjoining boreal regions of the United States) was considered as a classic cultural area within modern Americanist anthropology (e.g., Hallowell 1960). Nevertheless, generally speaking, the study of northern Alberta's Indigenous Peoples was not of high profile in such ethnographic endeavours. With the exception of a relatively small number of mostly preliminary studies by early Boasians—among the first generation of anthropologists trained in North America—at places such as Fort Chipewyan and Cold Lake (mainly focused on language but also on oral traditions), the ethnology and ethnohistory of northern Alberta (and particularly Western Woods Cree and Métis populations) has long been under-researched (Lewis 1982; Smith 1981). Indeed, it would not be too much to say that between 1880 and 1960—the golden age of modernist anthropology—the most important linguistic and ethnographic research in northern Alberta was carried out by missionaries, rather than anthropologists (Grouard 2010; Vandersteene 1960). By the end of this period, if not before, Indigenous people from northern Alberta were speaking for themselves to a national and international audience (e.g., Cardinal 1969).

Things improved somewhat with the establishment of anthropology departments in Albertan universities beginning in the late 1960s. Still, this flourishing was relatively short-term and most notable within archaeology. In ethnological terms, the under-researched status of northern Alberta has largely continued through to the end of the twentieth century and beyond, in spite of some strong work by individual researchers (Goulet 1998; McCormack 2010). One exception has been the scholarly and public attention focused to a large extent on particular communities such as the Lubicon Cree and their land rights, often without much consideration for (or even with prejudice to) the related plight of neighbouring groups (Goddard 1991; Martin-Hill 2008; Smith 1987). Meanwhile, anthropologists working on faculty at Alberta's major universities have largely disengaged from the ethnographic study of northern Alberta, which had been a greater focus in previous decades (but see Baker, this volume, recently hired at Athabasca University). To whom Alberta's academic anthropologists are leaving the field is unclear, although scholars in related fields such as Indigenous studies, resource management, and archaeology have become increasingly active in the region and on topics related to Indigenous people and the oil sands (Parlee 2015; Ronaghan 2017). Indeed, in recent decades, historical and archaeological investigations into northern Alberta have hit something of a high point (Payne, Wetherell, and Cavanaugh 2006; Wetherell and Kmet 2000), although nearly all archaeological fieldwork in northern Alberta is conducted under the auspices of cultural resource management, which is paid for by industry to meet regulatory requirements. This has resulted in a more professionalized corps of archaeological consultants who often also carry out traditional land use consultations with living populations. In general, the quality of grey literature on oil sands social science, including archaeology (see Martindale 2014), is quite uneven (Joly and Westman 2017).

One important published account of a Métis person's lived experience with both the oil patch and prior yet ongoing Métis economic and cultural activities is that of Elmer Ghostkeeper (2007). Trained as an anthropologist and using anthropological perspectives to contextualize his own experience, Ghostkeeper presents a strong contrast between the values and practices of industry and Métis values and practices, particularly around themes such as spirituality and reciprocity (see Joly, Todd, this volume).

The lack of a sustained anthropological or ethnographic focus on northern Alberta has had negative consequences beyond the academy. Gaps in social science knowledge have played out in the regulatory realm, where environmental assessments provide only the thinnest of description for social practices and likely social impacts, while making erroneous statements and quoting inappropriate literature to support their claims that contiguous megaprojects have no significant, long-term, cumulative, cultural, or social impact (Baker and Westman 2018; McCormack 2016; Westman 2006, 2013; see also McCormack, this volume, on the historical trajectory of impact assessment research and its tenuous relation to the academy). In contrast, our approach is to work with and represent the experiences of Indigenous (and Euro-Canadian) people in an engaged, accountable manner founded on our regional expertise and community-engaged research approaches.

Our volume is significant given that despite the prominence and importance of the oil sands in the context of debates about climate change, energy futures, and the Anthropocene, there is no edited volume that focuses solely on critical social science research on the oil sands, or any book that makes extensive use of ethnographic perspectives on the oil sands. Significantly, major recent comparative contributions in the anthropology of oil generally do not mention the oil sands (or Canada) at all (Behrends, Reyna, and Schlee 2011; Rogers 2015; Strauss, Rupp, and Love 2013). Meanwhile, the small number of recent Canadian books that address energy politics in Alberta (Adkin 2016b; Shrivastava and Stefanick 2015; Urquhart 2018) are largely written or edited by political scientists, do not include anthropologists as participants or provide ethnographic investigations, and feature no more than a chapter or two on Indigenous issues (but see Black et al. 2014, which includes several Indigenous contributors and related commentary). We emphasize the value and importance of these contributions; nevertheless, recent books on Alberta energy topics are largely devoted to the politics of the petro-state, sometimes focused in part on downstream issues such as climate change and pipeline infrastructure in other jurisdictions, whereas our focus is on lived experience at the site of production. In fact, editors and contributors to this volume are among the leaders in the analysis of oil sands impacts and processes in relation to Indigenous Peoples, particularly where anthropological and ethnographic approaches are concerned.

Besides the work of contributors to this volume (referred to herein), we can point to at least three other distinct recent bodies of work that focus on the oil sands from social science and humanities perspectives: the political science/political economy traditions mentioned above; interdisciplinary scholarship on the increasingly mobile and multicultural milieu developing in the region, especially its urban centres; and energy humanities research and related fine art that touches on themes relevant to oil sands. Although these stand as separate bodies of literature, they are relevant for brief consideration here, as our concerns occasionally overlap.

To a great extent, social studies of resource management in Alberta have been led by political scientists, in keeping with a grand tradition of political economic study of a jurisdiction that has been a policy laboratory (MacPherson 1962; Richards and Pratt 1979; Pratt and Urquhart 1994; Urquhart 2018). Furthermore, activist, politically engaged scholars from multiple disciplines have either documented or were involved in struggles against pulp mill development (e.g., Richardson, Sherman, and Gismondi 1993), and/or for the land rights of the Lubicon Nation (e.g., Martin-Hill 2008), particularly during the 1980s and 1990s, struggles which in some ways provide models for contemporary engaged scholarship and activism.

Broadly speaking, political economic approaches remain strongly represented and highly relevant (Adkin 2016b; Bowness and Hudson 2014; Shrivastava and Stefanick 2015) in analyses of the contemporary Alberta context. Current studies of the oil sands from political scientists and allied disciplines often examine socioeconomic benefits and approvals in the context of neoliberalism (e.g., Urquhart 2018), either using the term critically or reinforcing neoliberal ideals. Laurie Adkin (2016a) describes neoliberalism as a global market-driven form of governance that prioritizes capital gains over labour concerns or environmental protection. Neoliberal, market-driven approaches to resource management and rents have become increasingly influential in Alberta energy governance since the 1970s (Steward 2017). In Alberta, neoliberalism is characterized by a model of development that is reliant on oil and gas production, providing revenue to governments alongside tax breaks and relaxed environmental regulations to incentivize rapid development (Adkin 2016a, 81, 100–1). Anna Zalik (2016) takes a critical stance, arguing that agreements Indigenous communities make with oil companies provide these companies a so-called social licence to operate, which may fracture communities while enabling the company to portray itself as responsible. On the other hand, Gabrielle Slowey (2008) suggests that participating in neoliberal systems can support self-determination for communities who are thus able to leverage financial benefits; however, we would caution that it is difficult to trace or research these economic gains, which are in any case not equally available to Indigenous communities or individuals. Anthropologists have adopted political economy techniques to analyse ethnographically the processes of regulatory capture evident in the oil sands (Wheatley 2018), and pointed to connections between neoliberal ideologies, evolutionary thinking, and environmental racism (Joly and Westman 2017). All of our contributors understand the power held by corporations over state actors in Alberta (and, perhaps to a slightly lesser degree, Canada); chapters engaging most directly with political economy here include Gross, Longley, Lee-Jones, and Wanvik.

A second body of literature, in part linked to the above, explores the increasingly multicultural and globalized nature of oil sands communities and workforces. This body of literature, particularly a 2013 special issue of the *Canadian Journal of Sociology* called "Fort McMurray, Wood Buffalo, and the Oil/Tar Sands: Revisiting the Sociology of 'Community'" (Dorow and O'Shaughnessy 2013), problematizes concepts of community. At stake is the multi-ethnic, changing, and growing nature of cities such as Fort McMurray. Issues of mobility and education (Asselin 2014), labour rights and diversity (Barnetson and Foster 2012; Foster and Barnetson 2015; Foster and Taylor 2013; see Gross, this volume), and the maintenance of minority linguistic/ethnic identities (Heller et al. 2016) are highlighted through this work. Read together, and alongside media reports focusing on topics such as

Islamic life in Fort McMurray, Grande Prairie, and Lac La Biche, one focus here is on the creation of new forms of Canadian identity (as with Spady, this volume). Related to the deployment of ideas about community, jobs, and opportunity has been the cultural problem of "assembling consent" (Haluza-DeLay 2014) within Albertan and Canadian society for the large-scale exploitation of bitumen deposits, a nationalist hegemonic undertaking akin in some ways to the controversial and pugnacious claim by some on Canada's right that the country is producing "ethical oil" (Levant 2010). In our volume, Joly, Lee-Jones, and Spady engage most directly with Canada's culture of complacency around the oil sands and the corresponding performance of corporate ethics and citizenship.

The third body of work current in the oil sands is also linked to the first two but stands more on its own through its engagement with humanities and fine arts, while examining Indigeneity, the politics of colonialism, whiteness, and masculinity, as well as the nature of new communities and work experiences. Scholars and artists working in this area combine an ironic appreciation for the geotechnical spectacular of oil sands extraction with a subtle consideration of its meanings for race, gender, class, regional, and national identities. Perhaps most notable here is the work of Indigenous scholars and artists such as Warren Cariou (e.g., McArthur and Cariou 2009) and Alex Janvier (e.g., his painting *Oil Patch Heartbeat*, 2013). Also worth mentioning is recent sociological/cultural studies research on "petro-cultures" (Gordon 2015; Wilson, Carlson, and Szeman 2017), working through the social implications of oil and extraction in ways that connect with the literature on community mentioned previously. Finally, an increasingly diverse body of work including short stories, plastic arts, and other forms has been devoted to the oil sands; internationally, among the best-known interventions here are those of Canadian photographer Edward Burtynsky (e.g., *Oil Sands #2,* 2007). In this volume, such connections to the spectacular can perhaps be seen most clearly in Spady's, Wheatley and Westman's, and particularly Joly's contributions.

As a resource of Herculean scope, the oil sands present a rich field for ethnographic work on extraction, science studies, and the Anthropocene. The industry highlights issues of environmental change, colliding ontologies, race, gender, inequality, and state–Indigenous relations. This is true for most major extractive industries, especially if they take place in (settler) colonial spaces like Canada. In many countries and across differences, extractive industries play a prominent role in shaping new relations between Indigenous Peoples, the state, newcomers, corporations, plants, animals, and the land (e.g., Li 2015). Nevertheless, due to the sheer scale of the oil sands, and as the largest proven crude oil deposit under the jurisdiction of a liberal democratic state, the Canadian context of bitumen extraction stands out. Thus, the oil sands present an ideal critical framework for studies embracing (and in some cases, blending) theories of post-humanism, political ecology, settler colonialism, and race within extractive contexts. Still, we are convinced that our findings have relevance to other regions within extractive settings.

The insights we draw from ethnographically theorizing settler colonialism, sentient landscapes, and multispecies relations in northern Alberta within a critical political ecology framework are hence of interest for an international scholarly audience.

## Settler Colonialism, Extraction, and Multilocal/Multivocal Landscapes

Together, the contributors to this volume show a multiplicity of ways Indigenous and non-Indigenous peoples negotiate across territorialities (Dussart and Poirier 2017) in the context of an extreme form of extraction (Jalbert et al. 2017)—extreme due to the colossal magnitude of the deposit, the massive scale of its extracting and refining plants, the rapid pace of its resource rush, and the huge sums of capital at stake. Northern Alberta is, as mentioned above, often represented in popular media as an extractive zone, presented solely in the image of the commodity—in this case, bitumen—rendering certain (often Indigenous) socio-ecological histories invisible (Bridge 2001), while extractive futures are considered inevitable (Westman 2013). Through the goal of obtaining oil and the capital that comes with it, the landscape becomes a thing to be used, laboured, and overcome by technological advancements. However, for many Indigenous Peoples in northern Alberta, the landscape is a homeland, full of knowing, intentional beings with whom humans are responsible for entering into just relationships. These perspectives—one of a commodified landscape and the other of a sentient landscape—entangle and interact in place, each narrating and materially shaping the land in complex, often uneven, ways.

In the context of extreme extraction, the power to tell certain stories about environmental change is a central concern for this volume. Who can define a home? Who owns the land? What is a bison? Which berries can we eat? How does one define pollution? What does it mean to be "good" in a resource town? Who decides the future of a bog? What is a wasteland? What is a resource? What is development? And which (human and non-human) meanings and agencies do we contend with when facing these boreal forest homelands? Such questions coalesce around the crucial issues of making and remaking places or territories. The chapters in this volume describe northern Alberta at once as Indigenous territory, a field for creating and enacting new forms of Canadian identity, extractive space, temporary residence, agricultural home place, oil sands lease, trapline, berry patch, reclaimed lake district, and bison habitat.

In regions of extreme extraction, layers of rights and multiple geographies entangle in one space. Herein, Longley describes how attempts to reconstruct Indigenous homeland as oil sands territory arrange conditions for ongoing extraction. Lee-Jones looks at the "everyday" experience of industrial pollution in a region that borders on (white) agricultural space and (Indigenous) forest lands, showing how contamination affects all inhabitants of the region. Spady shows that urban spaces may be simultaneously constructed by predominantly white settlers as family towns, temporary residences, or places of permanent settlement. Conversely, Wanvik examines the politics of Indigenous communities in the region, looking at a regional-municipal dispute (with corresponding Euro-Canadian/Indigenous dimensions) over community infrastructure resource allocations in the wake of a major wildfire. Other contributors, including Baker, Gross, Joly, and Wheatley and Westman, demonstrate that northern Alberta remains, deeply and integrally, an Indigenous homeland, with attendant relations to other species and non-human persons (see Hallowell 1960). Yet these more cosmological and multi-species-focused chapters remain deeply engaged in political debates as well.

Focusing on home and territorialities in a place of extreme extraction necessitates a settler colonial analytical lens. Settler colonialism seeks to erase multiple stories of and claims to the land, specifically those rooted in Indigenous legal orders, with the colonial goal of perpetual access to and use of the land (see Wolfe 2006): creating settler home on Indigenous land. As Michael Asch (2014) states, settlers and Indigenous people are all "here to stay." So, what are the presently unfolding processes and consequences of settler attempts to redefine Indigenous homelands as a wasteland, a resource frontier, or an industrial space? This volume attempts to render these multiple, entangled, power-laden interpretations of the land visible ethnographically.

In an oft-quoted passage from which multiple contributors have taken inspiration, Patrick Wolfe (2006) states that settler colonialism is a structure, not an event. He sees settler colonialism as an ongoing process in the (attempted) elimination and dispossession of Indigenous Peoples from the landscape—an assertion this volume takes seriously. Settler colonialism has been called a unique form of colonialism that seeks to create a home for settler populations on lands that are already home to Indigenous Peoples (Rose 1991). Consequently, certain forms of citizenship, gender relations, ontologies, ways of living, and relations to humans and non-humans are enforced through legislation and biopolitics while others get erased or suppressed. Through hegemonic normalization and standardization—for example, heteronormativity and patriarchy through the implementation of the Indian Act (see Goeman 2017; Morgensen 2011; Simpson 2014, 2016), capitalist property laws, or the restriction of movement—settler colonialism is an ever-present condition of life. At the same time, we stress that Indigenous people have not disappeared or been assimilated in this region.

If settler colonialism is indeed an ongoing structure, then it cannot be relegated to the past. A collection of ethnographic works examining settler colonialism, therefore, demands a focused attentiveness on Indigenous Peoples. J. Kēhaulani Kauanui argues that settler colonial studies "necessarily [need] to tend to the question of indigeneity," seriously examining the effects of settler colonialism as an *ongoing* structure that endures *alongside* Indigeneity, and how Indigenous people "exist, resist, and persist" despite eliminatory forces (2016, n.p.). We also acknowledge that settler colonialism is entangled with related enduring yet changing structures such as capitalism and the nation state.

Turning to the land itself, anthropologists, geographers, and environmental historians have long acknowledged that landscape is not an inert backdrop for human action, but rather in part a construct of cultural and historical processes (Basso 1996; Hirsch and O'Hanlon 1995; Thornton 2008; Tilley 1994). The concept of home has comparably been theorized in anthropology as shaped by practice, phenomenological engagements, memory, senses of belonging, and identity (see Ingold 2000; Jackson 1995; Massey 1994). Home and domestic relations have been extended to the non-human in the context of northern sentient landscapes by David Anderson and his Arctic Domus research group, who understand landscape as tying different species together in relationships, signified by the term *domus* (Anderson et al. 2017, 401). Making a home with the land and with other species is of critical interest to many contributors to this volume.

Margaret Rodman describes places as polysemic, "politicized, culturally relative, historically specific, local and multiple constructions" (1992, 641). Landscapes are thus not simply ethnographic settings or locales in which actors are "incarcerated" (Appadurai 1988 in Rodman 1992, 652). They are spatially and temporally dynamic, requiring reflexivity on the part of those attempting anthropological representations, as well as attention to dimensions of power in the discursive and material performances of place making. In a sentient and storied landscape, stories, of course, hold power (Cruikshank 1998; Johnson 2010; King 2003; McLeod 2007; Palmer 2005). How then to represent such a place?

While most of us are anthropologists, some of us also have interdisciplinary degrees or are moored in other disciplinary traditions altogether. We use our different backgrounds to illuminate the problems of oil sands and home from different angles and within different periods of the (long) twentieth century (as well as the future) to give as comprehensive a picture as possible. Furthermore, we are speaking of three distinct oil sands deposits over a (mostly) boreal forest region larger than many nation-states, with several ecological transitions, complex demographic characteristics, and distinctive land use patterns, as well as differing extractive technologies. Thus, we encourage readers to take each chapter of this volume together to glean a clearer, if always incomplete, understanding of northern Alberta's oil sands industry and those living with it. This volume, then, is a study of a given locale, with global import, as a "patchwork" (Tsing 2005, xi). Anna Tsing uses this term to show how a given place can hold multiple meanings and encapsulate entanglements (see also Dussart and Poirier 2017) of social, political, and environmental change. The crossovers among our chapters—either in terms of field site, topic, or argument—demonstrate how seemingly disparate aspects of northern Alberta are in fact deeply entangled (see Lee-Jones, this volume). Furthermore, such ethnographic "fragments" (Tsing 2005, 271) disrupt the image of northern Alberta as a monolithic site of extraction, instead showing how the region is narrated and engaged with in multiple ways.

Currently, there is a paucity of scholarly literature on the lived experiences of Indigenous Peoples in the context of oil sands extraction (Joly and Westman 2017). This lack of social scientific literature stemming from work with Indigenous Peoples in the region is dangerous because it has perpetuated the erasure of Indigenous stories, presence, and territorialities (Westman 2006, 2013). In contrast, this volume is an attempt to document the persistence and presence of Indigenous Peoples in a region of extreme extraction. While the authors of the main chapters do not identify as Indigenous, the contributors to this volume aim to engage substantially with Indigenous thought, employing community-engaged methodologies here and/or in other contexts. With the exception of Spady and to some extent Lee-Jones, who examine Euro-Canadians' attempts at making home in extractive zones, the chapters primarily examine how Indigenous Peoples are impacted by settler colonial and capitalist processes of extraction in their homelands, but also how Indigenous communities are working to renew their connections to places on the landscape.

In 2015, Canada's Truth and Reconciliation Commission (TRC) issued a report stating that access to territory has been a primary motivation for the attempted cultural genocide of Indigenous Peoples in Canada. "The Canadian government pursued this policy of cultural genocide because it wished to divest itself of its legal and financial obligations to Aboriginal people and gain control over their land and resources" (TRC 2015, 2). Wolfe affirms that the "primary motive for [genocide] is not race (or religion, ethnicity, grade of civilization, etc.) but access to territory" (2006, 388). While this access to territory is often described as a requirement for *settlement*, we also suggest that settler colonial processes of acquiring territory are simultaneously processes of preparing the land for *extraction*.

Territory, of course, could also be read as "resources" (Voyles 2015, 25). Nonetheless, extractive landscapes in the North can be said to exemplify a unique kind of colonialism, one in which the settler does not always wish to stay (though many do), but rather mainly to extract wealth. This "mineral-led colonialism" (Sandlos and Keeling 2015, 18) can be characterized by transience and impermanence (see Wanvik, this volume). Longley's chapter demonstrates that the state is primarily interested in ensuring access to lucrative resources, such as the bitumen beneath trapline trails. But, as Spady and Lee-Jones show, many settlers *do* make or hope to make a long-term, intergenerational home in extractive spaces of northern Alberta—in both urban and rural settings. We suggest that extractivism in northern Alberta represents part of the broader agenda of settler colonialism: acquiring territory, eliminating (or containing) Indigenous presence, and controlling land and resources. In short, extreme extraction can be a product of and an agent of these settler colonial relations (cf. Sandlos and Keeling 2015, 8), which are also enmeshed in the dynamics of capitalism.

Resources are central to any articulation of territoriality within settler colonialism (Voyles 2015, 25). In her study of Diné responses to uranium mining in the United States, Traci Voyles argues that "settler colonialism is so deeply about resources that environmental injustices, whether on Native lands or lands of other others, must always be viewed through the lens of settler colonialism" (2015, 23). Extractive industries are thus a part of a larger settler colonial project that perpetuates loss of land and unequal power relations. And just as the project of settler colonialism is deeply about the land, decolonization also requires environmental justice (Ageyman et al. 2009; Black et al. 2014). As contributors to this volume show, Indigenous communities actively and creatively respond to, accommodate, resist, or refuse settler colonial forces that seek to disrupt their relations to the land.

Impacts to Indigenous and non-Indigenous communities who live in the oil sands region include contamination of land, air, and water as well as socio-economic changes. Indigenous Peoples in particular are faced with a difficult task of preserving their remaining land base, and the relationships integral to that sentient landscape, while also benefitting in some way from the extraction already occurring or proposed in their homelands.

As change in the non-human environment is central to analyses of settler colonial force and extraction, questions of multiple ontologies are also crucial to this volume. We understand ontologies as "ways of being and acting in the world of cultural and social subjects and agents, which are shaped by the subject's knowledge of what the world is and how it is constituted" (Dussart and Poirier 2017, 8). We do not seek to describe diverse worlds that are self-contained and separate, but rather seek to show how ontological constructions of extractive spaces can be both multiple and deeply entangled.

Another goal of this volume is to illuminate the power relations that tend to erase local knowledges and understandings of relationships to non-human beings. As multiple geographies overlap, scientific ways of knowing a given landscape predominate, rendering local knowledge less visible. Local knowledge, as Julie Cruikshank points out, is often tacit knowledge, embodied in life experiences, and reproduced through everyday behaviour and speech (2005, 9). For example, the disregard of this knowledge in environmental and social impact assessments for proposed oil sands projects (Westman 2013) shows the deep power imbalance that persists in Canada between Indigenous Peoples and Euro-Canadians. However, as Lee-Jones and Gross, among others, show herein, the results (pollution and other injuries) impact both Indigenous and non-Indigenous inhabitants of the region (and, we would add, beyond).

Scholars in Indigenous studies, anthropology, and geography have renewed interest in the disruption and persistence of Indigenous thought and ways of relating to the environment in the face of settler colonialism (Blaser 2013; Carroll 2015; de la Cadena 2015; Kohn 2013; Todd 2014, 2016). We intervene in recent circumpolar studies literature that calls for continued ethnographic focus on a storied North and on sentient landscapes of relations between human and non-human beings (Anderson 2017; Anderson et al. 2017). This is why some of us take an ecocentric approach to the study of the oil sands—shifting focus away from a socio-ecological study of bitumen extraction processes, to look at other entities (bears, bison, berries, fire, water, and oil itself, alone or as part of an assemblage) and how they relate to extractive processes and politics.

While most of us examine the present, some chapters focus on the past or future. Drawing through diverse approaches on fieldwork experiences in communities affected by the oil sands industry in the boreal forests of Alberta, our common concern is to provide a series of case studies that illuminate the complexities inherent in the entanglements of race, class, Indigeneity, gender, and ontological concerns in a regional context characterized by extreme extraction. Our contributors are among the handful of environmental social scientists currently conducting long-term research in the region. Composed mainly of early career scholars who recently have conducted fieldwork, our contributors draw from years working in the region and offer innovative examples informed by new scholarly perspectives. The majority of us have (as of late 2018) completed a doctorate. Several contributors (Baker, Joly, Longley, McCormack, Westman, Wheatley) have worked as consultants or researchers in the region's burgeoning applied social science industry. Some of us (Baker, McCormack, Spady, Todd, Westman) are from Alberta and thus bring to the project a long-term familiarity with the province and its energy industry.

While the authors of the main chapters do not identify as Indigenous and do not claim here to speak for any Indigenous community, we are grateful to Zoe Todd, a Métis scholar, for agreeing to contribute the foreword. Todd's deep connections to Alberta are evident in her highly personal contribution, which puts the accent on entanglements between people and land, evoking the complex and changing relations between Indigenous people, settlers, and non-humans in a particular place. She thus sets the stage for our examinations of dwelling in the oil sands region.

Longley's chapter examines the historical legal processes that transformed the Athabasca region from a primarily Indigenous space into a resource extraction zone. Focusing on the treaty land entitlement claim of the Mikisew Cree First Nation, Longley argues that state ownership of land and mineral rights dispossessed Indigenous Peoples, disrupted Indigenous landscapes, and redefined the region as an industrial space. Indigenous communities have contested Crown ownership of bitumen-rich land in the Athabasca with land claims and interventions in regulatory processes.

Lee-Jones brings readers to the Peace River Country, an often-overlooked region in analyses of oil sands extraction. Lee-Jones shows the contradictory ways the Peace Country is oriented towards oil sands extraction. He compares two days of fieldwork: one spent with Indigenous council members documenting unmarked burial grounds and one spent with a farmer living adjacent to the oil patch. The burden of development's deleterious consequences can move across racial boundaries, impacting both Indigenous and farming communities.

Returning to Fort McMurray in the Athabasca region, Spady analyses the perceptions of the oil industry among people employed by that industry in her home city. This chapter examines how such workers make sense of their industry. Drawing on the contributions of critical whiteness scholars, Spady considers how whiteness and particular forms of Canadian nationalism are at play in this region, given that oil has become crucial to not only the Canadian economy but also Canadian imaginaries.

Based on ethnographic research in the Lac La Biche region (and addressing both Cold Lake and Athabasca oil sands deposits), Gross focuses on accidents as illuminating features of life in the region. She examines work-related accidents that harm the human body, ongoing industrial pollution as a structural "accident," and infrastructure failure events such as oil spills. Gross argues that these three types of accidents must be seen in a close connection to settler colonialism and attitudes about the resource frontier. She documents accidental and purposeful acts of destruction.

While keeping the focus south of Fort McMurray, Wanvik explores the micro-politics of Métis–municipal government relations in the Athabasca region. By considering the notion of "disaster politics" in conjunction with pragmatism and assemblage theory, Wanvik explores the effectiveness of Métis advocacy strategies. Through the case study of the catastrophic 2016 wildfire near Fort McMurray and the deferral of infrastructure investment in a multipurpose community complex in Conklin, Alberta, Wanvik portrays the strategic but elusive benefits of the industry for Indigenous communities.

Remaining somewhat focused on wildfire, Baker relies on Cree indicators for detecting disturbances resulting from industrial development of the Athabasca oil sands deposit. Crees tend to their relationships with the sentient landscape through respectful speech and behaviour, including harvesting, cultivating, and burning practices. Bears and berries gift themselves with agency and decide whether or not humans can encounter, harvest, and share their substance. Baker discusses how non-humans experience and respond to the disturbance in cycles of ecology, relations, respect, reciprocity, and reincarnation due to oil sands extraction.

Joly examines Métis–bison relationships in the Athabasca region. Oil sands impact mitigation often involves plans to create or reclaim bison habitat on a transformed landscape, but such reclaimed habitats reflect a disruption of ongoing relationships to bison. Drawing on Métis scholarship and regional ethnography, Joly traces historic and contemporary human–bison relations to show the imposition of settler-industrial management practices and the ongoing work of Métis people to maintain relationships with bison into the future.

Besides providing studies from all three oil sands zones of industrial pollution in existing water bodies and tailings disposal systems, Wheatley and Westman consider future hydrological transformations, specifically new lakes proposed as part of the reclamation of industrial sites. By looking at current and future lakes in northeastern Alberta, they explore how industry proposals reshape regional landscapes from sentient ecologies, where Indigenous people hunt and forage, into a cyborg watershed. Lakes provide a window onto a future characterized by altered relations between humans and non-humans in a transformed Anthropocene nature.

McCormack has been conducting research in northern Alberta for decades. She graciously provided comments and suggestions throughout this process. In her conclusion, she focuses on the trajectory of applied and community-engaged research in the oil sands region and our book's place in that literature. Her concluding chapter both historicizes our topics and renders clear the relevance of our work for contemporary debates in Alberta and beyond. She highlights the importance of community-based scholarly research in the oil sands, in the context where much of the research takes the form of grey literature, and calls for scholars to address their findings to decision makers.

The chapters in this volume describe the discursive and material elements of extraction, settler colonial histories, and Indigenous survival and renewal. Themes of gender, race, and violence prevalent in the critical settler colonial literature are captured herein. In the oil sands region, extractive forces have been described as examples of environmental racism (Joly and Westman 2017), racial extractivism (Preston 2017), and neoliberal or capitalist ideology (Shrivastava and Stefanick 2015; Slowey 2008; Taylor and Friedel 2011). Each contributor here develops his or her case studies in slightly different ways, using these theoretical framings and others, including those taught to them by their Indigenous interlocutors. We advocate the importance of multiple representations to challenge and critique settler colonial erasure of stories or the attempted silencing of particular land-based relationships.

## Notes

1 In this volume, contributors predominantly follow standard Canadian English usage in referring to bitumen deposits as oil sands. *Oil sands* is a widely used and analytically neutral term, in contrast with the now more pejorative (though historically normative) *tar sands* usage. We use *tar sands* and other terms for bitumen mainly when quoting other sources.

2 Portions of the Cold Lake and Athabasca deposits lie in Saskatchewan, although the latter deposit is not currently being extracted within that province.

## References

Adkin, Laurie. 2016a. "Alberta's Neoliberal Environment." In *First World Petro-Politics: The Political Ecology and Governance of Alberta*, edited by Laurie E. Adkin, 78–113. Toronto: University of Toronto Press.

Adkin, Laurie, ed. 2016b. *First World Petro-Politics: The Political Ecology and Governance of Alberta*. Toronto: University of Toronto Press.

Agyeman, Julian, Peter Cole, Randolph Haluza-DeLay, and Pat O'Riley. 2009. *Speaking for Ourselves: Environmental Justice in Canada*. Vancouver: UBC Press.

Alberta Energy. 2018a "Facts and Statistics." https://www.energy.alberta.ca/OS/AOS/Pages/FAS.aspx (accessed August 30, 2018).

Alberta Energy. 2018b. "Oil Sands." https://www.energy.alberta.ca/OS/Pages/default.aspx (accessed August 30, 2018).

Anderson, David G. 2017. "Humans and Animals in Northern Regions." *Annual Review of Anthropology* 46 (1): 133–49. https://doi.org/10.1146/annurev-anthro-102116-041556.

Anderson, David G., Jan Peter Laurens Loovers, Sara Asu Schroer, and Robert P. Wishart. 2017. "Architectures of Domestication: On Emplacing Human-animal Relations in the North." *Journal of the Royal Anthropological Institute* 23 (2): 398–416. https://doi.org/10.1111/1467-9655.12613_1.

Appadurai, Arjun. 1988. *The Social Life of Things: Commodities in Cultural Perspective*. Cambridge: Cambridge University Press.

Asch, Michael. 2014. *On Being Here to Stay: Treaties and Aboriginal Rights in Canada*. Toronto: University of Toronto Press.

Asselin, Gabriel. 2014. "Next Stop, Cold Lake: Patterns of Mobility, Military Brats and Oil-Patch Kids." *Anthropologica* 56 (2): 423–34.

Baker, Janelle Marie, and Clinton N. Westman. 2018. "Extracting Knowledge: Social Science, Environmental Impact Assessment, and Indigenous Consultation in the Oil Sands of Alberta, Canada." *The Extractive Industries and Society* 5 (1): 144–53.

Barnetson, Bob, and Jason Foster. 2012. "Bloody Lucky: The Careless Worker Myth in Alberta, Canada." *International Journal of Occupational and Environmental Health* 18 (2): 135–46.

Basso, Keith. 1996. *Wisdom Sits in Places: Landscape and Language among the Western Apache*. Albuquerque, NM: University of New Mexico Press.

Behrends, Andrea, Stephen P. Reyna, and Gunther Schlee, eds. 2011. *Crude Domination: An Anthropology of Oil*. Oxford: Berghahn Books.

Black, Toban, Stephen D'Arcy, Tony Weis, and Joshua Kahn Russell. 2014. *A Line in the Tar Sands: Struggles for Environmental Justice*. Toronto: Between The Lines.

Blaser, Mario. 2013. "Ontological Conflicts and the Stories of Peoples in Spite of Europe: Toward a Conversation on Political Ontology." *Current Anthropology* 54 (5): 547–68. https://doi.org/10.1086/672270.

Bowness, Evan, and Mark Hudson. 2014. "Sand in the Cogs? Power and Public Participation in the Alberta Tar Sands." *Environmental Politics* 23 (1): 59–76.

Bridge, Gavin. 2001. "Resource Triumphalism: Postindustrial Narratives of Primary Commodity Production." *Environment and Planning A* 33: 2149–73.

Cardinal, Harold. 1969. *The Unjust Society: The Tragedy of Canada's Indians*. Edmonton, AB: M.G. Hurtig.

Carroll, Clint. 2015. *Roots of Our Renewal: Ethnobotany and Cherokee Environmental Governance*. Minneapolis, MN: University of Minnesota Press.

Coates, Ken S., and Bill Morrison. 1992. *The Forgotten North: A History of Canada's Provincial Norths*. Toronto: James Lorimer & Company.

Cruikshank, Julie. 1998. *The Social Life of Stories: Narrative and Knowledge in the Yukon Territory*. Lincoln, NE: University of Nebraska Press.

Cruikshank, Julie. 2005. *Do Glaciers Listen? Local Knowledge, Colonial Encounters, and Social Imagination*. Vancouver and Toronto: University of British Columbia Press and University of Washington Press.

De la Cadena, Marisol. 2015. *Earth Beings: Ecologies of Practice across Andean Worlds*. Durham: Duke University Press.

Dorow, Sara, and Sara O'Shaughnessy. 2013. "Fort McMurray, Wood Buffalo, and the Oil/Tar Sands: Revisiting the Sociology of 'Community'." *Canadian Journal of Sociology / Cahiers Canadiens de Sociologie* 38 (2): 121–40.

Dussart, Françoise, and Sylvie Poirier, eds. 2017. *Entangled Territorialities: Negotiating Indigenous Lands in Canada and Australia*. Toronto: University of Toronto Press.

Foster, Jason, and Bob Barnetson. 2015. "Exporting Oil, Importing Labour and Weakening Democracy: The Use of Foreign Migrant Workers in Alberta." In *Alberta Oil and the Decline of Democracy in Canada*, edited by Meenal Shrivastava and Lorna Stefanick, 249–73. Edmonton, AB: Athabasca University Press.

Foster, Jason, and Alison Taylor. 2013. "In the Shadows: Exploring the Notion of 'Community' for Temporary Foreign Workers in a Boom Town." *Canadian Journal of Sociology/Cahiers Canadiens de Sociologie* 38 (2): 167–90.

Ghostkeeper, Elmer. 2007. *Spirit Gifting: The Concept of Spiritual Exchange*. Raymond, AB: Writing on Stone Press.

Goddard, John. 1991. *The Last Stand of the Lubicon Cree*. Vancouver: Douglas & McIntyre.

Goeman, Mishuana R. 2017. "Ongoing Storms and Struggles. Gendered Violence and Resource Exploitation." In *Critically Sovereign: Indigenous Gender, Sexuality, and Feminist Studies*, edited by Joanne Barker, 99–126. Durham: Duke University Press.

Gordon, Jon. 2015. *Unsustainable Oil: Facts, Counterfacts and Fictions*. Edmonton, AB: University of Alberta Press.

Goulet, Jean-Guy. 1998. *Ways of Knowing: Experience, Knowledge, and Power among the Dene Tha*. Lincoln, NE: University of Nebraska Press.

Grouard, Émile. 2010. *The Beginning of Print Culture in Athabasca Country: A Facsimile Edition and Translation of a Prayer Book in Cree Syllabics, Prepared and Printed at Lac La Biche in 1883 with an Introduction by Patricia Demers*. Edmonton, AB: University of Alberta Press.

Hallowell, A.I. 1960. *Ojibwa Ontology, Behavior, and World View*. New York: Columbia University Press.

Haluza-DeLay, Randolph. 2014. "Assembling Consent in Alberta: Hegemony and the Tar Sands." In *A Line in the Tar Sands: Struggles for Environmental Justice*, edited by Stephen D'Arcy, Toban Black, Tony Weis, and Joshua Kahn Russell, 36–44. Toronto: Between the Lines.

Heller, Monica, Lindsay A. Bell, Michelle Daveluy, Mireille McLaughlin, and Hubert Noël. 2016. *Sustaining the Nation: The Making and Moving of Language and Nation*. Oxford: Oxford University Press.

Hirsch, Eric, and Michael O'Hanlon, eds. 1995. *The Anthropology of Landscape: Perspectives on Space and Place*. Oxford: Oxford University Press.

Ingold, Tim. 2000. *The Perception of the Environment: Essays on Livelihood, Dwelling, and Skill*. London/New York: Routledge.

Jackson, Michael D. 1995. *At Home in the World*. Durham: Duke University Press Books.

Jalbert, Kirk, Anna Willow, David Casagrande, and Stephanie Paladino. 2017. *ExtrACTION: Impacts, Engagements, and Alternative Futures*. London: Routledge.

Johnson, Leslie Main. 2010. *Trail of Story, Traveller's Path: Reflections on Ethnoecology and Landscape*. Edmonton, AB: Athabasca University Press.

Joly, Tara, and Clinton N. Westman. September 11, 2017. "Taking Research Off the Shelf: Synthesizing Existing Sources of Knowledge about Impacts, Benefits, and

Participatory or Consultative Processes around Extractive Industry in Northern Alberta." Final Report for the Social Sciences and Humanities Research Council of Canada Imagining Canada's Future Initiative, Knowledge Synthesis Grants: Aboriginal Peoples. https://artsandscience.usask.ca/profile/CWestman#/profile.

Kauanui, J. Kēhaulani. 2016. "'A Structure, Not an Event': Settler Colonialism and Enduring Indigeneity." *Lateral* 5 (1). https://doi.org/10.25158/L5.1.7.

King, Thomas. 2003. *The Truth about Stories: A Native Narrative*. Toronto: House of Anansi.

Kohn, Eduardo. 2013. *How Forests Think: Toward an Anthropology beyond the Human*. Berkeley, CA: University of California Press.

Leonard, David. 1995. *Delayed Frontier: The Peace River Country to 1909*. Calgary, AB: Detselig.

Levant, Ezra. 2010. *Ethical Oil: The Case for Canada's Oil Sands*. Toronto: McClelland and Stewart.

Lewis, Henry T. 1982. *A Time for Burning: Traditional Uses of Fire in the Western Canadian Boreal Forest*. Edmonton, AB: Boreal Institute for Northern Studies.

Li, Fabiana. 2015. *Unearthing Conflict: Corporate Mining, Activism, and Expertise in Peru*. Durham: Duke University Press.

MacPherson, C.B. 1962. *Democracy in Alberta: Social Credit and the Party System*. Toronto: University of Toronto Press.

Mair, Charles. 1999. *Through the Mackenzie Basin: An Account of the Signing of Treaty No. 8 and the Scrip Commission, 1899*. Edmonton, AB: University of Alberta Press.

Martindale, Julie. 2014. "Mobility and the Distribution of Beaver River Sandstone in Northeastern Alberta and Northwestern Saskatchewan." MA thesis, University of Saskatchewan.

Martin-Hill, Dawn. 2008. *The Lubicon Lake Nation: Indigenous Knowledge and Power*. Toronto: University of Toronto Press.

Massey, Doreen B. 1994. *Space, Place and Gender*. London: Polity Press.

McArthur, Neil, and Warren Cariou. 2009. *Land of Oil and Water: Aboriginal Voices on Life in the Oil Sands. 45 minutes*. Canada: Winnipeg Film Group.

McCormack, Patricia A. 2010. *Fort Chipewyan and the Shaping of Canadian History, 1788–1920s: "We like to be free in this country"*. Vancouver: University of British Columbia Press.

McCormack, Patricia A. 2016. "Doing Credible Cultural Assessment: Applied Social Science." *Environmental Practice* 18: 148–56.

McLeod, Neil. 2007. *Cree Narrative Memory: From Treaties to Contemporary Times*. Saskatoon, SK: Purich Publishing.

Morgensen, Scott Lauria. 2011. *Spaces between Us: Queer Settler Colonialism and Indigenous Decolonization*. Minneapolis, MN: University of Minnesota Press.

Nikiforuk, Andrew. 2010. *Tar Sands: Dirty Oil and the Future of a Continent*. Vancouver: Greystone Books.

Ominayak, Chief Bernard, with Kevin Thomas. 2009. "These are Lubicon Lands: A First Nation Forced to Step into the Regulatory Gap." In *Speaking for Ourselves: Environmental Justice in Canada*, edited by Julian Ageyman, Peter Cole, Randolph Haluza-DeLay, and Pat O'Riley, 111–22. Vancouver: University of British Columbia Press.

Palmer, Andie Diane. 2005. *Maps of Experience: The Anchoring of Land to Story in Secwepemc Discourse*. Toronto: University of Toronto Press.

Parlee, Brenda L. 2015. "Avoiding the Resource Curse: Indigenous Communities and Canada's Oil Sands." *World Development* 74: 425–36.

Payne, Michael, Donald Wetherell, and Catherine Cavanaugh, eds. 2006. *Alberta Formed –Alberta Transformed*, 2 vols. Edmonton, AB/Calgary: University of Alberta Press/University of Calgary Press.

Pratt, Larry, and Ian Urquhart. 1994. *The Last Great Forest: Japanese Multinationals and Alberta's Northern Forests*. Edmonton, AB: NeWest Press.

Preston, Jen. 2017. "Racial Extractivism and White Settler Colonialism: An Examination of the Canadian Tar Sands Mega-Projects." *Cultural Studies* 31: 1–23. https://doi.org/10.1080/09502386.2017.1303432.

Richards, John, and Larry Pratt. 1979. *Prairie Capitalism: Power and Influence in the New West*. Toronto: McClelland and Stewart.

Richardson, Mary, Joan Sherman, and Mike Gismondi. 1993. *Winning Back the Words: Confronting Experts in an Environmental Public Hearing*, 1st ed. Toronto: University of Toronto Press.

Rodman, Margaret C. 1992. "Empowering Place: Multilocality and Multivocality." *American Anthropologist* 94 (3): 640–56.

Rogers, Douglas. 2015. "Oil and Anthropology." *Annual Review of Anthropology* 44: 365–80.

Ronaghan, Brian M., ed. 2017. *Alberta's Lower Athabasca Basin: Archaeology and Palaeoenvironments*. Edmonton, AB: Athabasca University Press.

Rose, Deborah Bird. 1991. *Hidden Histories: Black Stories from Victoria River Downs*. Canberra: Aboriginal Studies Press.

Sandlos, John, and Arn Keeling, eds. 2015. *Mining and Communities in Northern Canada: History, Politics, and Memory*. Calgary, AB: University of Calgary Press.

Schindler, David. 2010. "Tar Sands Need Solid Science." *Nature* 468 (November 25): 499–501.

Shrivastava, Meenal, and Lorna Stefanick (eds.). 2015. *Alberta Oil and the Decline of Democracy in Canada*. Edmonton, AB: Athabasca University Press.

Simpson, Audra. 2014. *Mohawk Interruptus: Political Life across the Borders of Settler States*. Durham: Duke University Press.

———. 2016. "The State is a Man; Theresa Spence, Loretta Saunders and the Gender of Settler Sovereignty." *Theory & Event* 19 (4): 1–16. https://muse.jhu.edu/article/633280.

Slowey, Gabrielle. 2008. *Navigating Neoliberalism: Self-Determination and the Mikisew Cree First Nation*. Vancouver: University of British Columbia Press.

Smith, James G.E. 1981. "Western Woods Cree." In *Handbook of North American Indians*, vol. 6, Subarctic, edited by June Helm, 256–70. Washington, DC: Smithsonian.

Smith, James G.E. 1987. "The Western Woods Cree: Anthropological Myth and Historical Reality." *American Ethnologist* 14 (3): 434–48.

Steward, Gillian. 2017. *Betting on Bitumen: Alberta's Energy Policies from Lougheed to Klein*. Edmonton, AB: Parkland Institute and Canadian Centre for Policy Alternatives. https://www.parklandinstitute.ca/betting_on_bitumen.

Strauss, Sarah, Stephanie Rupp, and Thomas Love. 2013. *Cultures of Energy: Power, Practices, Technologies*. Walnut Creek, CA: Left Coast Press.

Taylor, Alison, and Tracy Friedel. 2011. "Enduring Neoliberalism in Alberta's Oil Sands: The Troubling Effects of Private-Public Partnerships for First Nation and Metis Communities." *Citizenship Studies* 15 (6–7): 815–35.

Thornton, Thomas F. 2008. *Being and Place among the Tlingit*. Seattle, WA: University of Washington Press.

Tilley, Christopher. 1994. *A Phenomenology of Landscape: Places, Paths and Monuments*, 1st ed. Oxford: Bloomsbury Academic.

Todd, Zoe. 2014. "Fish Pluralities: Human-Animal Relations and Sites of Engagement in Paulatuuq, Arctic Canada." *Études/Inuit/Studies* 38 (1–2): 217–38. https://doi.org/10.7202/1028861ar.

Todd, Zoe. 2016. "From a Fishy Place: Examining Canadian State Law Applied in the Daniels Decision from the Perspective of Métis Legal Orders." *TOPIA: Canadian Journal of Cultural Studies* 36 (Fall): 43–57. http://topia.journals.yorku.ca/index.php/topia/article/view/40398.

Truth and Reconciliation Commission of Canada (TRC). 2015. "Honouring the Truth, Reconciling for the Future: Summary of the Final Report of the Truth and Reconciliation Commission of Canada." http://www.trc.ca/websites/trcinstitution/File/2015/Findings/Exec_Summary_2015_05_31_web_o.pdf.

Tsing, Anna Lowenhaupt. 2005. *Friction: An Ethnography of Global Connection*. Princeton, NJ: Princeton University Press.

Urquhart, Ian. 2018. *Costly Fix: Power, Politics, and Nature in the Tar Sands*. Toronto: University of Toronto Press.

Vandersteene, Roger. 1960. *Wabasca: Dix ans de vie indienne*. Gemmenich, Belgium: Editions O.M.I.

Voyles, Traci Brynne. 2015. *Wastelanding: Legacies of Uranium Mining in Navajo Country*. Minneapolis, MN: University of Minnesota Press.

Westman, Clinton N. 2006. "Assessing the Impacts of Oilsands Development on Indigenous Peoples in Alberta, Canada." *Indigenous Affairs* 2 (3): 30–39.

Westman, Clinton N. 2013. "Social Impact Assessment and the Anthropology of the Future in Canada's Tar Sands." *Human Organization* 72 (2): 111–20.

Wetherell, Donald Grant, and Irene Kmet. 2000. *Alberta's North: A History, 1890 to 1950*. Edmonton, AB: University of Alberta Press.

Wheatley, Katherine. 2018. "Oil Sands Energy Governance: An Ethnography on Negotiating Development and Indigenous Rights in Northern Alberta." MA thesis, University of Saskatchewan.

Wilson, Sheena, Adam Carlson, and Imre Szeman, eds. 2017. *Petrocultures: Oil, Politics, Culture*. Montreal/Kingston: McGill-Queen's University Press.

Wolfe, Patrick. 2006. "Settler Colonialism and the Elimination of the Native." *Journal of Genocide Research* 8 (4): 387–409. https://doi.org/10.1080/14623520601056240.

Zalik, Anna. 2016. "'Duty to Consult' or 'License to Operate'? Corporate Social Practice and Industrial Conflict in the Alberta Tar Sands and the Nigerian Niger Delta." In *First World Petro-Politics: The Political Ecology and Governance of Alberta*, edited by Laurie E. Adkin, 356–84. Toronto: University of Toronto Press.

# 1 Uncertain Sovereignty

## Treaty 8, Bitumen, and Land Claims in the Athabasca Oil Sands Region

*Hereward Longley*

### Introduction

In the mid-1970s the Fort Chipewyan Cree Band sought to fulfill part of its Treaty Land Entitlement (TLE) claim by selecting bitumen-rich lands within the Athabasca oil sands region (Crown-Indigenous Relations and Northern Affairs Canada 2015).[1] On January 30, 1975, Alberta's minister of federal and intergovernmental affairs, Don Getty, wrote to cabinet proposing three approaches the government could take: co-operation, refusal, or conditional co-operation. Alberta ultimately adopted conditional co-operation: the province would agree to transfer land to settle the outstanding claim "on the condition that the Band agrees not to claim any or certain portions of the Alberta Oil Sands area when selecting the remainder of its land entitlement."[2] Getty wrote that imposing this condition allowed the province to settle the claim, while protecting provincial ownership of the Athabasca bitumen deposits and ensuring the area remained under provincial control. He acknowledged that the Fort Chipewyan Cree claimants would not be happy with the response:

> Traditionally, and in the popular image, Indians[3] have been relegated to the worst and least economically productive areas. This condition would serve to perpetuate this situation by depriving the Indian Band of its right to choose the best lands available. The Band has been choosing land at least partially on an economic basis, and this condition would deny it access to the most economically advantageous property in the Treaty area.[4]

For the Alberta government, land claims posed an unacceptable threat to its bitumen deposits. By the mid-1970s, industry and government efforts to build the oil sands industry, combined with global energy and economic crises, Indigenous rights, land claims, and strained federal–provincial relations became interconnected points of conflict as the Cree Band of Fort Chipewyan (today the Mikisew Cree First Nation, MCFN) sought bitumen-rich lands to settle its outstanding TLE claim.

This chapter asks, through what processes did Indigenous space in the Athabasca region become the Province of Alberta and a place where bitumen could be extracted? What role did bitumen, and the potential for its extraction, play in Treaty 8 and land claims in the Athabasca region? I trace the gradual increase in legal colonial control through several major events, including the sale of Rupert's Land and the North-West Territories to the new Dominion of Canada in 1870, Treaty 8 in 1899, a treaty through which Canada claimed over five hundred thousand square kilometres of the North-West Territories; the creation of the Province of Alberta in 1905; the Natural Resources Transfer Agreement (NRTA) in 1930, which transferred ownership of Crown lands to Alberta as implemented by federal and provincial natural resources transfer acts; and the settlement of TLE claims through the late twentieth century, which some First Nations used to claim reserve lands. With the Mikisew Cree TLE claim as a case study, I show how TLE claims became one avenue through which First Nations have challenged industrial colonization in the oil sands region. From there, I show how the political economy of oil sands influenced the TLE claim process in the 1970s, as the Government of Alberta refused to grant mineral rights or oil sands deposits to the MCFN to settle its TLE claim (Price 1993).[5] I argue that Canadian extensions of sovereignty over the Athabasca region were a fragmented and incomplete process that laid the foundations for a range of dispossessions of Indigenous lands through the development of the oil sands industry, and remain contested by Indigenous Peoples.

In the twentieth century, northern Canada became the site of widespread industrial colonization through hard-rock mining, commercial fishing, hydroelectric dam projects, and hydrocarbon extraction, which affected the land use of Indigenous Peoples (Carlson 2008; Desbiens 2013; Keeling and Sandlos 2015; Loo 2007; Peyton 2017; Piper 2009). The 1970s were a key point of emergence for land claims and energy conflicts. As communities faced industrial projects in their traditional territories, they worked to leverage the political process in various ways to advance the settlement of their land claims and to protect their societies, cultures, and ways of life. Literature examining land claims and industrial development conflicts has focused on comprehensive claims, such as the 1975 James Bay and Northern Quebec Agreement, which emerged from the conflict over the James Bay hydroelectric project, and the Inuvialuit and Dene agreements in the Northwest Territories, which followed Justice Thomas Berger's inquiry into the proposed Mackenzie Valley Pipeline (Carlson 2004; Morantz 2002; Page 1986; Sabin 1995). Less has been written about the connections between energy development conflicts and specific claims such as the TLE claims in the Treaty 8 region (but see Westman 2010, 2017).

Northern Alberta is significant as a provincial north—an internal colony of the province, a space politically and economically controlled for resource extraction by institutions in urban centres, that remains an Indigenous homeland (see Lee-Jones, this volume) (Coates and Morrison 1992; Mochoruk 2004; Wetherell and Kmet 2000).[6] Since Treaty 8 claimed the region as Crown land, and since the province has controlled the Athabasca bitumen deposits since 1930, the construction of the oil sands industry did not involve the federal government to the same extent as in areas where extraction or infrastructure projects crossed provincial, territorial, or international borders, or where the Crown had not signed treaties with Indigenous Peoples. Initially, the oil sands industry was much smaller and did not attract the same attention as other megaproject such as the James Bay Project, yet it was contested by Indigenous Peoples from the 1970s forward (Longley 2015).

This chapter applies historical geographer Cole Harris's position that to understand colonial power we must explain colonialism's geographic dispossession (2004, 165). Indigenous Peoples have inhabited northern Alberta for thousands of years, travelling by land and by water, creating a web of trails and cultural sites that both inform and embody their histories and relationships with the land (McCormack 1984, 2010, 2017). For Indigenous Peoples, landscapes are more than just biophysical environments from which they collect resources—landscapes embody culture, history, and identity mapped with toponyms (Eades 2015, 54). Imperial maps overlaid Indigenous geography with the territorial ambitions of the colonizing power (Edney 1996; Harley 2001; Weaver 2003). The accounts of early explorers travelling through the Athabasca River Valley described abundant bitumen and the potential for oil development, which played a role in motivating the Dominion government to sign a treaty with the region's Indigenous Peoples. The federal government reserved the richest deposits of bitumen from other land uses for the Crown and enveloped the region with Canadian law before the oil sands industry emerged as an economically viable industry (Gismondi and Davidson 2012; Longley 2016). While colonial maps presented the region as a mostly unoccupied space, the land remained blanketed with Indigenous land use and cultural geography (Joly et al. 2018). The Hudson's Bay Company's (HBC) claims to northwestern Canada, followed by the purchase of these lands by Canada and Canada's later program of treaties, extended formal Canadian sovereignty over Indigenous territories with a framework of rights and values that obfuscated Indigenous land rights. However, as historian Lauren Benton argues in her history of law and the geography of European empires, the imperial extension of sovereignty was never a clean and linear process; rather, it was messy, "contingent, and stubbornly incomplete" (Benton 2010, 4). In Canada the treaty-making process left territorial claims unsettled, economic benefits unpaid, and competing settler and Indigenous spatial conceptions of the Athabasca region intact. Treaty 8 did not at once change the lives of Indigenous Peoples or the physical space of the Athabasca region. Rather, it created a new geography of possibility, in which outsiders could enact new forms of industrial colonization for years to come.

## Extending Sovereignty

The foundations of Alberta's sovereignty in the Athabasca region are rooted in the gradual territorial expansion of Canada built on the lands that for two centuries fell within the jurisdiction of the HBC. In 1670 King Charles II gave the HBC a Royal Charter, which granted the company exclusive trading privileges, proprietary rights, and limited governance over Rupert's Land—the Hudson Bay watershed. The validity of the Royal Charter, the extent of the HBC's jurisdiction, and the geographical range of Rupert's Land are the subject of ongoing debate (Cavanagh 2011; McNeil 1999; Tough 1992). Following the 1821 merger between the HBC and its main rival, the North West Company, the HBC obtained a new trading licence for the lands to the north and west of Rupert's Land, which came to be known as the North-Western Territory.[7] Upon the expiry of the HBC licence in 1859, the British Parliament passed an act that named the North-West Territories and made provisions for regulating trade and administering criminal justice in "the *Indian* Territories" (McNeil 1982, 4).[8] Following Canada's 1867 confederation, in 1869 the HBC surrendered its rights and authority over Rupert's Land and the North-Western Territory to the Dominion government for £300,000 and other substantial benefits.[9] In June 1870 the Dominion government admitted Rupert's Land and the North-Western Territory into Canada with the Rupert's Land and North-Western Territory Order.[10] Term 14 of the Rupert's Land Order obliged the Canadian government to settle all Indigenous land claims (Tough 1992, 245). In 1875 the Dominion government passed the North-West Territories Act, creating the North-West Territories.[11] In 1882 the Dominion created four districts within the North-West Territories, including the two that came to comprise present-day Alberta: the District of Alberta, which formerly lay in Rupert's Land, and the District of Athabasca, which formerly lay in the North-Western Territory (Zaslow 1971, 72).

## Treaty 8

Treaty 8, signed in 1899, covered lands that became northern Alberta, northeastern British Columbia, northwestern Saskatchewan, and parts of the southern Northwest Territories. Indigenous Peoples had sought a treaty since the 1870s, but the Dominion government was reluctant to take on the expense and responsibility for a northern treaty before it desired the land for agricultural settlement, forestry, and mineral resource extraction (Madill 1986, 6). From the 1880s forward, the Government of Canada gained extensive knowledge of the potential mineral wealth of the Peace, Athabasca, and Mackenzie districts (Daniels 1979, 62). One of these resources was petroleum. The Geological and Natural History Survey of Canada reported that tar oozed from the banks of the Athabasca River as oil floated on the river surface (Bell 1884, 22). In 1891 Robert McConnell reported that "the Devonian rocks throughout the Mackenzie Valley are everywhere more or less petroliferous and over large areas afford promising indications of the presence of oil in workable quantities" (1891, 31). The news of such reserves of oil changed southern imaginings of northwestern Canada. A Senate Committee reported "the existence in the Athabasca and Mackenzie Valleys of the most extensive petroleum field in America, if not the World." The report envisioned a future importance for petroleum: "The uses of petroleum and consequently the demand for it by all Nations are increasing at such a rapid ratio, that it is probable that this great petroleum field will assume an enormous value in the near future and will rank among the chief assets comprised in the Crown Domain of the Dominions."[12] A Privy Council Report from 1891 stated that the expense and obligation of a treaty began to look minimal when compared to the mineral wealth of the region. The extraction of petroleum in the Athabasca and Mackenzie districts would "add materially to the public wealth, and...appear to render it advisable that a treaty or treaties should be made with the Indians who claim those regions as their hunting grounds, with a view to the extinguishment of the Indian title in such portions of the same."[13] Once the Geological Survey had documented the extent of mineral deposits in northwestern Canada, Canada planned Treaty 8 in the early 1890s, but did not pursue its signing until the discovery of gold in the Klondike region of the Yukon (Daniels 1979, 66).

Treaty Commissioners David Laird, J.H. Ross, and J.A.J. McKenna negotiated and signed Treaty 8 on June 20–21, 1899, at Lesser Slave Lake with Indigenous Peoples. After the signing at Lesser Slave Lake, the commissioners travelled throughout the region, gaining adhesions at various places, including at Fort McMurray and Fort Chipewyan (Laird, Ross, and McKenna 1899). The travelling commissioners could not uniformly cover the region. The commissioners travelled in a great hurry, were often late for meetings, and did not visit many important locations in the treaty area. The commissioners described mineral potential in the Athabasca region: "The country along the Athabasca River is well wooded and there are miles of tar-saturated banks. But as far as our restricted view of the Lake Athabasca and Slave River country enabled us to judge, its wealth, apart from possible mineral development, consists exclusively in its fisheries and furs" (Laird, Ross, and McKenna 1899, n.p.). This early remark highlights the later distinction between the perceived value of bitumen-bearing lands relative to the other lands within Mikisew Cree territory.

Although maps of Treaty 8 (Figure 1.1) and Crown interpretations of the Treaty suggest that it was a uniform surrender of a neatly defined territory, the journey of the commissioners was a variegated extension of sovereignty (Benton 2010, 2). The Treaty 8 map shows the region as neatly bounded by a red line encircling the District of Athabasca, extending from the District of Alberta through northern British Columbia and into the Northwest Territories along the southern shore of Great Slave Lake. However, the commissioners only travelled along major waterways, stopping for brief periods at certain points. Their journey was more a patchwork held together with threads than a blanket evenly covering the territory.

Treaty 8 resembled earlier treaties, with some changes that responded to local circumstances (Madill 1986, 37). In exchange for ceding title, rights, and privileges over the land to the Government of Canada, the treaty provided one square mile of land per family (128 acres per person) of reserve land or 160 acres of land per person who chose lands "in severalty" (which were to be neither formal reserves nor fee simple lands), as well as other benefits that included

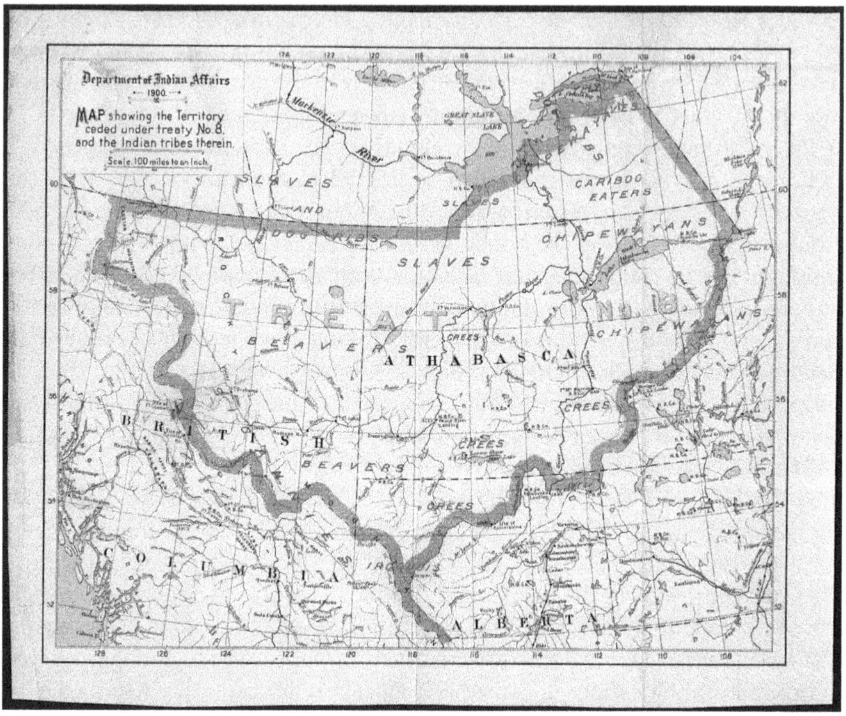


*Figure 1.1* Department of Indian Affairs, "Map showing the territory ceded under Treaty No. 8, and the Indian tribes therein," 1900, RG10M 78903/45, File 29858-10, Library and Archives Canada.

annuities, medals, clothing for the chiefs and headmen, an assortment of material goods for continued bush activities or for agriculture, and the promise of continued access to hunting and trapping.

The most frequently quoted passage of the treaty text reads,

> The said Indians DO HEREBY CEDE, RELEASE, SURRENDER AND YIELD UP to the Government of the Dominion of Canada, for Her Majesty the Queen and Her successors for ever, all their rights, titles and privileges whatsoever, to the lands included…And Her Majesty the Queen HEREBY AGREES with the said Indians that they shall have right to pursue their usual vocations of hunting, trapping and fishing throughout the tract surrendered as heretofore described, subject to such regulations as may from time to time,…and saving and excepting such tracts as may be required or taken up from time to time for settlement, mining, lumbering, trading or other purposes.[14]

In spite of the existence of arable land in the Peace River region, the Dominion's primary goal for Treaty 8, to secure ownership and access to resources, differed from its goals in southern treaties, such as Treaty 6 (which also covers substantial bitumen deposits) and Treaty 7, where it was more interested in clearing the lands for settlement and agriculture by moving Indigenous Peoples to reserves (Leonard 1995; Carter, First Rider, and Hildebrandt 1996; Cardinal and Hildebrandt 2000; Ray, Miller, and Tough 2000). In northern Alberta, by contrast, the treaty commissioners reported that "the extent of the country treated for made it impossible to define reserves or holdings, and as the Indians were not prepared to make selections, we confined ourselves to an undertaking to have reserves and holdings set apart in the future" (Laird, Ross, and McKenna 1899, n.p.). However, they also reported that Indigenous Peoples in the Treaty 8 region "were generally averse to being placed on reserves," because of the large land base needed to complete the seasonal rounds of hunting, fishing, and trapping, and the impracticability of farming in most areas. The commissioners wrote, "It would have been impossible to have made a treaty if we had not assured them that there was no intention of confining them to reserves. We had to very clearly explain to them that the provision for reserves and allotments of land were made for their protection, and to secure them in perpetuity a fair portion of the land ceded, in the event of settlement advancing" (Laird, Ross, and McKenna 1899, n.p.). While the treaty promised Indigenous rights to trapping and hunting on lands outside the reserve areas that had not been "taken up," it did not protect against competing land uses, which, following the influx of white trappers, and increasing industrial activity, began to compromise Indigenous land use in the Treaty 8 region through the twentieth century. The Crown offered the Métis land scrip of 240 acres or $240 (Madill 1986, 16). However, Métis scrip holders could not actually claim land in the region as the Dominion government had not completed township surveys or opened land offices (Larmour 2005, 104). Fraud and other problems plagued the scrip process, preventing many Métis people from claiming land or compensation (Tough and McGregor 2007).

While Canada and Alberta see Treaty 8 as a land surrender treaty, First Nations in the Treaty 8 region regard it as peace and friendship agreement. Treaty 8 Chief George Desjarlais explained the treaty to the Royal Commission on Aboriginal Peoples during the 1990s, "We did not sell or give up our rights to the land and territories. We agreed to share our custodial responsibility for the land with the Crown. We did not abdicate it to the Crown" (Asch 2014, 77). René Fumoleau argues that treaties 8 and 11 were fraudulently obtained by the Dominion of Canada, that Indigenous signatories signed without understanding all the terms and implications, as their primary concerns were about protecting traditional ways of life and ensuring their freedom to live from the land (2004, xxvi). Richard Daniels has suggested that Treaty 8 was a complex deal for Indigenous Peoples that was only made possible by a significant degree of trust between parties and the mutual need for an agreement (1979, 99). Treaty 8 had significant implications for Indigenous signatories. The government had pursued

Treaty 8 to extinguish Aboriginal title in the Peace and Athabasca regions, while Indigenous Peoples had sought peace and friendship.

## Alberta and the NRTA

With the HBC's shift from York boats to steamers for transportation in the 1880s, the Athabasca River emerged as an important transport corridor linking the southern economies with the industrializing northwest (Wetherell and Kmet 2000, 18; Piper 2009, 48). The Dominion of Canada created the provinces of Alberta and Saskatchewan in 1905, carved out of the North-West Territories.[15] Yet for the first twenty-five years of the province's existence, Canada retained control of natural resources and unoccupied land, which meant that northern Alberta remained the domain of the Dominion before it transferred ownership of Crown lands and resources to the provinces in 1930.

Beginning in 1922, Fort Chipewyan signatories to Treaty 8 began asking the government to set aside reserve lands, as their traditional fur economy was adversely affected by the arrival of outside trappers (McCormack 1984, 107). The Indian agent for Fort Chipewyan wrote, "To protect their interests, as guaranteed by treaty, both [the Chipewyan and Cree of Fort Chipewyan Bands] asked for a reserve, not for farming, as they had no wish to farm, nor is the land suited for that purpose, but for hunting and trapping. To make the matter definite, I requested both bands to apply for a reservation, naming the area selected. This application has been received and is herewith attached."[16] In 1922 the treaty annuity payment officer reported that both the Cree and Chipewyan bands were seeking reserve lands (Price 1993, 130). By 1928 reports from the Indian agent indicated that the Government of Canada had failed to meet the request.[17] During the following sixty-four years, the Fort Chipewyan Cree Band made over forty requests to settle the TLE, all of which were ignored, blocked, or denied (Selin 1999, 16; Slowey 2008, 10). In 1927 the federal government changed the Indian Act to prohibit First Nations from raising money or hiring lawyers to pursue land claims.[18]

In 1930 the Dominion Government promulgated the NRTA, which transferred ownership of natural resources and Crown lands to the western provinces.[19] The NRTA had two consequences for Indigenous people in northern Alberta. First, the NRTA involved the provincial government in fulfilling outstanding treaty obligations by obligating the province to transfer land to the federal government to fulfill land claims. This provision gave the province substantial power to control the amount and location of land that First Nations wanted to claim. In doing so, the NRTA created the potential for jurisdictional conflict over Crown lands, which led to significant political and bureaucratic obstacles for the Cree Band when it tried to obtain reserve lands. The NRTA was part of a process that limited Indigenous land rights, and encouraged settlement and resource extraction in northeastern Alberta.

Second, the NRTA limited Treaty 8 hunting rights to hunting for food. Under paragraph 12, Canada transferred the administration of wildlife to the province and changed First Nations' rights to hunt, trap, and fish. Whereas Treaty 8 refers to the right of the signatories to "pursue their usual vocations of hunting, trapping and fishing throughout the tract surrendered," the NRTA holds that "the Indians shall have the right…of hunting and fishing game and fish for food at all seasons of the year on all unoccupied Crown lands" (Tough 2004, 1001). With this change, the NRTA exchanged commercial treaty rights—that is, a right to practice commercial hunting—for rights to hunt only for food (Woodward 1989, 319). Although Alberta had been creating regulatory barriers to Indigenous land use since the Alberta Game Act of 1907 (McCormack 2010, 219), following the NRTA, Alberta defined trapping exclusively as a commercial activity, not related to subsistence treaty rights. The province implemented a trapper registration system in 1937 and established the Registered Fur Management Area ("trapline") system in 1941–1942 to accommodate outside trappers (McCormack 1984, 260). Between 1937 and 1944 the province did not charge First Nations trappers for licences, and from 1944 to 1968 the Department of Indian Affairs paid licence fees for First Nations trappers. Indian Affairs did not compensate Métis trappers for their licences. Once First Nations trappers had to start paying for trapping licences in 1968, many lost their traplines. Researcher Dawn Balazs argues that by the 1960s, wildlife and trapline management superseded Aboriginal and treaty rights, so that when trapping off the reserve, First Nations people "had to buy those rights that were supposed to be guaranteed" (1976, 134). By limiting Indigenous harvesting rights and monetizing the trapping system, Alberta curtailed treaty land use rights and erected regulatory barriers to Indigenous land use.

The NRTA created the legal basis for the layers of rights and jurisdictional conflicts that define contemporary land use in the Athabasca region. Alberta considers trapping and bitumen extraction both as commercial rights, which different people or companies can simultaneously hold to the same area of land. For instance, Figure 1.2 shows the extent of traplines on Crown lands in the region during the 1960s, most of which were held by First Nations and Métis trappers. Figure 1.3 shows a map of the same area outlining bitumen deposits that the Department of Mines and Minerals set aside, so that the province could not transfer these lands as reserve lands or sell them for other purposes. The Athabasca oil sands area map (Figure 1.3) presents a blank canvas for bitumen extraction, uncluttered by Indigenous land use, advertising the locations of the first projects, and welcoming future development.

The Alberta government has not put any limits on the "taking up" clause in Treaty 8, and since the 1960s Indigenous Peoples have lost much of their traditional territories to the oil sands industry. While many Indigenous Peoples perceived their traplines as part of their traditional territory, they only held commercial harvesting rights, while other companies or individuals held mineral rights (Brody 1981, 98; Passelac-Ross 2005, 37). Yet for Indigenous Peoples in northern Alberta, traplines are not simply commercial spaces: "The term 'trapline'…means more than just a place to harvest furs for sale on the

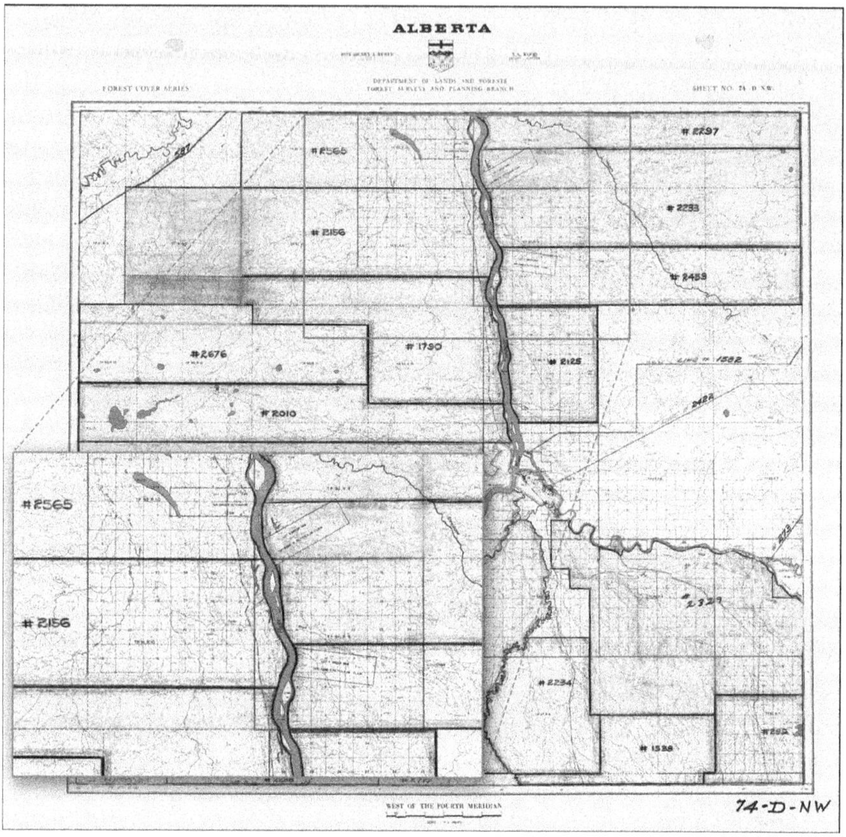


*Figure 1.2* Department of Lands and Forests: Surveys and Planning Branch, "Registered Fur Management Areas: Sheet No. 74-D-NW," Edmonton: Province of Alberta, 1967, GR1990.0377.0208, Provincial Archives of Alberta. Inset: Tar Sand Petroleum Claims faintly outlined within Registered Fur Management Areas.

commercial market. It means the territory where people hunted, fished, picked berries, gathered duck eggs and trapped for fur for local domestic consumption and trade. The trapline was the community food supply…It was and is synonymous with meat for the table; with stewardship of all natural resources; with extended family sharing; with the socialization of children; and with cultural sustainability" (Fort McKay First Nations 1994, 2). By defining trapping exclusively as a commercial right under the NRTA, Alberta and Canada privileged the possibility of resource extraction above the reality of Indigenous land use. In the Athabasca region, this structure has allowed bitumen extraction to destroy countless Indigenous traplines and other regions used for a variety of land uses. For many Indigenous people, the oil sands industry has undermined their ability to practice either commercial or subsistence traditional land use.

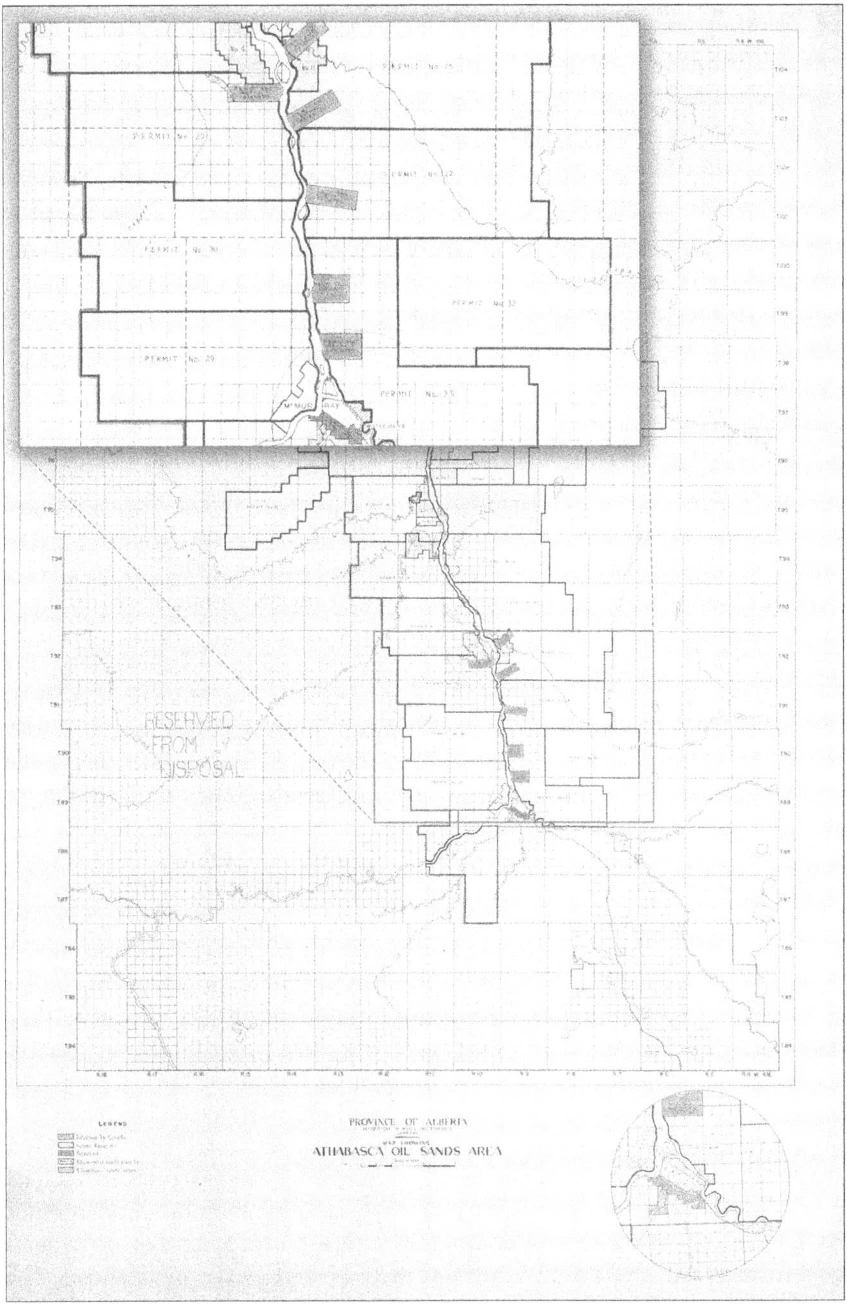


*Figure 1.3* Department of Mines and Minerals, "Map Showing Athabasca Oil Sands Area Reserved from Disposal," Edmonton: Province of Alberta, 1965, GR1965.0065.0022, Provincial Archives of Alberta.

## Land Claims and Energy Politics in the 1970s

The 1970s were a watershed in Indigenous and energy politics marked by legal challenges to Canada's appropriation of Indigenous lands, along with energy, financial, and political crises, including major disputes with provinces over energy jurisdiction. Policy debates, industrial development, and Supreme Court decisions brought relationships between Indigenous Peoples and the Crown to a boiling point in many places across the country. In 1969 the federal government put forward a policy paper widely known as the White Paper (Canada 1969). It proposed to eliminate treaties, the Indian Act, and the reserve system to create equality between settlers and Indigenous Peoples. Indigenous Peoples widely rejected the proposal, notably in a response publication *Citizens Plus*, also known as the Red Paper by the Indian Association of Alberta (1970). The fallout from the White Paper strengthened the resolve of Indigenous organizations across the country to fight for Indigenous rights and land claims (Weaver 1981, 173).[20] Following the 1973 *Calder v. British Columbia* decision that Aboriginal land rights had survived European settlement (Lambrecht 2013, 78), the federal government created the Office of Native Claims (ONC) in 1974.[21] The ONC's Specific Claims Branch had a mandate to both review claims of government failures to fulfill treaty obligations and to represent the government in negotiations.[22] The subsequent proliferation of land claims cases such as the 1975 James Bay and Northern Quebec Agreement, the Paulette Caveat in the Northwest Territories, the Mackenzie Valley Pipeline Inquiry, and claims in Manitoba and Saskatchewan influenced Alberta to begin the ongoing process of settling outstanding land claims in the province (Berger [1977] 1988; Coon Come 2004).[23]

In instances where First Nations did not receive all the land guaranteed to them by a treaty, they can use the TLE claims process to negotiate the outstanding land entitlement. For TLE claims (a type of Specific Claim), First Nations, the Government of Canada, and the relevant provincial government negotiate a settlement agreement. Once the parties reach an agreement, Canada and the province provide the First Nation with a negotiated amount of land (usually provincial Crown land) and a cash settlement (Indigenous and Northern Affairs Canada 2016). Given that much of Alberta has been widely settled and industrialized since the signing of the numbered treaties, TLE claims are a contested process. Many areas have been sold as private land, transected by infrastructure such as power lines, railways, or pipelines, or have valuable mineral deposits that have been leased by private companies and are owned by the provincial government. As the example of the MCFN TLE settlement shows, the province forces First Nations to choose from limited parcels of Crown land that the province is willing to part with or sue for damages based on the potential value of lands they could have secured during the treaty negotiations.

## Mikisew Cree First Nation's TLE Claim

The 1986 MCFN TLE settlement was the first TLE agreement in Alberta. While it is not the largest TLE settlement in the oil sands region, it is significant in that the Alberta government actively worked to limit the size and location of the Mikisew Cree claim to prevent the First Nation from securing bitumen reserves.[24] The Cree Band submitted its TLE claim in 1972. In 1973 a preliminary agreement with the federal government would have granted the band 97,280 acres based on the 128 acres per person using the 1973 population count of 760 people. The First Nation selected 42,000 acres at two locations in Wood Buffalo National Park and requested the remaining entitlement to be settled with land in the Athabasca bitumen deposits.[25] The Band Council reached a preliminary agreement with the provincial and federal governments in February 1975, but Alberta never complied with the transfer and began seeking to limit the size and location of the MCFN claim (Price 1993, 132; Slowey 2008, 32).

Alberta's response to the MCFN TLE was shaped by its investments in the oil sands industry amidst the energy and economic crises that defined the 1970s. Various experimental and small-scale oil sands operations came and went through the decades leading up to the 1960s. In 1967 the oil sands industry became a significant commercial endeavour when Great Canadian Oil Sands Limited, owned by Sun Oil, began mining and upgrading bitumen. The oil price and supply shocks of the 1970s—in conjunction with run-away inflation and plateauing conventional oil production in Alberta—propelled federal and provincial interest in the oil sands. In 1975 Atlantic Richfield Canada withdrew from the Syncrude consortium, which had planned to build a second synthetic oil plant.[26] To keep the project alive, the Alberta government purchased the outstanding position in Syncrude, along with Ontario and federal governments. Alberta's 10 percent, $200 million investment gave it the powerful new position of owner, developer, and regulator of bitumen.[27] The 1970s and early 1980s were marked by intense battles between the federal and provincial governments over the ownership and control of the Alberta energy industry, in which the federal government tried to exert more control over the energy flows and economic rents of the oil industry, and the province strongly resisted. Overall, during this period Alberta looked to maximize profits from the oil industry through active participation and management (Chastko 2004; Doern and Toner 1985; Pratt 1976; Richards and Pratt 1979).

Archival documents from Premier Peter Lougheed's papers show that the provincial government wanted to settle land claims quickly, although it was unwilling to cede mineral rights to First Nations or to settle TLE claims according to 1970s population counts, insisting instead on smaller 1899 population counts.[28] In October 1976 Alberta formed a special cabinet committee, consisting of the attorney general and ministers representing the departments of Federal and Intergovernmental Affairs, Energy and Natural Resources, and Native Affairs, to address land claims.[29] In the spring of 1977

Lou Hyndman, Alberta's minister of Federal and Intergovernmental Affairs, wrote to Hugh Faulkner, federal minister of Indian Affairs and Northern Development, that the provincial government would cooperate with the MCFN TLE claim only if the land base was calculated based on the band's population at the time of the 1899 treaty signing and if the provincial government retained the rights to all mines and minerals.[30] The Alberta government was concerned that granting mineral rights would set a precedent that would undermine investment certainty by allowing land claimants to take control of minerals.[31]

Minister Hyndman wrote to Premier Lougheed that the government should not support any claims that granted mineral rights to Indigenous Peoples, "based in part on the principle that Alberta would like to treat Indians in the same manner as other Albertans. In the same situation, an Albertan would not be given mineral rights." The provincial government's interpretation was that it had the power to determine which lands were acceptable for transfer to First Nations making TLE claims. The province required the band to submit a formal claim to the federal government. Canada would then consult with the province to agree on the specifics of the claim and validate it. The Alberta government, via the associate minister of Energy and Natural Resources, would review the claim and decide "whether the particular piece of land requested is acceptable."[32] If Alberta determined that the land requested was acceptable, it would then transfer it to Canada for settlement of the claim. If Alberta considered the land request unacceptable, it would return the claim to the federal government, or to the relevant First Nation, for revision. If Alberta rejected a claim, the band and the federal government would have to challenge the province in court. Hyndman acknowledged to Lougheed that both the Indian Association of Alberta and the federal government had rejected the Alberta process, its use of historic population to determine the size of the claim, and its refusal to transfer mineral rights.

A position paper submitted to the Alberta government in 1977 by the Indian Association of Alberta, a province-wide organization formed in 1939, contested Alberta's reluctance to settle the Fort Chipewyan Cree TLE claim. The report stated that Treaty 8 Elders believed they would be free to choose the size and location of their reserves, and that lands designated for a specific land use, but not occupied, should be available for selection, even when those lands were economically valuable. The report contended that the Crown should transfer mineral rights with reserve lands as it had done before the NRTA.[33]

The federal government did not challenge Alberta's refusal to transfer the lands sought by the Cree. Although Alberta was obligated under the NRTA to comply with the federal government in the settlement of TLE claims, it was the federal government's responsibility as signatory of Treaty 8 to settle claims, and in this case, take action against the Alberta government to settle the TLE claim. The change in the provincial government's negotiating position—to provide only 24,000 acres of land outside the oil sands region, based on an 1899 population of the 187 people—created a stalemate. MCFN left the negotiating table in 1977 (Price 1993, 132; Slowey 2008, 33).

## Settlement and New Lawsuits

In 1982, after several years of research, input from members and Elders, and consultations with academics from the University of Alberta, MCFN returned to negotiations with a revised proposal that no longer included bitumen-bearing lands (Slowey 2008, 35; Price 1993, 133). Over ten years after entering into TLE negotiations, MCFN, the Government of Alberta, and the federal government signed an agreement in 1986 that awarded MCFN 12,280 acres of land and $26 million.

By the 1980s a combination of droughts, low water levels due to hydroelectric projects, collapsing lynx and muskrat populations, animal rights campaigns, and disturbances on traplines from oil exploration and recreational land users weakened Indigenous trapping economies in the Athabasca region (Tattrie 1984). Meanwhile, the decline of oil prices weakened the economic rationale for the expansion of the oil industry, leading to project cancellations and layoffs. As such, Chief Archie Waquan told *Fort McMurray Today* that the deal was "the best package we can get," that "the band is tired and frustrated with the slow pace of negotiations that have been ongoing for over ten years. We want the land claim settled this year and we are taking the necessary steps to ensure that happens" (Younger 1986). The MCFN TLE settlement provided funding for the First Nation to move forward and develop essential administration and services that have been invaluable to its economic and social programs (Slowey 2008, 54). Yet the band was also desperate for a settlement, as it was impoverished and exhausted by the negotiation process.[34] MCFN was not a wealthy First Nation and did not have resources to fight the legal battle that would have ensued from pursuing its request for bitumen leases to settle its TLE. By the time the two governments finally agreed to settle MCFN's TLE claim, the Athabasca region had become a complex legal space where the First Nation had to negotiate with the provincial government as well as the federal government, with which it had signed Treaty 8. The Alberta government had already leased many areas to private companies for development. The land base of the settlement was less than half the acreage of the entitlement based on 1899 population numbers, and some disagreed with the strategic value of the settlement (Fort McMurray Today 1986; Pilon 1987). With the outstanding land claim resolved, the Alberta government could proceed with expansion of the oil sands industry and create a welcoming investment environment.

In 1996 the MCFN submitted a lawsuit against Alberta, claiming Alberta had defrauded MCFN of mineral rights and potential wealth by not disclosing the true value of bitumen rights and dissuading MCFN from claiming oil sands lands during TLE negotiations.[35] MCFN sought damages of $1 billion for loss of use and enjoyment of land. The MCFN statement of claim maintained that "Alberta agreed to set aside lands for Reserves in order to allow Canada to fulfill its Treaty obligations," and that "both of the Defendants (Alberta and Canada) have been consistently reluctant to abide by the terms of Treaty No. 8." MCFN argued that the government knowingly excluded valuable bitumen deposits from treaty land settlements and subsequently profited from the exploitation of Indigenous territory.[36] In its statement of defence, Alberta held that the 1986 agreement satisfied its obligations to provide land to Canada for MCFN under Treaty 8. It denied any obligation to provide land on the basis of modern population counts, and denied that MCFN was entitled to select lands in the oil sands or to damages or compensation.[37] When MCFN elected a new chief and council in 2005, the First Nation reached a confidential settlement agreement and dismissed the 1996 action. In 2015 the re-elected Chief Waquan initiated another lawsuit including many of the same claims as the 1996 action.[38]

Recent studies on the political economy of oil in Alberta focus on its impact on democracy and the role of neoliberalism (Adkin 2016; Shrivastava and Stefanick 2015). Gabrielle Slowey argues that neoliberalism motivated the provincial government to settle land claims, while the rollback of government involvement enabled the MCFN to use land claims settlement money to carve out space in the oil sands (Slowey 2008; Slowey and Stefanick 2015). Without dismissing this interpretation, I suggest the history of the MCFN TLE is an important window on the significance of resource extraction to colonization in northeastern Alberta. Industrial colonization is not a historic or complete process—it is an ongoing process of litigation and political economic conflict in which hydrocarbon extraction informs the ways that the Canadian state works to limit Indigenous claims to traditional territory in the north. Further, while Slowey emphasizes how neoliberalism impelled the Alberta government to settle land claims, it was Indigenous Peoples who brought the government and industry to the table with litigation. Slowey argues that the 1996 lawsuit was part of the MCFN's plan to benefit economically from the oil sands industry (2008, 69). While this is certainly one reason a First Nation might litigate a past land claim, such a perspective does not account for other significant reasons for pursuing land claims, such as increased territorial sovereignty: the power to influence and regulate development, minimize environmental impacts, and protect important cultural spaces. Attributing land claims resolution primarily to neoliberalism diminishes the importance of Indigenous Peoples who have fought to challenge the certainty of Canadian sovereignty and carve out cultural, political, and economic space in the new industrial economy.

MCFN's experience with the TLE claim laid the foundation for the First Nation's legal battles in the twenty-first century, including landmark cases in Indigenous law, making MCFN one of the most legally influential First Nations in the country. Most significantly, in *Mikisew Cree v. Canada (Minister of Canadian Heritage)* (2005), the Supreme Court of Canada ruling held that the federal government wrongfully failed to consult MCFN prior to the construction of a winter road. This decision, in conjunction with *Haida Nation v. British Columbia* (2004), established the duty of the Crown to consult with and accommodate Indigenous Peoples whose rights and title may be affected by the taking up of land for industrial development.[39] The duty to consult challenged the Alberta government's position that "it does not endorse a duty consult (whether *ex ante*, as maintained by Canada; or as part of a duty of fair dealing, as maintained by the Appellant) prior to the proof of Aboriginal title or rights."[40] In 2018, MCFN pursued a judicial review of omnibus budget bills C-38 and C-45, which restructured federal environmental law, limiting environmental assessments. MCFN appealed to the Supreme Court to overturn a Federal Court of Appeal decision that First Nations are not owed a duty to consult during the development of legislation (Canadian Press 2018). Although the appeal was unsuccessful, it was an important case in Aboriginal law. Chief Archie Waquan stated, "Law making is the most important form of Crown decision making. It is corrosive to the process of Reconciliation for the government to say that it does not need to consult with First Nations on legislation that may adversely affect our Treaty Rights" (JFK Law Corporation 2018). Taken together, these cases show how First Nations like MCFN are using litigation as one way they continue to increase their power to control activities in their traditional territories.

## Conclusion

For First Nations in northeastern Alberta, Treaty 8 (1899) legitimized a process of industrial colonization through which law became a primary tool of dispossession that affected all First Nations and Métis communities in the Athabasca region. By transferring Crown land and mineral rights to Alberta in 1930, the federal government—intentionally or not—created jurisdictional complexity that complicated the land claims processes. When the Alberta government invested in Syncrude in 1975, it became directly involved in the extraction process and simultaneously a party to the settlement of land claims between Canada and Indigenous Peoples. In this instance, Alberta was unwilling to adopt a sympathetic stance to First Nations and would not agree to the Mikisew Cree claim if it included a transfer of any bitumen-bearing lands. When MCFN, Alberta, and Canada eventually settled the TLE in 1986, it was for a fraction of what MCFN had initially claimed. The proceeds of the settlement nevertheless helped MCFN build investments and work towards economic independence, and MCFN has continued to litigate on treaty-related issues.

Indigenous communities in the oil sands region have had to balance competing priorities of sustaining their relationships with the land, carving out economic space in the industrial economy, and picking careful legal battles to try and protect their cultures, ecosystems, and well-being for future generations. While a community may have a promising claim, the huge cost and time needed to pay the armies of lawyers and expert witnesses necessary to fight these cases, which government contests with seemingly limitless resources, make many legal actions difficult to sustain (Taddese 2013). Alberta continues to champion its jurisdiction over Crown lands and minerals. The province takes a rigid interpretation of the treaties and Indigenous rights in the courts. It interprets Treaty 8 as a land surrender agreement that contemplates development. Overall, the province works to limit consultation with Indigenous communities (Laidlaw and Passelac-Ross 2016; Passelac-Ross and Potes 2007). The province stands thoroughly committed to the oil sands industry (Steward 2017). Although the government promotes the Athabasca bitumen deposits as "Alberta's oil sands," provincial sovereignty is not uniform and uncontroversial.[41] Rather, Alberta's ownership of the Athabasca region evolved from a gradual, patchwork extension of the Dominion of Canada, which remains contested by Indigenous Peoples.

## Notes

1 TLE claims are a type of Specific Claim. Generally, land claims in Canada are either Specific Claims (which address particular grievances of First Nations related to historical breaches of Canada's obligations under treaties, or in the management of First Nations lands, funds, and assets) or Comprehensive Claims (also known as modern treaties, which normally address Indigenous land claims in areas not covered by historic treaties). TLE claims are a type of Specific Claim, the mechanism through which First Nations seek land and benefits promised to them under a historic treaty, but never delivered.

2 Don Getty to Merv Leitch, Helen Hunley, Allan Warrack, and Allen Adair, January 30, 1975, accession no. 85.401, file 905, Provincial Archives of Alberta (hereafter PAA).

3 When describing Indigenous Peoples, I try to refer to specific First Nations or Métis peoples, for example the Mikisew Cree First Nation. When referring to Indigenous Peoples collectively, I use the term *Indigenous Peoples*, unless when quoting historical material or discussing legal terminology.

4 Getty to Leitch, Hunley, Warrack, and Adair, January 30, 1975.

5 This chapter relies exclusively on materials from the public record. It is not the product of community-based research and does not represent the views of the Mikisew Cree First Nation. The primary goal of this chapter is to show how MCFN challenged Canadian territorial sovereignty and how Alberta responded to these challenges. My research uses archival documents from Premier Peter Lougheed's papers, court documents, and historical newspaper articles from *Fort McMurray Today* and builds the research of Richard Price and Gabrielle Slowey on the 1986 settlement. While the Provincial Archives of Alberta hold some valuable material, which I present in this chapter, the Alberta government currently has a litigation block on all archival materials relevant to land claims.

6 Northern Alberta was an internal colony of Canada prior to 1905 and was in many ways controlled by the federal government until the 1930 Natural Resources Transfer Agreement.

7 The North-Western Territory was an ill-defined geographic entity that included the lands to the north and west of Rupert's Land. Canada combined these lands as the North-West Territories when it admitted them to the Dominion. Following the 1906 Northwest Territories Act, the North-West Territories lost its hyphen and became the Northwest Territories.

8 An Act to make further Provision for the Regulation of the Trade with the Indians and for the Administration of Justice in the North-Western Territories of America, 1859, 22 & 23 Victoria, Chapter 26 (UK).
9 The Rupert's Land Act, 1868, 31–32 Victoria, Chapter 105 (UK).
10 Rupert's Land and North-Western Territory Order (June 23, 1870), (UK), reprinted in R.S.C. 1985, App. II, No. 9.
11 Northwest Territories Act, 1875 (An Act to amend and consolidate the Laws respecting the North-West Territories), 38 Victoria, Chapter 49 (UK).
12 John C. Schultz, in Canada Senate, *Journals*, March 27, 1888, 14.
13 Canada Privy Council, O.C. 52, January 26, 1891, RG 10, vol. 3848, file 75236-1, Library and Archives Canada (hereafter LAC), cited in Madill 1986, 7.
14 Treaty No. 8 Made June 21, 1899, and Adhesions, Reports, Etc. Reprinted from the 1899 edition by Roger Duhamel, F.R.S.C. Ottawa: Queen's Printer and Controller of Stationery, 1966.
15 The Alberta Act, 1905, 4-5 Edward VII, c. 3 (Canada).
16 G. Card to Assistant Deputy Secretary of the Department of Indian Affairs, August 15, 1922, RG 10, vol. 6921, file 770/28-3 pt. 2, LAC, cited in Bellegarde, Prentice, and Corcoran 1997, 6.
17 1922–23 Annuity Payment Officer's Report, August 11, 1922, RG 10, vol. 6921, file 779/28-3 pt. 2, LAC; Constable R.A. Williams to Fitzgerald, Officer Commanding the Royal Canadian Mounted Police, August 6, 1923, RG 10, vol. 6921, file 779/28-3 pt. 2, LAC; 1927–28 Agent's Report on Annuity Payments, 1927, RG 10, vol. 6921, file 779/28-3 pt. 2, cited in Bellegarde, Prentice, and Corcoran 1997, 7.
18 Slowey (2008, 8) cites this block on land claims, but it is not clear whether it affected the Cree Band's claims. Parliament repealed the clause in 1951 but the Fort Chipewyan Cree were not able to begin negotiating a land claim before the 1970s. The 1951 Act dropped some clauses but did not formally repeal them.
19 Alberta Natural Resources Act, S.C. 1930, c. 3.
20 Harold Cardinal, Address to the Alberta All Chiefs Conference and Other Distinguished Representatives of Provincial Indian Associations, April 3, 1970, Lake Isle, AB, accession no. 72.59, file 187, PAA.
21 Calder et al. v. Attorney-General of British Columbia, [1973] S.C.R. 313; Canada, Statement Made by the Honourable Jean Chrétien, Minister of Indian Affairs and Northern Development on Claims of Indian and Inuit People, Department of Indian Affairs and Northern Development, August 8, 1973, http://publications.gc.ca/site/eng/9.850204/publication.html.
22 The ONC's dual mandate created a conflict of interest, which resulted in a revised process in 1982: *Outstanding Business: A Native Claims Policy—Specific Claims*. However, the ONC continued to control the new process. First Nations widely criticized the ongoing conflict of interest, and it remained controversial. See Specific Claims Tribunal Canada 2011.
23 Paulette et al. v. The Queen, [1977] 2 S.C.R. 628; Bob Bogle to Peter Lougheed, December 8, 1976, accession no. 85.401, file 904, PAA.
24 As of 2018, the biggest Specific Claim settlement is the 2010 Bigstone Cree Nation TLE agreement, which resulted in land and cash compensation totalling 567 square kilometres and $249 million. It reflects the increasing value of TLE settlements such as Woodland Cree Nation, Loon River Cree Nation, Mikisew Cree First Nation, and Fort McKay First Nation. Other communities who were not contacted by the Treaty 8 commissioners, most notably the Lubicon Lake Cree, have ongoing, unsettled claims and conflicts with Crown (Goddard 1991; Corcoran and Prentice 1995; Bellegarde et al. 1997, 2000; Martin-Hill 2008; Westman 2010, 2017).

25 Band Council Resolution, Council of the Cree Band of Fort Chipewyan, Fort Chipewyan, Saddle Lake/Athabasca District, Alberta, August 26, 1974, accession no. 85.401, file 905, PAA.
26 The Syncrude consortium consisted of Atlantic Richfield, Cities Service, Gulf Oil, and Imperial Oil.
27 The federal government spent $300 million for a 15 percent position, and Ontario $100 million for a 5 percent position. Syncrude Project, *Winnipeg Agreement*, Winnipeg, MB, February 3, 1975, accession no. 82.165, vol. 49, file 440, PAA.
28 Papers of Premier Peter Lougheed, accession no. 85.401, files 904, 905, and 915, PAA.
29 Bob Bogle to Peter Lougheed, December 8, 1976, accession no. 85.401, file 904, PAA.
30 Lou Hyndman to Warren Allmand, April 27, 1977, accession no. 85.401, file 904, PAA.
31 Subsequent TLE settlements in Alberta have often included mineral rights.
32 Lou Hyndman to Peter Lougheed, n.d. 1977, accession no. 85.401, file 904, PAA.
33 "Indian Land Entitlement," position paper of the Indian Association of Alberta, October 1977, accession no. 85.401, file 904, PAA.
34 Articles from *Fort McMurray Today* through the 1980s show that the Mikisew Cree First Nation encountered significant financial difficulties in part because of the travel and expenses band councillors incurred in pursuit of the TLE settlement. See Moralis 1984, for example.
35 Chief Archie Waquan v. Her Majesty the Queen (Canada and Alberta), Alberta Court of Queen's Bench, Calgary, Action No. 9601-18174 (1996).
36 Mikisew Cree First Nation v. Canada, "Amended Amended Amended Amended Amended (5th) Statement of Claim," Alberta Court of Queen's Bench, Calgary, Action No. 9601-18174 (2007).
37 Mikisew Cree First Nation v. Canada, "Amended Statement of Defence of the Defendant Her Majesty the Queen in Right of Alberta," Alberta Court of Queen's Bench, Calgary, Action No. 9601-18174 (2007).
38 Waquan v. Canada (Attorney General), 2017 ABCA 279. Waquan was re-elected chief in the summer of 2017, and in November 2017 Mikisew Cree reached a $136 million settlement, first sought in 1993, with the federal government for agricultural benefits from Treaty 8 that the government had never provided (Trochu 2017).
39 Mikisew Cree First Nation v. Canada *(Minister of Canadian Heritage)*, 2005 SCC 69, [2005] 3 S.C.R. 388, and Haida Nation v. British Columbia (Minister of Forests), 2004 SCC 73, [2004] 3 S.C.R. 511.
40 Taku River Tlingit First Nation v. British Columbia (Project Assessment Director), [2004] S.C.C. 74, [2004] 3 S.C.R. 550, Factum of the Intervener The Attorney General of Alberta, September 2003, para. 8, cited in Passelac-Ross 2005, 38.
41 For an example of how Alberta promotes its ownership of the Athabasca bitumen deposits, see Government of Alberta, 2009, *Responsible Actions: A Plan for Alberta's Oil Sands*, https://open.alberta.ca/publications/9780778580546.

## References

Adkin, Laurie E., ed. 2016. *First World Petro-Politics: The Political Ecology and Governance of Alberta*. Toronto: University of Toronto Press.

Asch, Michael. 2014. *On Being Here to Stay: Treaties and Aboriginal Rights in Canada*. Toronto: University of Toronto Press.

Balazs, Dawn. 1976. *A Short Analysis of the Transfer of Natural Resources to Alberta in 1930 and a Preliminary Study of the Registered Trapline System*. Ottawa: Treaty and Aboriginal Rights Research (T.A.R.R.) of the Indian Association of Alberta.

Bell, Robert. 1884. *Report on Part of the Basin of the Athabasca River, North-West Territory*. Montreal: Geological and Natural History Survey of Canada.

Bellegarde, Daniel J., James Prentice, and Carole T. Corcoran. 1997. *Inquiry into the Claim of the Mikisew Cree First Nation*. Ottawa: Indian Claims Commission.

———. 2000. *Bigstone Cree Nation Inquiry Treaty Land Entitlement Claim*. Ottawa: Indian Claims Commission.

Benton, Lauren. 2010. *A Search for Sovereignty: Law and Geography in European Empires, 1400–1900*. New York: Cambridge University Press.

Berger, Thomas R. 1977 1988. *Northern Frontier, Northern Homeland: The Report of the Mackenzie Valley Pipeline Inquiry* (Rev ed.) Vancouver: Douglas & McIntyre.

Brody, Hugh. 1981. *Maps and Dreams: Indians and the British Columbia Frontier*. Vancouver: Douglas & McIntyre.

Canada. 1969. "Statement of the Government of Canada on Indian Policy (The White Paper, 1969)." Presented to the *First Session of the Twenty-eighth Parliament by the Honourable Jean Chrétien*, Minister of Indian Affairs and Northern Development. Ottawa: Queen's Printer Cat. No. R32-2469. https://www.aadnc-aandc.gc.ca/eng/1100100010189/1100100010191.

Canadian Press. January 14, 2018. "Supreme Court Case Could Lead to First Nations Role in Law-Making." *CBC News*. http://www.cbc.ca/news/canada/north/supreme-court-case-could-lead-to-first-nations-role-in-law-making-1.4487029.

Cardinal, Harold, and Walter Hildebrandt. 2000. *Treaty Elders of Saskatchewan: Our Dream is That Our Peoples Will One Day Be Clearly Recognized As Nations*. Calgary, AB: University of Calgary Press.

Carlson, Hans M. 2004. "A Watershed of Words: Litigating and Negotiating Nature in Eastern James Bay, 1971–75." *The Canadian Historical Review* 85 (1): 63–84.

———. 2008. *Home is the Hunter: The James Bay Cree and Their Land*. Vancouver: University of British Columbia Press.

Carter, Sarah, Dorothy First Rider, and Walter Hildebrandt. 1996. *The True Spirit and Original Intent of Treaty 7*. Montreal and Kingston: McGill-Queen's University Press.

Cavanagh, Edward. 2011. "A Company with Sovereignty and Subjects of Its Own? The Case of the Hudson's Bay Company, 1670–1763." *Canadian Journal of Law and Society* 26 (1): 25–50. doi: 10.3138/cjls.26.1.025.

Chastko, Paul. 2004. *Developing Alberta's Oil Sands: From Karl Clark to Kyoto*. Calgary, AB: University of Calgary Press.

Coates, Ken, and William Morrison. 1992. *Forgotten North: A History of Canada's Provincial Norths*. Toronto: James Lorimer & Company.

Coon Come, Matthew. 2004. "Survival in the Context of Mega-Resource Development: Experiences of the James Bay Crees and the First Nations of Canada." In *In the Way of Development: Indigenous Peoples, Life Projects, and Globalization*, edited by Mario Blaser, Harvey A. Feit and Glenn McRae, 153–64. London: Zed Books.

Corcoran, Carol T., and James Prentice. 1995. *Inquiry into the Treaty Land Entitlement Claim of the Fort McKay First Nation*. Ottawa: Indian Claims Commission.

Crown-Indigenous Relations and Northern Affairs Canada. 2015. "Specific Claims." https://www.aadnc-aandc.gc.ca/eng/1100100030291/1100100030292 (accessed August 4, 2018).

Daniels, Richard. 1979. "The Spirit and Terms of Treaty Eight." In *The Spirit of the Alberta Indian Treaties*, edited by Richard Price, 47–100. Montreal: Institute for Research on Public Policy.

Desbiens, Caroline. 2013. *Power from the North: Territory, Identity, and the Culture of Hydroelectricity in Quebec*. Vancouver: University of British Columbia Press.

Doern, G. Bruce, and Glen B. Toner. 1985. *The Politics of Energy: The Development and Implementation of the N.E.P.* London: Methuen.

Eades, Gwilym Lucas. 2015. *Maps and Memes: Redrawing Culture, Place, and Identity in Indigenous Communities*. Montreal/Kingston: McGill-Queen's University Press.

Edney, Matthew H. 1996. "Theory and the History of Cartography." *Imago Mundi* 48: 185–91.

Fort McKay First Nations. 1994. *There Is Still Survival Out There: A Traditional Land Use and Occupancy Study of the Fort McKay First Nation*. Calgary, AB: Arctic Institute of North America.

Fort McMurray Today. December 30, 1986. "Lawyer Says Fort Chip Settlement 'a Ripoff'." *Fort McMurray Today*.

Fumoleau René. 2004. *As Long as This Land Shall Last: A History of Treaty 8 and Treaty 11, 1870–1939*. Calgary, AB: University of Calgary Press.

Gismondi, Mike and Debra J. Davidson. 2012. "Imagining the Tar Sands 1880–1967 and beyond." *Imaginations* 2 (3): 68–103.

Goddard, John. 1991. *Last Stand of the Lubicon Cree*. Vancouver: Douglas & McIntyre.

Harley, J.B. 2001. *The New Nature of Maps: Essays in the History of Cartography*. Baltimore, MD: Johns Hopkins University Press.

Harris, Cole. 2004. "How Did Colonialism Dispossess? Comments from an Edge of Empire." *Annals of the Association of American Geographers* 94: 165–82. doi: 10.1111/j.1467-8306.2004.09401009.x.

Indian Association of Alberta. 1970. *Citizens Plus*. Edmonton, AB: Indian Assocation of Alberta.

Indigenous and Northern Affairs Canada. 2016. "Lands and Economic Development: Treaty Land Entitlement." http://www.aadnc-aandc.gc.ca/eng/1100100034822/1100100034823 (accessed July 27, 2016).

JFK Law Corporation. January 16, 2018. "Mikisew Cree First Nation Challenge at the Supreme Court of Canada." *JFK Law News*. http://jfklaw.ca/mikisew-cree-first-nation-challenge-supreme-court-canada/.

Joly, Tara, Hereward Longley, Carmen Wells, and Jennifer Gerbrandt. 2018. "Ethnographic Refusal in Traditional Land Use Mapping: Consultation, Impact Assessment, and Sovereignty in the Athabasca Oil Sands Region." *The Extractive Industries and Society* 5 (2): 335–43.

Keeling, Arn, and John Sandlos, eds. 2015. *Mining and Communities in Northern Canada: History, Politics, and Memory*. Calgary, AB: University of Calgary Press.

Laidlaw, David and Monique Passelac-Ross. 2016. *Alberta First Nations Consultation and Accommodation Handbook*. Occasional Paper #53. Calgary, AB: Canadian Institute of Resources Law.

Laird, David, J.H. Ross, and J.A.J. McKenna. 1899. *Report of Commissioners for Treaty No. 8*. Winnipeg, Manitoba. Reprinted from original by Roger Duhamel, FRSC. Ottawa: Queen's Printer and Controller of Stationery, 1966.

Lambrecht, Kirk N. 2013. *Aboriginal Consultation, Environmental Assessment, and Regulatory Review in Canada*. Regina, SK: University of Regina Press.

Larmour, Judy. 2005. *Laying Down the Lines: A History of Land Surveying in Alberta*. Victoria, BC: Brindle and Glass Publishing.

Leonard, David. 1995. *Delayed Frontier: The Peace River Country to 1909*. Calgary, AB: Edmonton & District Historical Society and Detselig Enterprises Ltd.

Longley, Hereward. 2015. "Indigenous Battles for Environmental Protection and Economic Benefits during the Commercialization of the Alberta Oil Sands, 1967–1986." In *Mining and Communities in Northern Canada: History, Politics, and Memory*, edited by Arn Keeling and John Sandlos, 207–32. Calgary, AB: University of Calgary Press.

———. 2016. "Bitumen Exploration and the Southern Re-Inscription of Northeastern Alberta: 1875–1967." In "*Environmental Knowledge, Environmental Politics: Case Studies from Canada and Western Europe*," edited by Piper, L. and Clapperton, J., 17–24. Special issue of RCC Perspectives: Transformations in Environment and Society. Munich: Rachel Carson Center for Environment and Society. https://www.jstor.org/stable/e26241381.

Loo, Tina. 2007. "Disturbing the Peace: Environmental Change and the Scales of Justice on a Northern River." *Environmental History* 12: 895–919.

Madill, Dennis F.K. 1986. *Treaty Research Report Treaty Eight (1899)*. Ottawa: Indian and Northern Affairs Canada, Treaties and Historical Research Centre.

Martin-Hill, Dawn. 2008. *The Lubicon Lake Nation: Indigenous Knowledge and Power*. Toronto: University of Toronto Press.

McConnell, Robert G. 1891. *Report on an Exploration in the Yukon and Mackenzie Basins, N.W.T.* Montreal: Geological and Natural History Survey of Canada.

McCormack, Patricia. 1984. "How the (North) West was Won: Development and Underdevelopment in the Fort Chipewyan Region." PhD diss., University of Alberta.

———. 2010. *Fort Chipewyan and the Shaping of Canadian History, 1788–1920s: "We Like to Be Free in This Country"*. Vancouver: University of British Columbia Press.

———. 2017. "Walking the Land: Aboriginal Trails, Cultural Landscapes, and Archaeological Studies for Impact Assessment." *Archaeologies* 13 (1): 110–35.

McNeil, Kent. 1982. "Native Claims in Rupert's Land and the North-Western Territory: Canada's Constitutional Obligations." *Studies in Aboriginal Rights No. 5*. Saskatoon: University of Saskatchewan Native Law Centre.

———. 1999. "Sovereignty and the Aboriginal Nations of Rupert's Land." *Manitoba History* 37: 2–8.

Mochoruk, Jim. 2004. *Formidable Heritage: Manitoba's North and the Cost of Development, 1870 to 1930*. Winnipeg, MB: University of Manitoba Press.

Moralis, Michael. July 31, 1984. "Waquan Wants to Run a Tight Ship." *Fort McMurray Today*.

Morantz, Toby. 2002. *The White Man's Gonna Getcha: The Colonial Challenge to the Crees in Quebec*. Montreal and Kingston: McGill-Queen's University Press.

Page, Robert J.D. 1986. *Northern Development: The Canadian Dilemma*. Toronto: McClelland and Stewart.

Passelac-Ross, Monique M. 2005. *The Trapping Rights of Aboriginal Peoples in Northern Alberta*. Calgary, AB: Canadian Institute of Resources Law.

Passelac-Ross, Monique, and Verónica Potes. 2007. *Crown Consultation with Aboriginal Peoples in Oil Sands Development: Is it Adequate, Is it Legal?* Occasional Paper #19. Calgary, AB: Canadian Institute of Resources Law.

Peyton, Jonathan. 2017. *Unbuilt Environments: Tracing Postwar Development in Northwest British Columbia*. Vancouver, BC: University of British Columbia Press.

Pilon, Bernard. January 6, 1987. "Fort Chip Settlement: Former Chief Says His Family Will Pursue Separate Deal." *Fort McMurray Today*.

Piper, Liza. 2009. *The Industrial Transformation of Subarctic Canada*. Vancouver, BC: University of British Columbia Press.

Pratt, Larry. 1976. *The Tar Sands: Syncrude and the Politics of Oil*. Edmonton, AB: Hurtig Publishers.

Price, Richard. 1993. "Contemporary Land Claims Negotiations and Settlement: The Political Leadership Challenge of Alberta's Fort Chipewyan Cree." In *The Uncovered Past: Roots of Northern Alberta Societies*, edited by Patricia McCormack and R. Geoffrey Ironside, 127–148. Edmonton, AB: University of Alberta Press.

Ray, Arthur J., J.R. Miller, and Frank Tough. 2000. *Bounty and Benevolence: A History of Saskatchewan Treaties*. Montreal and Kingston: McGill-Queen's University Press.

Richards, John, and Larry Pratt. 1979. *Prairie Capitalism: Power and Influence in the New West*. Toronto: McClelland and Stewart Limited.

Sabin, Paul. 1995. "Voices from the Hydrocarbon Frontier: Canada's Mackenzie Valley Pipeline Inquiry, 1974–1977." *Envrionmental History Review* 18 (1): 17–48.

Selin, Ron. 1999. *Into the New Millennium, Our Story: The Mikisew Cree First Nation*. Edmonton, AB: Western Communications.

Shrivastava, Meenal, and Lorna Stefanick, eds. 2015. *Alberta Oil and the Decline of Democracy in Canada*. Edmonton, AB: Athabasca University Press.

Slowey, Gabrielle. 2008. *Navigating Neoliberalism: Self Determination and the Mikisew Cree First Nation*. Vancouver, BC: University of British Columbia Press.

Slowey, Gabrielle, and Lorna Stefanick. 2015. "Development at What Cost?: First Nations, Ecological Integrity, and Democracy." In *Alberta Oil and the Decline of Democracy in Canada*, edited by Meenal Shrivastava and Lorna Stefanick, 195–224. Edmonton, AB: Athabasca University Press.

Specific Claims Tribunal Canada. 2011. "A Brief History of Specific claims Prior to the Passage of Bill C-30: The Specific Claims Tribunal Act." http://www.sct-trp.ca/hist/hist_e.htm (accessed August 16, 2018).

Steward, Gillian. 2017. *Betting on Bitumen: Alberta's Energy Policies from Lougheed to Klein*. Edmonton, AB: The Parkland Institute and the Canadian Centre for Policy Alternatives.

Taddese, Yamri. November 11, 2013. "Feds Pouring Big Money into Aboriginal Litigation." *Law Times*.

Tattrie, Doug. March 15, 1984. "Trapping Season Hits Rock Bottom." *Fort McMurray Today*.

Tough, Frank. 1992. "Aboriginal Rights versus the Deed of Surrender: The Legal Rights of Native Peoples and Canada's Acquisition of the Hudson's Bay Company Territory." *Prairie Forum* 17 (2): 225–50.

———. 2004. "The Forgotten Constitution: The Natural Resources Transfer Agreements and Indian Livelihood Rights, ca. 1925–33." *Alberta Law Review* 41 (4): 999–1048.

Tough, Frank, and Erin McGregor. 2007. "'The Rights to the Land May Be Transferred': Archival Records as Colonial Text—A Narrative of Métis Scrip." In *Natives and Settlers Now and Then: Historial Issues and Current Perspectives on Treaties and Land Claims in Canada*, edited by Paul W. DePasquale, 33–63. Edmonton, AB: University of Alberta Press.

Trochu, Melinda. October 17, 2017. "Mikisew Cree Vote to Accept $136M Treaty 8 Settlement from Federal Gov't." *CBC News North*.

Weaver, John C. 2003. *The Great Land Rush and the Making of the Modern World, 1650–1900*. Montreal/Kingston: McGill-Queen's University Press.

Weaver, Sally M. 1981. *Making Canadian Indian Policy: The Hidden Agenda, 1968–1970*. Toronto: University of Toronto Press.

Westman, Clinton N. 2010. "The Making of Isolated Communities in the Lesser Slave Lake Interior, Alberta." In *Papers of the Rupert's Land Colloquium 2008*, edited by M.A. Lindsay and M.A. Richard, 223–41. Winnipeg, MB: Centre for Rupert's Land Studies, University of Winnipeg.

———. 2017. "Cultural Politics of Land and Animals in Treaty 8 Territory (Northern Alberta, Canada)." In *Entangled Territorialities: Negotiating Indigenous Lands in Australia and Canada*, edited by Francoise Dussart and Sylvie Poirier, 117–39. Toronto: University of Toronto Press.

Wetherell, Donald G., and Irene R.A. Kmet. 2000. *Alberta's North: A History,* 1890–1950. Edmonton, AB: University of Alberta Press.

Woodward, Jack. 1989. *Native Law*. Toronto: Carswell.

Younger, Ken. February 26, 1986. "Cree Band to Hold Vote on Proposed Reserve Deal." *Fort McMurray Today*.

Zaslow, Morris. 1971. *The Opening of the Canadian North*. Toronto: McClelland and Stewart.

# 2 Living and Dying through Oil's Promise

## The Invisibility of Contamination and Power in Alberta's Peace River Country

*Tristan Lee-Jones*

### Introduction

For a phenomenon that activists, scholars, and the media alike have so thoroughly sensationalized, daily life amid oil sands extraction in and around the town of Peace River, Alberta, is remarkably mundane.[1] Like other places in Canada, shopkeepers open their doors every morning; the drive-through line around Tim Hortons ebbs and flows throughout the day; and the museum and municipal government offices see a steady movement of residents and visitors coming to and fro each hour. Although Peace River is a busy regional economic and governmental centre, it is easy to describe this town of 6,800 as quiet, wholesome, and close-knit. It is a place where locals were typically puzzled by my presence there: What could "a researcher" have to study in a place that was so "*boring*?" How could I stand being in a place with so little to do when not engaged and working in government services, forestry, or the oil and gas industry—the big games in town?

Yet this rendering of the region as a place where "nothing happens"—a place where boredom structures the experience of everyday life (Jervis et al. 2003, 38–41)—only barely conceals from the town the invisible contaminations, health impacts, and structural violence that nearby farmers and Indigenous communities experience in their daily lives. A mere twenty kilometres up the road, a large oil sands field ("the patch") is allegedly leaking unknown and invisible pollutants into the air and water, which are finding their way into human and animal bodies. And though most of the operations within this patch—around a thousand production tanks and an in situ plant,[2] besides hundreds of conventional gas wells and pump jacks (Alberta Energy Regulator [AER] 2014)—were hidden among the boreal forest, the people I spoke to who live in adjacent Indigenous and farming communities witness mysterious health impacts and were always keenly aware of the "slow violence" just outside their doors and inside their homes (Nixon 2011). These dissenters to unimpeded extraction, whose numbers have dwindled to barely a handful in recent years, defy projections of cosy community coherency with which the town presents itself. Having stirred up press and activist interest in their struggle to force an inquiry and regulatory review of oil and gas emissions in 2014, many research participants from these affected areas described town residents, government, and industry as indifferent or hostile to their claims of illness. In other words, participants described the town as having turned away from them, refusing to acknowledge the bodily and social suffering their neighbours vocally decry (Kleinman, Das, and Lock 1997).

This chapter is based on nineteen months of fieldwork conducted from 2012 to 2016, throughout Alberta and British Columbia, but primarily in the town of Peace River. The town itself is seated on a dike-protected flood plain at the bottom of a broad and deep valley carved out by the collapse of a glacial dam millennia ago. Standing at the river banks, gazing towards the top of the valley, it's easy to imagine looking across a mountainous landscape. From the top of the valley, however, the observer is greeted by a mix of cultivated parkland and boreal forest stretching beyond view. As a governmental and economic hub, the town draws daily visitors from numerous villages, hamlets, and other small towns dotting the agricultural landscape, including from two Indigenous communities: Cadotte Lake and Little Buffalo (home to Woodland Cree First Nation, Lubicon Lake Band, Region VI Métis Nation settlements, and others).

In this chapter, to understand and differentiate diverse regional experiences of everyday contamination in northern Alberta on a finer-grained level, I put two days of fieldwork in concert with one another: each only a single day, a year apart, spent in the bush where leaders from neighbouring farming and First Nations communities generously invited me on guided tours. In the former, downwind of the patch, air and health concerns took priority; in the latter, water and game contamination were of central concern. Consequently, I argue that each of these communities, though both surrounded by extractive industry, experience subtle but important differences of environmental contamination in their daily lives.

Additionally, comparing these two days moves anthropologists and activists alike beyond essentialist narratives of Indigenous political resistance against oil sands extraction. This approach forces a more nuanced understanding of how different communities live with the environmental contaminations of oil sands extraction in specific ways, at the intersections of Indigeneity, class, and race. Allowing concerned readers to apprehend Indigenous and farming community engagements with the state and industry in ways that are not solely recognizably "resistant" demonstrates that social actors in northern Alberta are engaged in strategic and savvy negotiations with oil sands encroachment, locally perceived as an unmovable fact of daily life in the province (Blaser 2004; Ramos 2003; Wanvik and Caine 2017).

One challenge before this material is the failure of current analytical frameworks to capture the complexities of everyday life in the Peace River oil sands. Settler colonialism, as a structure and not an event (Wolfe 2006), inarguably shapes social relations between white and Indigenous communities in the region—a point to which I return subsequently. Indeed, the entire area has been part of a decades-long struggle by the Lubicon Cree and other Indigenous communities to establish formal land claims over their traditional territories, despite the ubiquity of oil, gas, agriculture, and forestry activity on those lands.[3] Yet, as an analytic, settler colonialism fails to capture the complicated effects extraction has on adjacent non-Indigenous communities, including migrant and agricultural workers. That is, Peace River oil sands operations efface a reductive binary of settler versus Indigenous. It is true that Indigenous communities and people of colour generally bear the greatest burdens of oil, gas, and mining extraction (Joly and Westman 2017), and given that these projects proximate to the town occur on lands that have been subject to claim negotiations, the situation takes on moral and ethical dimensions that pull it squarely into the realm of a colonial environmental injustice.[4] The slow violence of contamination and dispossession here is especially egregious given the historical context of treaty breaking, or treaty absence, and endemically high rates of poverty experienced in local Indigenous communities (Amnesty International 2010). But contamination refuses to remain confined to the social and spatial boundaries with and through which humans live. Contamination is unruly and acts in unexpected ways that spill over the technical and social limits we impose upon it. This situation, then, is an ongoing disaster, the "accident" of which is not truly a disruption of norms, but always present within the invention of extraction's technologies, manifested in material ways that spell the destruction of human and natural lifeways, thus revealing crude operations of power (Barrios 2017; Blaser 2004; see Gross, this volume). My purpose then is not to diminish the significance of continuing violence inflicted upon Indigenous communities or their farming neighbours, but to expand and nuance our view of how the slow violence of contamination moves across boundaries, whether social or biophysical (Kosek 2006; Shapiro 2015; see Wheatley and Westman, this volume).

Historically, if Alberta's north ever held allure for Europeans settling westward and northward from urban metropoles, it was nearly always for its natural resources: its furs, forests, or the agricultural potential of the land and what's beneath it. Yet long before settlers' agricultural ambitions, missionaries and trappers from a handful of fur companies, including the Hudson's Bay Company, had long-established posts with small plot agriculture dating to the 1700s that suggested the viability of crop growth in the region. By the late nineteenth century, colonial promoters argued that the Peace River Country was perfect for agricultural settlement. Until the railways arrived, the wide navigable rivers could support steamboat transportation, and the open mix of boreal forest and parkland possessed "more land suited for agriculture than there was west of Winnipeg—probably more than 65,000,000 acres" (Kaiser and Aubrey 2006, xvii)—despite the fact that this land itself was only marginally suited for cultivation. Indeed, many early agricultural experiments ended in failure (Leonard 2000, 175–95).

Desiring land and fearful of conflict, the federal government in Ottawa sought to strike a treaty that would cover a vast area extending from Lake Athabasca in the east to the Rocky Mountains in the west (Fumoleau 2004, 36–49). A treaty commission was organized and set out from Edmonton in May of 1899. Heading the commission was the former lieutenant governor of the Northwest Territories, David Laird. Previously, Laird had helped negotiate several of the "Numbered Treaties,"[5] a series of agreements extending across western Canada intended to obtain land for settlement from any First Nations already living there (see Longley, this volume). He arrived at the treaty grounds on the shores of Lesser Slave Lake, near present-day Grouard. Missionaries supporting the treaty had already circulated fliers among many of the area's Indigenous communities. On the day of the treaty's signing, several hundred members of nearby Indigenous communities assembled for the commission's arrival.

Representatives at the signing agreed to either treaty or scrip certificates, and between 1899 and 1901 adhesions of First Nations that had been missed at the initial negotiation were made throughout the Athabasca district, mostly along large navigable rivers like the Peace. From the perspective of colonial officials, the Peace River Country was now open for European settlement—a historical rendering of the region and its unique microclimate as a space promotional materials called "the Last Great West," and historian David Leonard describes as a "delayed frontier" (2000), "the last major region on the North American continent to have been thrown open for agricultural settlement on a broad scale" (2005, 8). Excluding railroads, every piece was in place: the North-West Mounted Police, trading posts, and ferry crossings. All that remained was a matter of state promotion and financial enticement for settlers to begin moving into place en masse, which they did once the railroad reached the tiny settlement of Peace River Crossing in 1912. While the forested areas surrounding the town (Figure 2.1), particularly those to the northwest around Cadotte and Little Buffalo lakes, were not settled agriculturally, by the 1970s, the area was a hotbed of oil exploration, regardless of promises commissioners provided during treaty negotiations to protect the hunting economy.

## Day One: Carmen

The proud grandson of an early homesteader, Carmen was a bearded middle-aged man, tall and strong. Yet, while he spoke, he was consumed with a racking, wet cough. His language was coarse but direct. When I told an interlocutor in town that I was meeting with Carmen on his farm for an interview, he responded, "Oh, yeah, Carmen! He's a tough guy…a little rough around the edges."

Carmen's life had been upended through the explosive growth of the extractive industry that occurred in the region in the early 2000s. Sitting at his kitchen table near the hamlet of Three Creeks on a frost-covered September morning, he detailed a lengthy chronicle of his attempts to force provincial regulators to stop the odours that had saturated both his body and his farmland with some invisible *thing*. Having worked in industry for decades, and more recently navigated regulatory red tape, he had an educated guess as to what that *something* is: volatile organic compounds, hydrogen sulphide,

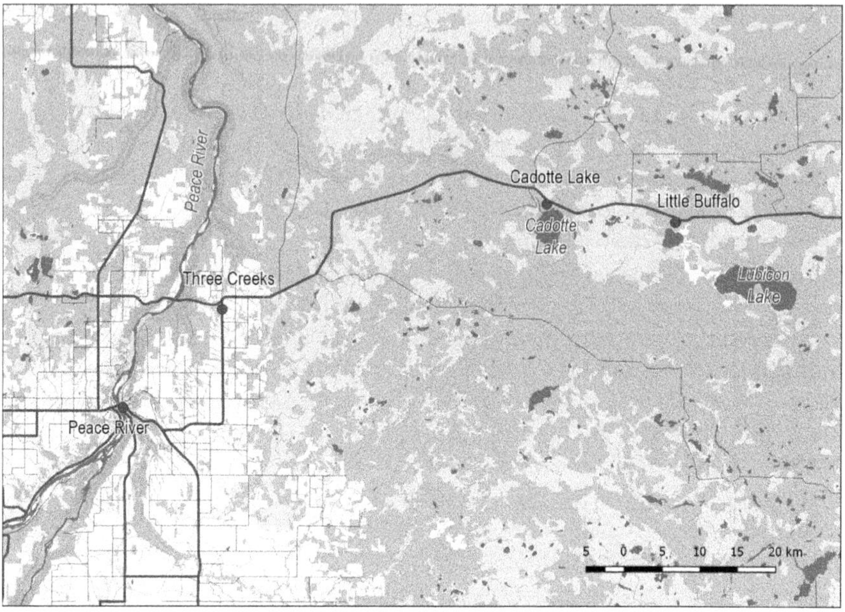


*Figure 2.1* Map showing agricultural and forested areas around the town of Peace River. Map by Alessandro Pasquini.

benzene, toluene, or other invisible chemicals (AER 2013, 91), which manifested in his body most perceptibly through his coughing. Worse than his cough, however, were his accounts of leaning over a toilet vomiting blood, or the double vision with which he sometimes struggled after nights of a "heavy dose" from the patch. He suspected that emissions from the nearby pulp mill were mixing with airborne particulate matter from off-gassing oil production tanks, synergistically acting on his body in ways that are worse for him than even for his neighbours. In the last decade, Carmen's cattle have all died, he said, and most of his friends and family have either left the area or died of "undiagnosable" illness: "I think [in] this community…everybody, is really, really sick. People have passed away, people are currently in the hospital." At the time of my first interview with him, he was in the process of relocating his parents to places where they might escape the health impacts of living adjacent to the patch.

Carmen is not alone in his experience of bodily ailments that neither regulatory nor industry representatives acknowledge as the result of production tank emissions. Two other farming communities, both near francophone hamlets south of Three Creeks, began to issue complaints to Alberta's energy regulator in the mid-2000s. In 2010, facing continuing health issues, area residents formalized an action committee, the Three Creeks Working Group, described by local reporters as "a collaborative effort between residents, industry, and government that meets on a monthly basis [to address] issues relevant to industrial development in the area" (Steele 2011). The working group began with roughly thirty members and included representatives from several oil operators in the region: Shell, Penn West, Baytex, Husky, Murphy, as well as officials from the regulator (then, the Energy Resources Conservation Board, which reformed in 2014 as the Alberta Energy Regulator [AER]), Alberta Environment, Alberta Health, and local government agencies. This multistakeholder group "met monthly to discuss the concerns and issues relating to the heavy oil production operations...and allowed for education and awareness presentations on various aspects" (AER 2014, 65). The group's stated goal was to alleviate both the environmental and public health concerns of local residents, hopefully establishing a new set of best practices with which the industry could reduce its tank emissions and ease tension between industry and farming families.

By 2013, local concerns about emissions had not abated. Between 2010 and 2013, over 710 complaints were filed to the AER, and affected families were already relocating to avoid the odours that wafted from the patch (Toledano 2014; Young 2013). Symptoms continued to appear in residents' bodies: headaches, sore joints, exhaustion, sinus congestion, skin rashes, nausea, and changing hair colour. Consequently, in early 2014, the AER convened a panel inquiry into these health concerns. The inquiry, an eight-day event, reviewed data and collected testimony from landowners, scientists, medical consultants, and industry operators. The transcripts of this event are indicative of the politics of oil sands extraction in Alberta: one doctor's critical testimony was dismissed as biased; only a handful of companies sent representatives, typically asserting that they were already capturing emissions and needed no new regulation; and residents noted discrepancies between official reports and their own sensorial experience. One resident stated at the inquiry that "there is some incongruence in between our feeling better and their trying to do something about it because we continue to experience ill health. We want to know if it's related to emissions; there's not enough study to indicate one way or another, but clearly there's an association in our mind we want reviewed" (Steele 2014). On March 31, the AER released its *Report of Recommendations on Odours and Emissions in the Peace River Area* (2014), covering several thematic areas: geological surveys, health concerns, better industry monitoring, regulatory revisions, and stakeholder engagement. One company, whose name is emblazoned on the town ice rink, was ordered to cease operations until they could resolve several of these emissions problems, but had resumed activity by the time of my arrival to the region in 2015.

On the second morning I spent with Carmen, the unmistakable smell of oil production lingered over Carmen's farm. The odour was something like the mingling of rotten eggs and freshly poured asphalt. Carmen's cough had worsened from the day before. That morning we drove my truck around the patch together—Carmen's "tour," on which he had already taken numerous members of government, activists, and press—along a grid of high-grade gravel roads that extend throughout the boreal forest from Carmen's farm northward to Cadotte Lake and other Cree-Métis communities. Signs on the forest edge marked a turn from an agricultural landscape to an extractive one: "NO HUNTING: workers in area," "No Unauthorized Access," "DANGER: H2S POISONOUS GAS," "Warning: High Pressure Sour Gas." This, despite the road's passage through public Crown land, is Indigenous territory that is still regularly used for hunting, trapping, and fishing. On both sides of us, spruce and aspen gave way to open areas of muskeg, streams, beaver ponds, and industrial sites—pipelines, pump jacks, and well pads alongside prefabricated trailer offices, work camps, parking lots, and pumping stations.

The extractive landscape of the Peace River oil sands is distinct from that of its more infamous counterpart, the Athabasca oil sands surrounding Fort McMurray. The latter's bitumen deposits are usually nearer to the surface, and thus may be accessible to industry through massive strip-mining projects. Images of the Athabasca mines are often what come to mind even if one has only a passing familiarity with the oil sands, thanks to activists and journalists. Peace River bitumen, however, has its own unique materiality that shapes the aesthetics of this landscape, too far beneath the ground to extract through strip mining. For these deposits, industry relies primarily on two in situ methods to extract the resource: steam-assisted gravity drainage (SAGD, "sag-dee") and cold heavy oil production with sand (CHOPS). The former method is typically used on heavier, thicker bitumen, in which a mixture of steam and chemicals are injected under high pressure into the ground, heating and softening the oil to permit pumping it through wells to the surface. CHOPS is used instead when bitumen is viscous enough to flow without the assistance of steam, pumping both oil and sand to the surface where they are then separated. The waste sand is spread on municipal roads—a contribution to community infrastructure, industry states—and the bitumen is stored in batteries of black tanks, each two stories tall, until tanker trucks haul it to pipeline terminals. To ensure the extra-heavy crude oil remains viscous, heating elements are installed along the side of the tanks, keeping the oil warm but also likely causing the odours residents noted during the AER inquiry.[6] We passed a dozen of these batteries as we drove through the patch. As we approached one to photograph it, several white company pickup trucks parked across the road or drove by slowly. Despite being on public land, we were non-industry and Carmen is a known critic, frequently reporting odours to regulators and the press; the company men in their pickups were clearly surveilling us. Carmen said, "Every time we go to stop a fucking vehicle is on our ass…And it's going to get really, a lot of traffic out here after I call the AER, 'cause they have to call all six companies [to inform them of the complaint]…and you'll see how they'll be reacting, and then they're going to call back within two hours and say there was [no odour]. They always do. Oh, he's got to smell that. But you can't smell it after you work with it for years…Until you get away from it again, eh?"

Such are the problems of addressing emissions from the Peace field: not everyone agrees that the odours even exist. On the town's Facebook general forum in 2015, one member posted a *VICE Magazine* article regarding ongoing odour problems. What followed were a litany of comments denying that any such smells existed—some from oil workers themselves; people claimed that the smells were the product of nervous people's overactive imaginations. If emissions did exist, said others, surely industry could be trusted to ensure that there were no negative health impacts. Some wrote that industry had provided such tremendous economic benefits to the region that even to speak about potential contaminations could irrevocably damage the town's good relationship with industry. But after passing through a large dip in the road through a patch of muskeg, both Carmen and I could certainly sense the odours. As a friend working in reclamation told me, these low spots are where heavier gases such as $H_2S$ (hydrogen sulphide) flow. A wall of smell filled my truck's cabin, and Carmen immediately began coughing. Even after such a momentary exposure, my eyes began to water, a wave of nausea overcame me, and my skin itched.

These types of symptoms are often more common, and intense, for people who are routinely exposed to chemical vapours in their homes (Shapiro 2015, 370–71). One chilly spring morning I sat at the kitchen table of another Three Creeks resident, M., sick from exposure just like her neighbour, who would pass away from an undiagnosed illness only a few weeks later. Like Carmen, M. rattled off a list of the symptoms she experienced after a "bad night." "You feel it [in your body] before you smell it," she said, and apologized for being out-of-sorts and dizzy; the night before had been a bad one. Her small ranch home sat on a beautiful acreage, close to where the open farmland ended and the forested oil patch began; on the road in front of her house, gargantuan tanker trucks rumbled past every few minutes.

M. had been a government worker and active citizen in the town. After she and her neighbours began experiencing their shared symptoms, they began a good-faith effort to engage with industry and the regulator to both discover and control what affected their health. Over the years and building up to the inquiry, her soft-spoken advocacy began to consume more and more of her time and energy, even as symptoms of fatigue began to set in. Like Carmen, when I spoke to her in 2015 and again in 2016, M. was frustrated with the circumstances in which she found herself: ignored by the regulator, feeling isolated as neighbours moved or passed away. These two addressed the situation differently, though. Whereas Carmen continued his press campaign and ceaseless calls to government officials, M. began recording detailed notes of her symptoms and the frequency of their occurrence—a citizen scientist.

Nearly every month, M. emails her reports to relevant parties, which I receive in a blind carbon copy. The numbers and symptoms are strikingly consistent. In October 2017, she reported joint stiffness and pain, sinus congestion, shortness of breath and nausea; the same symptoms appear in every other report. The percentage of days during which symptoms appeared are likewise curious: 29 per cent of all days in February 2017, 36 per cent in May, 26 per cent in August, 40 per cent in September, and 32 per cent in October. Her quarterly averages are telling: 30 per cent of all days for Q1 in 2017, 30 per cent for Q2, 32 per cent for Q3. One hundred per cent of these days resulted in "extensive negative health effects." Yet these reports seem to go unheeded—by everyone. A note on an April email states, "Please be advised that I have received only an out-of-office reply to my email of March 27/17 requesting additional information, and I redirected the request to another representative in the company. I have received NONE of the information requested." Such a refusal on behalf of government, regulators, and public health officials to acknowledge these reports is discouraging; as each report claims, residents have "completely lost confidence in the AER investigative process and are no longer calling the AER with emissions complaints." Given that, apart from the inquiry, Three Creeks residents' concerns have largely gone unaddressed in the eight years since reports to the AER spiked, their lack of confidence is understandable. The AER's official website for operator compliance reports three year-to-date emissions/odour complaints for Q1 to Q3 in 2017, indicating that the meticulous data M. supplies are disregarded.

Once, M. and I had planned to meet up at an industry open house, meant to inform residents of an already-approved project. When I arrived at the community hall, the building was locked with a letter taped to the door announcing the postponement of the meeting for four months. I had heard that only a few days before M.'s friend passed away and, out of sensitivity, I did not contact her. Later, I asked Carmen about it during our tour of the patch: "Well, I got that cancelled." "How'd you get it cancelled?" I asked. He replied,

> [The open house] was just a bunch of bullshit and lies and they weren't prepared and, uh, we got gassed really bad right before that. And [our neighbour] just died, right…like, ten days before that. And I said, if you fucking rotten fucking terrorists want to do this and lie to people right after we buried a neighbour—*that you guys killed*—gassed. Like, [some of us] went crazy in their minds over this stuff as well as being gassed. It was so traumatizing…Yeah, so [our neighbour] had just died and they wanted to have this thing a few days later and I said, "there's no fucking way that's gonna happen." Respect the dead.

Eventually, we tired of avoiding the white company trucks that appeared every time we passed a well pad. I drove Carmen back to his cattleless farm, past the industrial landfill, past rows of harvested canola. On the horizon, a blue haze hung over the forest. I was still dizzy, and Carmen was still coughing. He spent the rest of his day on bed rest.

## Day Two: Chief Isaac

Chief Isaac Laboucan-Avirom is a young man, the chief of the Woodland Cree First Nation (WCFN). On the phone, in October 2015, he invited me to join him and several other council members on a trip into the bush to identify important historical sites, including abandoned trapline cabins and an unmarked graveyard. The area of the survey, north of the main WCFN community of Cadotte Lake, was slated for a new gas pipeline and compressor stations. It was crucial, Chief Isaac said, that we recorded these places to protect them from the aggressive expansion of the patch, which would thereby require industry to work more collaboratively with the community. Critical of both uncontrolled development and the light touch of Alberta's regulators, at the time of our meeting, he also hoped for the economic opportunities industry could provide the WCFN; he had worked as a tradesman in the industry and found his own life in some ways improved by the experience.

While I sat beside him in his large black pickup truck on the way to meet our group, Chief Isaac detailed the issues his community members face: poverty, domestic violence, unemployment, health problems, a lack of infrastructure and adequate housing, and a lack of access to both educational and vocational opportunities (see Harper and Thompson 2017). As he talked, his expression turned from pained to determined and back again—someone who had witnessed social suffering in his community, but with a resolve to fix it. Like many people I met from Cadotte, he had a keen critical analysis of this state of affairs, noting that it was the consequence of decades of state policy that forcibly removed Indigenous children from their families to place them in residential schools, breaking generational cycles of grandparents' knowledge transmission, along with the hunting and trapping skills historically passed from parents to their children. Moreover, industrial development had reduced the very possibility of returning to a "prior" livelihood. He told me what many hunters in the region had also reported: game animals, especially moose, are rarer now and the ones that are cleaned are often diseased. A widely circulating account describes how, when a moose's organs were being removed to prepare the body for skinning, its liver was green and mottled. Other moose in the area, after being processed into drymeat, tasted "off," unwell. In addition, ceremonial medicines in the bush were becoming scarcer, and trapping was becoming more limited as development encroached upon traplines. In a 2015 letter to the National Energy Board regarding the permit for a gas project expansion, Chief Isaac wrote,

> One of the things our Nation has learned, particularly since the industrialization of our Traditional Territory began in the 1960s, is that all developments have permanent and profound impacts on our members…Our members are particularly wary of pipelines and associated infrastructure…due to recent examples of pipeline failures (at least 5 in the past 5 years), including the largest spill in Alberta's history. We have concerns

> about the possibility of an explosion and/or a forest fire…We are also concerned about what a gas leak would do to the environment and waterways—would the leak kill plants, contaminate the soil, poison our air, water and fish? We do not have any confidence that this Project is safe… The Project will reduce the lands available to us for the exercise of our treaty and aboriginal rights.
>
> Laboucan-Avirom (2015)

Although supporters of the oil industry in Alberta consistently assert that spills and environmental damages are overreported, Isaac's skeptical line of questioning is clearly informed, measured, and reasonable. Despite this, and as noted above, he remained open to collaboration with industry for the purpose of economic improvement. Such a position was corroborated by other comments people made to me during the course of fieldwork, captured succinctly in the remarks of a development officer in the Treaty 8 offices during an interview in Edmonton: "We don't want to stop development. We [First Nations peoples] don't want to shut down the oil sands. We just want to make sure it works [equitably] for everyone." For Chief Isaac, with little economic opportunity in the region outside of oil, gas, and forestry, industry remains one of the only pathways for his community to bring itself out of the legacy of residential schools, harmful child welfare policies, and the constraints of the Indian Act. Yet even such a moderate position is stymied at every turn. "Look at all the people I got here," he said, while driving around the reserve. "I could get these guys [working] on site tomorrow. But industry flies people in from [British Columbia], Nova Scotia…and they're on *our* land." Compounding this bind is a lack of access to the basic safety permits industrial workers are required to have to operate equipment on site (see Gross, this volume). These safety tickets require the equivalent of a high school diploma, and given the high dropout rate at the WCFN's school—the consequence of structural racism embedded in Canada's educational system, participants told me—the possibility to earn even the basic prerequisites for employment in oil and gas are limited. But, Chief Isaac asks, why doesn't Shell or another company establish more educational and training programs to move more First Nations workers into local employment? Recognizing that decades of inequitable and uncontrolled development are progressively foreclosing the possibility of a return to "traditional livelihood," what Chief Isaac and others like him desire is opportunity—the very same thing homesteaders, like Carmen's grandparents, came to the Peace River Country to find.

In 2013, at an anti–oil sands gathering near Fort McMurray, the chief of the Athabasca Chipewyan First Nation delivered a speech to an assembly of several hundred Indigenous and environmental activists from across North America. Participants had arrived to bear witness to and pray for the healing of the land disturbed by the open-pit bitumen mines of northwest Alberta. Chief Adam Allan began, "We're not like…the environmentalists. We don't want to protect the land just because it's beautiful; we use the land to feed our families and communities." He asserted himself, and those on whose behalf he spoke, as land users, rather than conservationists or environmentalists. Like Chief Isaac and others with whom I've spoken throughout Alberta, they contend that preserving the land is important because it preserves *both* the land and the people. This is why, for many, traditional subsistence and wage economies can work together—a mixed economy (Angell and Parkins 2011, 72–73)—and perhaps why the total shutdown of extractive industry is often excluded from the discourse of Indigenous leaders. Oil and gas, in remote places, can provide heating, light, and fuel to power the vehicles used to access hunting, fishing, and trapline areas. Often what I have heard in the province was a desire to have legitimate and sustained participation in the development process—not simply the Traditional Land Use Impact reports that are legally required for the approval of industrial projects, the thing for which consultants "come for just so they can check a box," in the words of one Métis Elder I spoke with.[7] What people wanted was an equitable share of industry's bounty and a more robust regulatory and environmental monitoring apparatus, given its multiple historic failures. Knowing that the Peace deposits lie beneath traditional Indigenous lands, then—the very thing that brings extraction to this region—isn't this request both reasonable and fair?

## Looking Ahead

In the province of Alberta, where often even opponents view the oil and gas industry as "here to stay" given its deep economic, political, and cultural entrenchment, both critical and cooperative engagements are vital to the survival of the very communities that extraction impacts most. Actors in the Peace River Country, like Carmen, M., and Chief Isaac, deliberately choose when, where, and how to engage in critique, cooperation, or to strike out on an altogether new path. Each is caught up in a set of political conditions structured through law and policy, adapting their engagement in response to the contingencies of these arrangements over time. Through ethnographic work with persons living among these contingencies, then, we can look more carefully at their particularities, including when they disrupt the expectations produced via reductive binaries of passive victimhood or militant resistance of both Indigenous and settler communities the oil sands extraction impacts (Wanvik and Caine 2017, 2).

The arrangements that produce these extractive zones run deep and are foundational to the formation of the modern settler states. The cases above demonstrate not only political arrangements between farmers, First Nations, industry, and the state, but relations of power that work to dispossess peoples of the land *from* their land (West 2017)—a "colonial relation" that in settler societies is an "inherited background field within which market, racist, patriarchal, and state relations converge to facilitate [the] power effect…[of] hierarchical social relations [facilitating] dispossession" (Coulthard 2014, 6–7; see also Povinelli 2016, 7–33). This stratified working of power is inescapably violent.[8] Indeed, violence, both ecological and social, often accompanies oil and gas extraction; such violence has been documented and analyzed more generally (Angell and Parkins 2011; Ballard and Banks 2003; Watts 2001) as well as in Canada, and the oil sands more specifically (Preston 2013; Sandlos and Keeling 2016; Westman 2013a). Such power effects are evident not only in the ethnographic evidence recounted above, but appear even at the moment of Treaty 8's imagining, designed as it was to order bodies and space, and render the land settleable. Thus, industry's violent effects upon bodies—whether of farmers, Indigenous communities, or moose—are neither coincidental nor accidental. For Chief Isaac, this means that new projects "reduce the lands available for the exercise of treaty and Aboriginal rights." For Carmen, without the revenue his formerly lucrative ranch provided, he is dispossessed not only of his family's homestead land but of his own body, its health, and senses: "they bankrupt everybody," he said. While Carmen meant the bankrupting specifically of his finances, a deeper working of fields of power moved within his body, stirred up by coughing and bouts of vomiting. Surely, the violence of oil sands extraction denies him of more than his livelihood alone—even when that agricultural livelihood was itself historically produced by and productive of a colonial arrangement of power.

The experiences of Carman and Chief Isaac also illuminate the threshold where the invisible becomes visible—or better, collapses any such distinction altogether. Like "the state," in its diffusiveness power seems to be an unseen force, akin to gravity or magnetism: something that binds the world together, seemingly intangible. So too with the unseen contaminants people in Three Creeks and Cadotte face: pollution not known immediately through the *sensorium* per se, but through changing landscapes and bodily illnesses. Like colonial power, we may wish to term this unseen pollution "invisible," but this would be inaccurate: while the particulates themselves may be unseen, they are made to manifest in bodies (human and non-human) in ways that *are* felt or seen. The unseen thus emerges in the bodily sensorium as the seen. Pollution and power are thus known on a secondary order, as experienced in the body and land, but "made visible" through the technologies of a positivist science—denied to neighbours of the Peace River oil sands through inadequate environmental monitoring and public health interventions. The illusion of the intangibility of power and contamination may then be why violence and dispossession in the area are routinely normalized by those non-Indigenous residents who are not directly impacted by extraction in the region, permitting their "[decoupling] from [their] original causes" (Nixon 2011, 11), and indexing local violence instead to racist narratives of Indigenous sloth and criminality, as Euro-Canadians often recounted to me during fieldwork. This, I suspect, is one constituent cause of the town of Peace River's turning away from the social suffering of their neighbours mere kilometres away: it ensures continued dispossession through the relegation of Indigenous suffering—now coupled with farmers' suffering—to personal or community failures. Turning away denies responsibility, marking the limits of who does or does not belong to the Canadian polity, and who is thus then expendable, abandonable, or "sacrificial," in M.'s words.

There may then be a simple and elegant solution to the problems of extraction in the Peace River Country: the collaborative development of a shared definition of community, or at the very least, a more sustained effort by settlers to understand human differences wherever they are perceived (Dunk 2003; Furniss 2000), paving a path to a genuine reconciliation between Indigenous and settler peoples. As long as neighbours in the Peace River Country are turned away from these issues, though—as long as, in the words of many of this research's participants, there remains a "gap" between Indigenous and non-Indigenous people, and all those suffering amid the patch—it is difficult to see how this situation will resolve itself collaboratively for all parties involved. Likewise, it remains to be seen how alleged contaminants impacting Indigenous people and settlers alike can ever be fully understood, left meanwhile to drift on the water and wind into human and non-human bodies. Can this arrangement change? Lives and lifeways are at stake, and so it must. At work already are citizen scientists like M. and agitators like Carmen; leaders in the Indigenous communities such as Cadotte Lake, as well as those dedicated few in town working to create spaces for reconciliation and collaboration between Indigenous and non-Indigenous peoples. Each of these actors ruptures the sedimentation that seeks to entrench arrangements of dispossession, power, and violence. But are such ruptures able to achieve sustained and permanent changes to the political and spatial order of this place, and of Canada, and even the colonized world more broadly?

## Acknowledgements

This project was funded through the Society for Economic Anthropology, the Wenner-Gren Foundation, the Social Sciences Research Council, and Rutgers University. Sponsorship in the field was provided by Dr. Brenda Parlee, Faculty of Native Studies, University of Alberta. Local implementation was facilitated through the generosity of the Sagitawa Friendship Centre, Aboriginal Interagency Council, and the Peace River Museum, Archives and Mackenzie Centre.

## Notes

1 On terminology: while international activist, academic, and journalist accounts of northern Alberta's bituminous sands typically refer to the *tar sands* (the historical normative designation [Finch 2007, 99]), both local and Canadian academic convention on terminology refer to this unconventional fossil fuel as the *oilsands* or *oil sands*. In this chapter, I deploy the latter term.

2 Cold heavy oil production with sand (CHOPS) is an oil extraction technique developed in the 1990s that intentionally injects sand into oil wells to increase their productivity. Its key feature are batteries of eight-metre-high black tanks on production sites, heated to raise the viscosity of the oil. In situ refers to oil sands production technologies that do not or cannot utilize strip mining due to the depth of the bitumen deposit. Strip-mining techniques, like those used near Fort McMurray, are typically not found in Alberta's other bitumen deposits.

3 Because treaty commissioners failed to reach every Indigenous community in northern Alberta, the Lubicon Cree were not provided an opportunity to sign a treaty adhesion until late 2018. For works covering the political struggle of the Lubicon Cree's land claims, see Goddard (1991) and Martin-Hill (2008). For a broader regional perspective on this history, see Westman (2010).
4 Distinguished from a normative environmentalism, environmental justice recognizes "that poor and minorities have been especially damaged by societal threats such as environmental pollution, runaway development, and resource depletion" (Shrader-Frechette 2002, 6).
5 Specifically, Treaties 4 and 7, and Treaty 6 adhesions.
6 Indeed, one of the AER's recommendations to industry operators was to lower the temperature of CHOPS battery tanks (AER 2014, 64).
7 For further information on land use reports and their problems, see Westman 2013b, 111; and Joly and Westman 2017.
8 Although the anthropological literature on violence is vast, for my purposes I define violence as that which impedes the full flourishing of both human and non-human life.

## References

Alberta Energy Regulator (AER). 2013. Decision 2013 ABAER 018: Proceeding into Odours and Emissions in the Peace River Area; Organizational Meeting Report, October 23, 2013. https://aer.ca/documents/decisions/2013/2013-ABAER-018.pdf.

———. 2014. Decision 2014 ABAER 005: Report of Recommendations on Odours and Emissions in the Peace River Area, March 31, 2014. https://aer.ca/documents/decisions/2014/2014-ABAER-005.pdf.

Amnesty International. 2010. *Canada: 20 Years' Denial of Recommendations Made by the United Nations Human Rights Committee and the Continuing Impact on the Lubicon Cree*. London: Amnesty International Publications. https://amnesty.org/download/Documents/36000/amr200032010en.pdf.

Angell, Angela C., and John R. Parkins. 2011. "Resource Development and Aboriginal Culture in the Canadian North." *Polar Record* 47 (1): 67–79. doi: 10.1017/S0032247410000124.

Ballard, Chris, and Glenn Banks. 2003. "Resource Wars: The Anthropology of Mining." *Annual Review of Anthropology* 2003 (32): 287–313.

Barrios, Roberto E. 2017. "What Does Catastrophe Reveal for Whom? The Anthropology of Crises and Disasters at the Onset of the Anthropocene." *Annual Review of Anthropology* 46: 151–66. https://doi.org/10.1146/annurev-anthro-102116-041635.

Blaser, Mario. 2004. "Life Projects: Indigenous Peoples' Agency and Development." In *In the Way of Development: Indigenous Peoples, Life Projects and Globalization*, edited by Mario Blaser, Harvey A. Feit, and Glenn McRae, 26–44. New York: Zed Books.

Coulthard, Glen Sean. 2014. *Red Skin White Masks: Rejecting the Colonial Politics of Recognition*. Minneapolis: University of Minnesota Press.

Dunk, Thomas W. 2003. *It's a Working Man's Town: Male Working-Class Culture*. Montreal and Kingston: McGill-Queen's University Press.

Finch, David. 2007. *Pumped: Everyone's Guide to the Oil Patch*. Calgary, AB: Fifth House Publishers.

Fumoleau, René. 2004. *As Long As This Land Shall Last: A History of Treaty 8 and Treaty 11*, 1870–1939. Calgary, AB: University of Calgary Press.

Furniss, Elizabeth. 2000. *The Burden of History: Colonialism and the Frontier Myth in a Rural Canadian Community*. Vancouver: University of British Columbia Press.

Goddard, John. 1991. *Last Stand of the Lubicon Cree*. Vancouver: Douglas and McIntyre.

Harper, Anita Olsen, and Shirley Thompson. 2017. "Structural Oppressions Facing Indigenous Students in Canadian Education. *Fourth World Journal* 15 (2): 41–66.

Jervis, Lori L., Paul Spicer, Spero M. Manson, and The AI-SUPERPFP Team. 2003. "Boredom, 'Trouble,' and the Realities of Postcolonial Reservation Life." *Ethos* 31 (1): 38–58.

Joly, Tara, and Clinton N. Westman. 2017. *Taking Research Off the Shelf: Synthesizing Existing Sources of Knowledge about Impacts, Benefits, and Participatory or Consultative Processes around Extractive Industry in Northern Alberta*. Final Report for the Social Sciences and Humanities Research Council of Canada Imagining Canada's Future Initiative, Knowledge Synthesis Grants: Aboriginal Peoples. September 11, 2017. https://artsandscience.usask.ca/profile/CWestman#/profile.

Kaiser, Ken, and Merrily Aubrey, eds. 2006. *In the Promised Land of Alberta's North: The Northern Journal of Katherine Hughes (Summer 1909)*. Calgary, AB: Alberta Records Publication Board, Historical Society of Alberta.

Kleinman, Arthur, Veena Das, and Margaret Lock, eds. 1997. *Social Suffering*. Berkeley: University of California Press.

Kosek, Jake. 2006. *Understories: The Political Life of Forests in Northern New Mexico*. Durham, NC: Duke University Press.

Laboucan-Avirom, Isaac. 2015. "Written Evidence of Woodland Cree First Nation Chief and Council." Letter submitted by Witten LLP obo Woodland Cree First Nation to Secretary of the Board, National Energy Board, and Tisha Homer, Regulatory Project Manager, NOVA Gas Transmission Limited. https://apps.neb-one.gc.ca/REGDOCS/File/Download/2825516.

Leonard, David W. 2000. *Delayed Frontier: The Peace River Country to 1909*. Calgary, AB: Detselig Enterprises Ltd.

———. 2005. *The Last Great West: The Agricultural Settlement of the Peace River Country to 1914*. Calgary, AB: Detselig Enterprises Ltd.

Martin-Hill, Dawn. 2008. *The Lubicon Lake Nation: Indigenous Knowledge and Power*. Toronto: University of Toronto Press.

Nixon, Rob. 2011. *Slow Violence and the Environmentalism of the Poor*. New Haven, CT: Yale University Press.

Povinelli, Elizabeth. 2016. *Geontologies: A Requiem to Late Capitalism*. Durham, NC: Duke University Press.

Preston, Jen. 2013. "Neoliberal Settler Colonialism, Canada and the Tar Sands." *Race & Class* 55 (2): 42–59. doi: 10.1177/0306396813497877.

Ramos, Alcida Rita. 2003. "Pulp Fictions of Indigenism." In *Race, Nature, and the Politics of Difference*, edited by Donald S. Moore, Jake Kosek, and Anand Pandian, 356–79. Durham, NC: Duke University Press.

Sandlos, John, and Arn Keeling. 2016. "Aboriginal Communities, Traditional Knowledge, and the Environmental Legacies of Extractive Development in Canada." *The Extractive Industries and Society* 3 (2): 278–87. doi: 10.1016/j.exis.2015.06.005.

Shapiro, Nicholas. 2015. "Attuning to the Chemosphere: Domestic Formaldehyde, Bodily Reasoning, and the Chemical Sublime." *Cultural Anthropology* 30 (3): 368–93. doi: 10.14506/ca30.3.02.

Shrader-Frechette, Kristin. 2002. *Environmental Justice: Creating Equality, Reclaiming Democracy*. New York: Oxford University Press.

Steele, Erin. 2011. "Three Creeks Working Group a Collaboration between Industry, Gov't and Residents to Ensure Highest Standard of Living for All." *Peace River Record-Gazette*, October 11, 2011. https://www.prrecordgazette.com/2011/10/11/three-creeks-working-group-a-collaboration-between-industry-govt-and-residents-to-ensure-highest-standard-of-living-for-all.

———. 2014. "Baytex Hearings Slated for Eight Days." *Peace River Record-Gazette*, January 29, 2014. https://www.prrecordgazette.com/2014/01/29/baytex-hearings-slated-for-eight-days.

Toledano, Michael. 2014. "Albertans Are Abandoning Their Homes Due to Toxic Air." *Vice News*, February 20, 2014. https://www.vice.com/en_ca/article/4w57ed/albertans-are-abandoning-their-homes-to-toxic-air.

Wanvik, Tarje Iversen, and Ken Caine. 2017. "Understanding Indigenous Strategic Pragmatism: Métis Engagement with Extractive Industry Developments in the Canadian North." *The Extractive Industries and Society* 4 (3): 595–605. doi: 10.1016/j.exis.2017.04.002.

Watts, Michael. 2001. "Petro-Violence: Community, Extraction, and Political Ecology of a Mythic Commodity." In *Violent Environments*, edited by Nancy Lee Peluso and Michael Watts, 189–212. Ithaca, NY: Cornell University Press.

West, Paige. 2017. "Dispossession." *Cultural Anthropology*, June 28, 2017. https://culanth.org/fieldsights/1150-dispossession.

Westman, Clinton N. 2010. "The Making of Isolated Communities in the Lesser Slave Interior, Alberta." In *Papers of the Rupert's Land Colloquium 2008*, edited by Margaret Anne Lindsay and Mallory Allyson Richard, 223–41. Winnipeg, MB: University of Winnipeg.

———. 2013a. "Cautionary Tales: Making and Breaking Community in the Oil Sands Region." *Canadian Journal of Sociology* 38 (2): 211–31.

———. 2013b. "Social Impact Assessment and the Anthropology of the Future in Canada's Tar Sands." *Human Organization* 72 (2): 111–20.

Wolfe, Patrick. 2006. "Settler Colonialism and the Elimination of the Native." *Journal of Genocide Research* 8 (4): 387–409. doi: 10.1080/14623520601056240.

Young, Leslie. 2013. "Ill Wind: Alberta Families Leaving Homes for Health Reasons Blame Oil Giants Next Door." *Global News*, October 16, 2013. https://globalnews.ca/news/784583/ill-wind-alberta-families-leaving-homes-for-health-reasons-blame-oil-giants-next-door/.

# 3 Northern Respectability

## Whiteness and Improvement in Fort McMurray

*Sam Spady*

## 1 Introduction

The Alberta oil sands (also known as the tar sands or bituminous sands) are a crucial site to study the intersections between neoliberal capitalism and the white settler colonialism of contemporary North America. The term *white settler colonialism* describes the foundational role of whiteness and white supremacist logics that are integral to the creation of the settler colonial project in Canada. In her book *The Intimacies of Four Continents* (2015), Lisa Lowe discusses how white supremacist logics, including anti-blackness and the transatlantic slave trade, as well as Orientalism and indentureship, structured and informed settler colonialism in the Americas, and the rise of the European colonial period. Lowe argues that we can understand the emergence of global capitalism through studying these disparate histories of colonization, and she points to the foundational role that race held in these histories for creating the present-day configurations of capitalism. Neoliberalism has been described as an "economic configuration" (Harvey 2007, 1–2) and doctrine built upon the foundations of classical liberalism where laissez-faire free markets dominate and the individual is the central political/economic actor. Unangax̂ theorist Eve Tuck describes neoliberal thought as "epistemology, economic strategy, and moral code rolled into one, neoliberalism refers to the reliance on market-based relationships to explain how the world works, or how it should work" (2012, 27). Key to neoliberalism are the ideas that the market is the most efficient way to organize society and "that economic growth equals human improvement. These rest on particular assumptions about people, including indigenous peoples" (Bargh 2007, 2). These ideas are crucial to understanding modern settler colonialism. As Māori scholar Maria Bargh argues, neoliberalism "continue[s] to perpetuate the spread of older ideas about the degrees of civilisation and techniques of civilising, although now more covertly" (2007, 13). In this way, neoliberalism functions as the "latest configuration of colonial imperialism" (Tuck 2012, 29) and offers important insights into how contemporary liberal democracies, such as Canada, can espouse liberal beliefs while engaging in colonial dispossession and violence.

In this chapter I attempt to understand how logics of improvement—that is, the settler colonial desire to improve and "uplift" the use of land—underpins how the industry and those who work in it defend oil sands extraction (Veracini 2010, 20). From the beginning of European presence in what is now Canada, the notion of uplifting or improving the use of land has been used as part of the "doctrine of discovery" to facilitate the dispossession of Indigenous Peoples from their lands to make way for Euro/Canadian settlement (Lindberg 2010). As Edward Said puts it, "You're not just robbing the people…You're improving them in some way" (1993). Improvement, progress, and aspirations for respectability have all been racially coded ways to dispossess people from lands and justify theft.

My research takes place in Fort McMurray, Alberta, the nearest urban centre to the main projects in the Athabasca oil deposit. I grew up in Fort McMurray and my family worked in the oil sands for over thirty years. I am white and grew up as a settler on Treaty 8 lands, and in this research I interviewed white settler workers. There are significant populations of Indigenous Peoples, black people, and other people of colour living and working in Fort McMurray, but their experiences are not the focus of this work. I am interested in how white settlers understand their place in this region, and how they make sense of the work they do in relation to the nation. I understand this experience to be different from the experience of those who migrate from other places, or whose place in the nation is always contingent on race and/or the conditions of their arrival into the Canadian nation.

Recruitment took place through personal networks, including neighbours, co-workers, friends, and family members. In this chapter I draw from fifteen semi-structured qualitative interviews conducted in Fort McMurray in October and December 2016. All participants worked in the oil industry and lived in Fort McMurray full time, as opposed to the population of people who work in the oil sands but commute from long distances and live in employer-provided camps during their shifts. Participants were all under the age of forty. Two-thirds of participants migrated to Fort McMurray from other places across Canada for work in the oil industry. Many came here right out of university and have spent most of their working lives in Fort McMurray. One-third of participants grew up in this community and remain here because of work opportunities and because they consider it home. Most people I spoke to were professionals, including accountants, engineers, business specialists, and executives. Only six participants of this sample of fifteen were tradespeople or office workers who did not have a university education. In these interviews, I asked participants about their work in the oil industry, their reasons for coming to the region, their relationship to this place, and the ways in which they understood and responded to the common critiques levelled at the oil development by Indigenous groups and environmentalists.

While much research on this oil deposit has asked important questions about culture (Heller et al. 2015; Major and Winters 2013), labour mobility (Thorne 2012), and neoliberalism (Adkin 2016), it is less common to find research on questions of the white settler state.[1] I argue that the framework of white settler colonialism is indispensable for understanding this region and the contradictions that emanate from it. While internationally criticized for its dirty image, the Athabasca oil deposit has also come to hold an important role for the Canadian state economically and in its imaginary. The migrations for work in this place make this story a national one as well. As many participants told me, "everyone in Canada knows at least one person working up in Fort McMurray." In tracing the political economy of the frontier, and of settler colonialism more specifically, it is possible to understand how this oil deposit functions for the nation. Furthermore, the oil sands are an important site for thinking about the racial-colonial project of the contemporary Canadian state and the economic logics that structure it.

Whether or not the people I spoke to felt complicated or conflicted about their role in the oil industry, they all drew from well-worn discourses of the Canadian national imaginary: seeking to carve out a modern city in the northern frontier, doing respectable work for the nation, and being a good citizen. These themes are all easily identifiable with the Canadian project of improvement and goodness articulated by many critical race scholars, including Sunera Thobani (2007), Sherene Razack (2015), Carol Schick (2014), and Barbara Heron (2007). Through these accounts, I argue that it is important to examine how whiteness and particular forms of Canadian nationalism are at play in this region in order to understand how oil has come to been seen as foundational not only to the Canadian economy but also the Canadian imaginary (Barney 2017). In this chapter I explore three themes that arose from interviews conducted with Fort McMurray residents employed in the oil industry: (1) opportunity, and the political economy of interprovincial migration in Canada; (2) corporate culture, the ways in which people identify with their employment; (3) improvement discourses and the way these discourses structure white Canadian national identity.[2] Thinking through whiteness in this chapter allows me to pay attention to the ways in which the logics and desires that sought to found the Canadian state as a white nation continue to function in the present day through objectives of improvement, civility, and good citizenship (Berger 1966; Thobani 2007). To understand extractive economies under settler colonialism, it is important to trace how the logics of improvement make extraction a logical and desired objective, even as this oil deposit is the site of conflict over access to Indigenous land use, environmental degradation, and a place of incredible industrial growth, and mass migration of labour to feed the industry (Athabasca Chipewyan First Nation 2010; Nikiforuk 2010; Thorne 2012).

## 2 Opportunity on the Frontier

The first theme emerging from these interviews is economic migration and the political economy of resource extraction in Canada. Many of my participants left the places they called home for the lucrative wages offered by the oil and gas sector. Historical and ongoing depressed economic conditions in many parts of Canada have fuelled migration to oil and gas regions for decades. One participant in her thirties, originally from Cape Breton, Nova Scotia, made the choice to move to Fort McMurray a few years after graduating university. She and her husband, suffering under the weight of their student loan payments, realized they were heading towards bankruptcy. Working retail and living in her father's basement after university and marriage, she said moving to Fort McMurray made independence, financial stability, and the chance to work towards a career (as opposed to working in the increasingly precarious retail labour force) possible for the first time. This was a story shared by many of my participants, particularly by those from the Maritimes and other economically depressed regions in the country. For these individuals, a "real" job was at least ten years away. The economically driven migration from the Maritimes and Newfoundland has become a central feature of Fort McMurray's demographics (Heller et al. 2015; Major and Winters 2013; Thorne 2012). This migration has been ongoing since the late 1980s, leaving Fort McMurray importantly shaped by East Coast culture (Thorne 2012). For this participant, migration first felt as a failure: "I didn't want to be another East Coaster in the Mac," but soon the opportunities, the money, and life possible there made her "Fort Mac proud" and a self-appointed "ambassador for the city."

One participant in her mid-twenties, from southwestern Ontario, where her employer also has operations at an oil refinery, said she could have moved home during the wildfire evacuation of Fort McMurray in May 2016. While her company would have found her a job at the Ontario office, she decided to return to Fort McMurray despite losing her home and possessions. She reasoned that staying in Ontario would have left her locked into an administrative role for the rest of her career, whereas in Fort McMurray, she continues to advance and enjoys a more dynamic environment. She sees Fort McMurray as a place where her incomplete university education does not harm her chances for career advancement. Moreover, she can continue to work while her company pays for her to finish her college certificate and has offered to pay for her business degree if she decides to continue. This is a common story in Fort McMurray, where companies big and small often pay for their employees' education, and many employees pursue an MBA or upgrade their college diplomas into full four-year bachelor's degrees.

Because of these opportunities, many participants described experiencing high personal fulfillment in their careers. Their work environments provide financial security and the possibility of accumulating wealth. It is common to hear employees share immense gratitude for having a career of which they are proud. Thus, criticisms of the oil sands in the Athabasca region challenge the means through which these participants have become fulfilled and financially secure—in their words, "real adults." With a lack of economic opportunity in many regions, there has been widespread interprovincial migration to oil-and-gas-rich regions. Though this migration is not new (Newfoundlanders have been travelling west for decades, particularly after the cod fishery collapsed in the 1990s; see Thorne 2012), migration intensified in the early to mid-2000s as oil prices rose dramatically. Oil projects expanded, offering lucrative wages and other financial incentives to meet the boom-driven labour shortage. However, it is also important to note that as manufacturing, forestry, and other export industries in Canada suffered during the mid-2000s, it became the de facto policy of the Canadian government to encourage interprovincial migration to Alberta to deal with job losses. As opposed to addressing regional and sector-based unemployment, former Finance Minister Jim Flaherty famously argued that employment insurance did not need to be expanded because out-of-work Canadians could relocate to Alberta to find a job (Curry 2012). Relocation became the strategy through which to deal with economic crises, and entire remittance-based economies now exist in some regions of the Maritimes (Heller et al. 2015).

Similarly, one participant, who works in supply chain management for a large oil company, explained how moving to Fort McMurray radically altered his life. Stuck in lower-paid jobs in the Maritimes and then again when he moved to Ontario, the ability to find meaningful, "adult" work in Fort McMurray completely improved his well-being. He told me,

> [Working here has] made me…It's changed a lot of things about me…It's given me a sort of direction and a means to do the things I want to do. Before I was, like I said, when I was at the bank [in Ontario], I didn't like what I was doing, I didn't like the environment, I was just barely making enough money to get by, then I went Ottawa, and I couldn't get a decent job, so again I was scraping by. And I came here, and now I have the means to do things I couldn't do before. So it's changed me in a sense, I feel more complete, I have more confidence, before I was just sort of—I would shrink away from things. Because all of my friends who lived out here, worked out here would go on vacation and meet together, and I was just kind of like, well I'm working at a kitchen at a restaurant, and let's talk about what you're doing instead. So it definitely gave me more confidence. And I even noticed that in my relationship. Before I was depressed, I didn't want to talk about the future because I didn't really have a present. Whereas now we can plan, we have a baby on the way, coming in a few months.

These kinds of concerns are common for young people in Canada: a university education leading to unemployment or underemployment has become a generational consequence of contemporary neoliberal precarity.

Though, taking a longer view of history, settler desire for the "good life" has both facilitated colonialism while alleviating the problems and crises of capitalism for centuries. The colony served to offer the landless and the working and entrepreneurial classes alike wealth that was unattainable in the metropole. Much like economic migration patterns in Fort McMurray over the last forty years, Richard Slotkin (1985) has described a similar pattern as being a crucial feature of the American Frontier. Tracing the opening of new frontiers in the United States from 1800 to 1890, Slotkin argues that a frontier theory of development allowed the problem of scarcity and inequality to go unsolved. He writes, "the Frontier theory of development offers both a theory of capital development and a theory of social relations. It sees the sources of wealth as lying outside society, an unappropriated natural wilderness, rather than as the products of social labor: it sees acquisition of that sort of wealth as an antidote to social [class/race] conflicts within the Metropolis" (1985, 45). As cities in the American colony became filled with waged poor, the newly opened frontier of the historical moment offered the enterprising young man a place to stake his claim, addressing the scarcity of the colonial metropolis with the resources, opportunity, and open spaces of the frontier colony. Looking at Fort McMurray today, it is not hard to see this frontier theory in contemporary practice. Those on the periphery of the economy can relocate and stake their claim, get a good job (likely with a pension), and buy a house—the old markers of North American success, which are increasingly unavailable to young workers (see Gross, this volume). Again, this does not happen by accident, but instead by state policy to depend upon frontier development to ameliorate the scarcity of decent work, and economic security found elsewhere.

## 3 Petro-Nationalism and Corporate Social Responsibility

The second reoccurring theme in interviews with my participants is strong personal identification with the companies employing them. This identification was strong across different groups of workers: professionals identified the strongest, while some tradespeople and blue-collar employees shared marginally less identification with their employer. It was more common for tradespeople to have worked for multiple companies during different phases of their apprenticeship, and therefore they had a wider exposure to different corporate practices. Ray, a communications professional who works for a major pipeline company, told me that he is proud of the culture of inclusivity and corporate social responsibility his employer engenders. Ray remarked,

> I work on a diverse staff, I work with a very gender-balanced staff, I work with a management team that is made up of a number of different voices and collective focuses and common goals that are universal to all Canadians. We want the safety of our operations, we want the environment stewarded to in a way that is meaningful. And yet what it seems to come across as, in the larger discourse is "Oh yeah, that's the oil industry, this big, bad monolith of people who are heartless, and soulless and focused on nothing but the bottom line." And that is a very difficult us vs. them to break now because those attacks on the personal character

> of people who work in the industry or that kind of labelling them as being these kind of deviant, heartless, soulless people really doesn't aid in the conversation bringing out their ideas for improvement. And I think in a lot of cases when they work within the company they just discover opportunities to really enhance the way that we do business. And that's why I'm staying in the industry, I feel trusted and respected and valued.

Ray and many other participants describe what they see as the oil industry's desire for excellence, which makes them proud to work there and be a part of the oil industry. They identify with the company to the point that critiques of the sector are often rebutted defensively; then the integrity of the company reflects their own. This identification with corporate social responsibility was illustrated to me by participants praising the many volunteer initiatives run by companies (which are widely taken up by employees), rigorous environmental testing, and creating training and job opportunities for Indigenous Peoples. There is a real pride and belief in the work they do as having a positive impact on the Canadian economy in general and on their community in Fort McMurray in particular. Many pointed to the federal–provincial transfer payments program and spoke of pride in oil money funding universities and hospitals across the country. The markers of the progressive Canadian state—universal health care and publicly funded universities—are made possible through oil extraction and export.

Indeed, a new consensus on the place of oil as a pillar of the Canadian economy has emerged since 2008. This consensus is perhaps more obvious now that the Conservative government, which favoured oil and gas, has been replaced with Justin Trudeau's Liberal government, which campaigned on Indigenous approval for projects on their territories. However, Trudeau's December 2016 approval of the controversial Trans Mountain and Line 3 pipelines (both of which cross many Indigenous territories and are being protested by some of these nations) illustrates the continued dismissal of Indigenous assertion to sovereignty over development on their land, and the national consensus about the importance of oil in the nation. During the crash of oil prices in 2014, the calls for more pipelines to get "our oil to market" became the new economic solution for oil-dependent provinces as well as the federal government, as both suffered huge losses in their annual budgets. The subsequent approval of the Trans Mountain and Line 3 pipelines was described by Prime Minister Trudeau as a "major win for Canadian workers, for Canadian families and the Canadian economy now and into the future" (Tasker 2016). Linking the oil sands to the national well-being and economic prosperity for workers and their families, Trudeau affirms the role of resource extraction in the national imaginary.

A part of this consensus is achieved through social licence to operate. Forms of corporate charity and (particularly in Fort McMurray) corporate investments in communities including schools, infrastructure projects, and recreation centres seek to "create conditions of dependence upon the private sector which can help secure the social license needed for many corporations to operate" (Preston 2017, 367). These investments would have once been made by governments as part of the welfare state. With neoliberal restructuring, as Jen Preston argues, corporate social responsibility has become a strategic and important tool for extractive companies to "become associated with social good, particularly where extractive-sector workers live, the social, political and environmental costs of their operations are obscured from view" (2017, 368). More than just public relations, gaining corporate social licence to operate in these places is also about embedding and normalizing the extractive company in the everyday life of the community.

Fort McMurray is home to many examples of this social licensing technique. The new Catholic high school has a state-of-the-art performing arts centre sponsored and named after Suncor Energy. The impressive recreation centre and sporting facility at MacDonald Island features Shell Place, and again, the Suncor Community Leisure Centre (though all oil companies operating in the region are major sponsors of this facility). Sponsorship of social and sporting events is commonplace, as are scholarships and research funding. The social licensing project begins early targeting youth: Syncrude has children's mascots (Billy and Becky the Bison; see Joly, this volume), who entertain at social functions;[3] it is common for oil companies to sponsor summer camps and teaching materials for both elementary and secondary education. These sponsorships "all embed a variety of capital-driven corporations into the everyday of contemporary settler colonial life," further normalizing extractive economies (Preston 2017, 368).

My participants were quick to defend these practices as "civic pride." There is little cynicism about the true goals of these programs and sponsorships, as those I spoke to feel very strongly that the oil companies have made it part of their culture to give back, and argue this value is as much about community building as it is about the corporations' socially responsible values. Furthermore, this sense of civic spirit is something many participants told me makes Fort McMurray a community they are proud of and help to make this place feel like home. More than just creating social licence for the extractive operations, it also becomes a practice of community making and identity building for those who live and work in Fort McMurray. When placed alongside the ways in which people described their community, corporate identity fits into a larger conversation about respectability and goodness. Moving from how these feelings of community pride and corporate social practice are narrated by participants to the literature on colonialism, it becomes possible to trace how objectives of improvement and progress are not neutral or necessarily positive goals. These aspirations have instead long been an organizing principle of the colonial project and, as scholars have shown, in modern state initiatives and development projects (Li 2007; McClintock [1995] 2013; Razack 2015; Said 1993; Scott 1998; Stoler 1995).

## 4 Improvement

Improving the productivity of the Athabasca region is a goal with deep roots in the colonial project. Once the frontier has been settled, the mission then turns to improving the land, or uplifting it to a "higher purpose" (Veracini 2010, 20). As part of the national myth, the Canadian National earns his right on the land through labour, which supposedly makes our settlement a peaceful and hard-working one (Ignatieff 2000). Through the Lockean configuration to perform an act of "original appropriation," work forges both the settler's place on the land and his place in the nation. Value of and entitlement to land was only recognized through "productive" European practices. Cree legal scholar Tracey Lindberg has described how the Doctrine of Discovery codified racial superiority of European conquerors, and constructed Indigenous Peoples as in need of civilization, "as [the] rationale to take Indigenous lands on the basis of Indigenous peoples' constructed and Doctrinally defined deficiencies and inhumanity" (2010, 95). This doctrine includes the erasure and constructed deficiency of Indigenous property systems and land use. As Zapotec political scientist Isabel Altamirano-Jiménez argues, "Although Indigenous territories were imprinted by human actions and inhabitants were governed by complex systems of land use and ownership, disavowing Indigenous peoples and constructing them as 'hunter-gatherers' and their lands as being waste or 'wilderness' corresponded to a practice of eliminating Indigenous peoples. Moreover, these constructions justified the civilizing action of English settlers and the rejections of Indigenous land ownership" (2013, 32). Viewing land in relation to racially/doctrinally defined use placed European land use as superior. To make way for the transformation of land for so-called productive uses, the removal and erasure of Indigenous Peoples was justified under the banner of improvement and progress (see also Li 2007).

Sean K. Maher's (2011) historical account of the Treaty 8 commission, which sought to extinguish Indigenous title (in an area that now includes northern Alberta, northeastern British Columbia, northwestern Saskatchewan, and south-central Northwest Territories) through a predetermined treaty, is particularly helpful to explain how the application of these ideas worked in the Canadian Northwest. Maher charts the ways in which misapprehension of Indigenous practices of land use justified Canadian appropriation and then settlement of this land. Drawing extensively from the correspondence and travelogues of the Treaty 8 commissioners from the summer of 1900, Maher illustrates how the commissioners saw the land through the lens of *terra nullius*. According to the commissioners, "the forest appeared empty as seen from a passing boat moving slowly along the Athabasca River. There was an 'absence of life of any kind along the river,' and from the commission's vantage point, 'even fish seemed to be anything but plentiful'" (Maher 2011, 67). Descriptions of this empty land sought to depopulate the territory and depict Indigenous Peoples and communities as barely human and, in other cases, as a population quickly dying out (Maher 2011, 67–68). Maher characterizes the commission's view of the Treaty 8 land as a "transformative gaze" that sought to incorporate this region into the Canadian settler colonial project, which was predicated on European settlement and agriculture (2011, 71). Making land productive through labour becomes a form of emplacement or place making for the settler (Blomley 2003). Labour, through its value and role in the imaginary of "building the nation," becomes an important practice for developing identities in the colony for the National subject—what Shona Jackson has called a "technique of settler belonging" (2012, 61). Capitalism's and colonialism's entangled structures co-create these discourses of working to earn one's place on the land and in the nation.

In Fort McMurray today, this process also resembles city making: building schools, new recreation centers, new shopping facilities, offering affordable public transit with heated bus shelters. Research participants constantly remarked to me how much the city has been changing for the better. I found myself constantly commenting to participants how I barely recognized the place. The Tim Hortons coffee shop in which many of my research meetings took place had been a dense forest only six years before. This rapid change reflected our own imaginaries of the place, including constant growth and work. A commonly held imaginary of Fort McMurray is a town of hard-working people, employed in an industry that itself is constantly improving. This contrasts with the imaginary widely held of the city as a boomtown. Many social problems plagued the city during the boom in the early 2000s; this bad version of Fort McMurray was referenced many times by participants.

This boomtown version of Fort McMurray is one filled with young people who have access to quick money but must deal with the loneliness of working long hours away from family and friends, and spend their cash on drugs and sex workers. Substance abuse, criminal activity, and high divorce rates as a result of long hours, and loneliness in the work camps for commuting workers soon became a powerful narrative used to describe the social problems the city faced during the protracted boom of the early and mid-2000s (see Gross, this volume). This particular imaginary was one my participants were quite sensitive to. The negative views of their new home held by many of their families and friends back home made participants quick to defend the reputation of the city and to highlight its best attributes. Describing a time she felt judged for living and working in Fort McMurray, one participant, originally from Nova Scotia, told me,

> I think it's just that it's [the town] pictured as dirty site workers, men, and just the dirty…I think what it is, is that a lot of people from home, go back and tell those stories, and they are the ones who have stayed in camp, and they go back and forth. And so I think a lot of people get those kind of stories…camp, that doesn't sound great, but camp isn't Fort McMurray, and that's what a lot of people don't realize. That those are two totally separate things. That's not the community of Fort

> McMurray, and that has nothing to do with camp life, that's two different lives. That's part of it, and just, the media doesn't give it the best name, and it's just seen as dirty and remote...So it's constantly, I feel like I'm constantly fighting for Fort McMurray.

Repeatedly in the interviews my participants insisted on their respectability, and on the town's transformation. They see themselves and the community in general as responsible, hard working, and caring. They recounted stories of neighbours who know each other, have barbecues together on the weekend, and help each other out with childcare. These are people who volunteer and have boundless civic pride. The re-branding, for people who live here at least, seems to be complete.

Participants narrated how, although Fort McMurray was once a town ravaged by the social issues of its transient populations, the city has emerged as a stable suburb in which to raise families. One participant, an engineer and now executive, describes the city in overwhelmingly positive terms:

> As far as living in Fort McMurray, itself, I wish people could see the community that we do have here. Not just the negativity that the media seems to portray. It seems that whenever you see a clip of Fort McMurray, it's the downtown strip, when you see, you know they talk about drugs, and homeless people, and shift workers working fourteen hours a day and not getting to see their families, and they talk about divorce, they don't talk about the vast majority of people here who are making a good living for themselves, giving a great living to their family. And that community that we have here.

The version of a community that counts, which is desired, is the community as defined by white middle-class values (Dorow and O'Shaughnessy 2013). Citing the recent economic downturn and wildfire (see Wanvik, this volume), many told me the silver lining of these hardships was that people who were not committed to the city did not come back. The people who loved the city and who wanted to put down roots came back to rebuild.

My participants see themselves in a very different light than the way they are portrayed by the media and in the collective Canadian imagination of the oil industry. Ray, the communications professional mentioned above, told me, "I'm not a good old boy from Texas." He holds multiple university degrees and is deeply critical of both the former Conservative Harper government and former Progressive Conservative provincial governments. Many participants saw themselves in similar ways, and reconciled their more liberal values within their roles in the oil industry in a number of interesting ways, partially through their claim to civility as demonstrated by their tolerant attitudes attained through education. Ray explained,

> One of the most disdainful things I witness is the framing of Fort McMurray as a blue-collar community. It's not that I have anything

> against the blue-collar work that happens there; it's an essential part of the process, but I think it's been framed as, you know, all of the backwater attitude, that very conservative focus on things, that hasn't necessarily been accurate. If you look at the make-up, the demography of Fort McMurray itself, it's one of the most diverse and educated cities in Canada. You have a huge proportion of the population university educated because they're engineers, and they are technical specialists who are looking at the very scientific aspects of the oil sands process. Extraction, tailings management, engineering of mines, engineering of water intake sources of water management and environmental considerations. So you have that very white-collar aspect to the community, you have a very diverse community with a number of new Canadians who have contributed a tremendous amount to the community and to Canada as a whole through their work in the industry.

Through the appeal to education and diversity (and the assumed acceptance of diversity), many of my participants see themselves as living a moral life. They are not like the Texans who own the companies they work for, and they are not the presumed racists, or holders of "backwater attitudes" stereotypically associated with less educated blue-collar workers. Theirs is a claim to civil, respectable whiteness: one that is responsible, pragmatic, and hard working.

This particular version of civility is described by many participants who describe how their environmentally concerned friends do not judge them for their roles in the oil industry. One engineer told me, "I have friends who work in solar energy, and a friend who's a lawyer—an environmental lawyer. Most of the people I know understand oil's place in the world and understand the necessity." His friends' ability to be pragmatic and respectful of his work despite their personal beliefs references the type of Canadian civility that Daniel Coleman describes in his 2006 book, *White Civility*. White civility, or the common Canadian stereotype of extreme politeness, is important to understanding how Canadian culture sanctions and accepts settler colonialism while it aspires to a morality that would otherwise come into conflict with settler colonialism. The norm of English Canadian cultural identity has developed around the "conflation of whiteness and civility" a civility built upon ideas of "Britishness" distinguishing British Canadian colonialism from the violence of American settlement, as well as the excess and lassitude of upper-class English gentlemen and European elites (Coleman 2006, 5). Central to making a racial and moral Canadian project was the idea that the best qualities of British masculinity could be improved upon and strengthened through the hard work of settlement and fortitude nurtured by the northern climate (Coleman 2006, 24). Goodness *and* whiteness are thus placed at the heart of the Canadian national imaginary (see also Lee-Jones, this volume).

Significantly, civility is built on both "*the temporal notion* of civilization as progress that was central to the idea of modernity and the colonial mission with the *moral-ethical concept* of a (relatively) peaceful order" (Coleman 2006, 10). In these ways, civility, and a racialized definition of the civil, came to become both an organizing principle for the nation-building project throughout the early twentieth century, but also a method of self-management and definition (Coleman 2006, 12). This idea is useful to think of in relation to how many people who work in the oil industry see their work as making the world a better place. Ray sees his work at the pipeline company in this way. As he explained,

> I like my career. One of the other things I fully stand behind, and it's something that a colleague of mine at another oil company had mentioned once, but it's how is change going to happen within companies if we don't have good people in them. And I honestly think, if you have people who care, who are passionate, who are driven to do better and to move forward addressing a number of different needs that are not just bottom lines and profits, but also social needs and finding ways, and making things more efficient and more intelligent in their design—we need those people in all aspects of life. Which means we need them in oil companies to affect change, we need them working in government to affect change, and I think my role in the oil and gas sector right now…is perfect for me.

This perspective is shared by many in the industry: there are good people working to improve an industry that is already striving for excellence. However, this type of individualization of the problem and solutions from people inside the industry ignores the structures of the state and the industry. While money is spent on reclamation projects (Joly, this volume) and research to clean up tailings ponds, the question of the state's right to destroy Treaty lands for these extractive projects remains unaddressed (see Wheatley and Westman, this volume). In making the focus on individuals, the question about what to do about the oil sands becomes a problem of individual solutions, motivations, or morality. The fact that many participants saw themselves as doing good in the industry further demonstrates how this problem can become individualized. Indeed, the conversation about goodness allows us to bypass the material considerations of land and the structures of the state, which authorize extractive land use. Cris Mayo describes a similar tendency in anti-racism education initiatives that focus on the individual. Mayo writes that to "overcome the political distances without actually altering the material conditions that structure those differences" creates conditions for individualizing the solutions to racism, which in turn protects whiteness and the structures that produce it (2002, 179). These personal solutions become a civil attempt to achieve a more educated or cosmopolitan attitude, a civility that performs a particular form of whiteness that is made anew. Similarly, the focus on the impact the individual can make on the larger structures of the oil industry bypasses the material consideration of what must be sacrificed for this industry to exist.

For example, many of the people I interviewed believe the water quality in the downstream Indigenous community of Fort Chipewyan is better now than before the oil industry arrived in the region, despite overwhelming scientific evidence to the contrary (e.g., Kelly et al. 2010) and Indigenous activism to protect the Athabasca River. These participants' logic is that, as the tarry oil naturally seeps from the riverbank into the river, the pollution predates industrial oil extraction. Now that state of-the-art water monitoring systems have been implemented and oil companies are actively taking the oil out of the ground, they suggest, less bitumen is getting washed downstream. Indeed, the oil industry's environmental self-promotion is widely adopted by those I interviewed. They see the industry as actively engaged in and improving its impact on the environment (see Wheatley and Westman, this volume; Gross, this volume).

As a result, it is perhaps understandable that many of those with whom I spoke felt unfairly attacked by environmental movements and national media outlets that cover the environmental impacts of the industry. They see themselves as part of a project that is entirely respectable, legal, and voluntarily operating under corporate social responsibility frameworks. Critiques of the liberal project and its connection with settler colonialism, however, routinely point to the use of respectability as a way to distinguish between the subject and the Other, the settler and the native. Ann Laura Stoler's (1995) thesis is significant here; she argues that from the beginning, goodness and respectability were a racial and class-based colonial project of distinguishing who would rule and who would be ruled. Focusing on how the industry might be improved from the inside by well-meaning employees, or through its own internal social responsible ethics, falls too easily into this logic of respectability and goodness. For this reason, the oil sands demand to be studied as a racial-colonial project of late capitalism. The use of land, its productivity and value, and how this ideology operates through notions of progress, race, and civility are deeply tied together in the structures of extractive capitalism and settler colonialism. Attending to how these logics and structures push and pull people into extractive futures brings our attention back from looking at individual people and their choices as either problem or solution.

In this chapter I have argued that understanding the role of improvement as a driver and logic of settler colonialism is important to make sense of the oil sands. Examining this place through the frameworks of white settler colonialism and improvement, it becomes possible to understand how industrial projects can be justified as a practice of productive land use and place making. Through the political economy of frontier development, resource extraction offers the state a temporary solution to the crises created by neoliberal precarity and regional economic disparity. However, as I have argued, there is more at work in this place than simple economic factors.

Through corporate social licensing techniques and both community and individual desires for improvement, oil extraction becomes a normalized feature of everyday life. Tracing how oil becomes an inevitable feature at both the scale of the local community but also on the macro level of nation building, it is possible to understand how logics of land use, progress, and improvement are woven into the colonial capitalist relations of contemporary Canadian resource extraction.

## Notes

1 See Preston (2013, 2017) for the exception.
2 *Canadian National* is a term developed by Sunera Thobani (2007) to discuss white Canadian subjectivity, and how this subject position (and racial formation) is created through a triangulation between Indigenous Peoples and the racialized immigrant Other. Thobani argues that through celebrating the "diversity" of immigrants who are not white, the Canadian National constructs itself as the legitimate "Canadian subject" who is also benevolent and tolerant enough to grant status to the Other, reproducing the superiority of the white subject's compassion.
3 My first job was wearing the Billy the Bison costume at local hockey games.

## References


Adkin, Laurie E. 2016. "Ecology and Governance in a First World Petro-State." In *First World Petro-Politics: The Political Ecology and Governance of Alberta*, edited by Laurie E. Adkin, 3–50. Toronto: University of Toronto Press.

Altamirano-Jiménez, Isabel. 2013. *Indigenous Encounters with Neoliberalism: Place, Women, and the Environment in Canada and Mexico*. Vancouver: University of British Columbia Press.

Athabasca Chipewyan First Nation. 2010. "ACFN Elders' Declaration on Rights to Land Use." *Athabasca Chipewyan First*, July 8, 2010. http://media.wix.com/ugd/58e3a4_dab1a7bbd76a482287fca0bdb29d3906.pdf.

Barney, Darin. 2017. "Who We Are and What We Do: Canada as a Pipeline Nation." In *Petrocultures: Oil, Politics, Culture*, edited by Sheena Wilson, Adam Carlson, and Imre Szeman, 79–119. Montreal and Kingston: McGill-Queen's University Press.

Bargh, Maria. 2007. "Introduction." In *Resistance: An Indigenous Response to Neoliberalism*, edited by Maria Bargh, 1–25. Wellington, NZ: Hula Publishers.

Berger, Carl. 1966. "The True North Strong and Free." In *Nationalism in Canada*, edited by Peter Russell, 3–26. Toronto: McGraw Hill.

Blomley, Nicholas. 2003. "Law, Property, and the Geography of Violence: The Frontier, the Survey, and the Grid." *Annals of the Association of American Geographers* 93 (1): 121–41.

Coleman, Daniel. 2006. *White Civility: The Literary Project of English Canada*. Toronto: University of Toronto Press.

Curry, Bill. 2012. "Sweeping EI Changes Usher in Three New Tiers of Jobless Workers." *Globe and Mail*, May 24, 2012. https://www.theglobeandmail.com/news/politics/sweeping-ei-changes-usher-in-three-new-tiers-of-jobless-workers/article4209603/.

Dorow, Sara, and Sara O'Shaughnessy. 2013. "Fort McMurray, Wood Buffalo, and the Oil/Tar Sands: Revisiting the Sociology of 'Community.'" *Canadian Journal of Sociology* [Cahiers canadiens de sociologie] 38 (2): 121–40.

Harvey, David. 2007. *A Brief History of Neoliberalism*. New York: Oxford University Press.

Heller, Monica, Lindsay A. Bell, Michelle Daveluy, Mireille McLaughlin, and Hubert Noël. 2015. *Sustaining the Nation: The Making and Moving of Language and Nation*. Oxford: Oxford University Press.

Heron, Barbara. 2007. *Desire for Development: Whiteness, Gender, and the Helping Imperative*. Waterloo, ON: Wilfrid Laurier University Press.

Ignatieff, Michael. 2000. *The Rights Revolution*. Toronto: House of Anansi Press.

Jackson, Shona N. 2012. *Creole* Indigeneity*: Between Myth and Nation in the Caribbean*. Minneapolis: University of Minnesota Press.

Kelly, E.N., D.W. Schindler, P.V. Hodson, J.W. Short, R. Radmanovich, and C.C. Nielsen. 2010. "Oil Sands Development Contributes Elements Toxic at Low Concentrations to the Athabasca River and Its Tributaries." *Proceedings of the National Academy of Sciences* 107 (37): 16178–183.

Li, Tania Murray. 2007. *The Will to Improve: Governmentality, Development, and the Practice of Politics*. Durham, NC: Duke University Press.

Lindberg, Tracey. 2010. "The Doctrine of Discovery in Canada." In *Discovering Indigenous Lands: The Doctrine of Discovery in the English Colonies*, edited by Robert J. Miller, Jacinta Ruru, Larissa Behrendt, and Tracey Lindberg, 89–125. Oxford: Oxford University Press.

Lowe, Lisa. 2015. *The Intimacies of Four Continents*. Durham, NC: Duke University Press.

Maher, Sean K. 2011. "Narrating Administrative Order: Treaty 8 and the Geographical Fashioning of the Canadian North." *Postcolonial Studies* 14 (1): 63–74.

Major, Claire, and Tracy Winters. 2013. "Community by Necessity: Security, Insecurity, and the Flattening of Class in Fort McMurray, Alberta." *Canadian Journal of Sociology* [Cahiers canadiens de sociologie] 38 (2): 141–65.

Mayo, Cris. 2002. "The Binds That Tie: Civility and Social Difference." *Educational Theory* 52 (2): 169–86.

McClintock, Anne. [1995] 2013. *Imperial Leather: Race, Gender, and Sexuality in the Colonial Contest*. New York: Routledge.

Nikiforuk, Andrew. 2010. *Tar Sands: Dirty Oil and the Future of a Continent*. Vancouver: Greystone Books.

Preston, Jen. 2013. "Neoliberal Settler Colonialism, Canada and the Tar Sands." *Race & Class* 55 (2): 42–59.

———. 2017. "Racial Extractivism and White Settler Colonialism: An Examination of the Canadian Tar Sands Mega-Projects." *Cultural Studies* 31 (2–3): 353–75.

Razack, Sherene. 2015. *Dying from Improvement: Inquests and Inquiries into Indigenous Deaths in Custody*. Toronto: University of Toronto Press.

Said, Edward. 1993. "Culture and Imperialism." Lecture delivered at York University, Toronto, ON, February 10, 1993. Accessed September 26, 2018. http://engres.ied.edu.hk/literature/E-lecture(Mat)/Week3(RudyardKipling)/Culture%20and%20Imperialism.pdf.

Schick, Carol. 2014. "White Resentment in Settler Society." *Race Ethnicity and Education* 17 (1): 88–102.

Scott, James. 1998. *Seeing like a state: How certain schemes to improve the human condition have failed.* New Haven: Yale University Press.
Slotkin, Richard. 1985. *The Fatal Environment: The Myth of the Frontier in the Age of Industrialization,* 1800–1890. New York: Atheneum.
Stoler, Ann Laura. 1995. *Race and the Education of Desire: Foucault's History of Sexuality and the Colonial Order of Things.* Durham, NC: Duke University Press.
Thobani, Sunera. 2007. *Exalted Subjects: Studies in the Making of Race and Nation in Canada.* Toronto: University of Toronto Press.
Thorne, Cory. 2012. "Mexicans with Sweaters, Working in the Oil/Tar Sands, in Newfoundland's Third Largest City: Regionalism, Narrative, and Imagination in Fort McMurray, (Texas?)." *Ethnologies* 34 (1–2): 29–58.
Tasker, John Paul. 2016. "Trudeau Cabinet Approves TransMountain, Line 3 Pipelines, Rejects Northern Gateway." *CBC News*, November 29, 2016. https://www.cbc.ca/news/politics/federal-cabinet-trudeau-pipeline-decisions-1.3872828.
Tuck, Eve. 2012. *Urban Youth and School Pushout: Gateways, Get-Aways, and the GED.* New York: Routledge.
Veracini, Lorenzo. 2010. *Settler Colonialism: A Theoretical Overview.* Basingstoke, UK: Palgrave Macmillan, 2010.

# 4 Wastelanding the Bodies, Wastelanding the Land

## Accidents as Evidence in the Albertan Oil Sands

*Lena Gross*

### Introduction

Since my interest in the Albertan oil sands started in 2010, reports about oil spills, pollution, and workplace accidents have dominated international news. While only workplace incidents fall under the traditional understanding of the umbrella term *accident*, I heard all of these undesired events commonly referred to as accidents both during fieldwork and in the news. I started to wonder if it would make sense to look at all three types of negative happenings collectively instead of analyzing each separately. Following this thought, I wondered if investigating the emic term *accident* could tell me something about the way people made sense out of destruction, death, or other negative impacts caused by oil sands extraction, which led me quickly to further questions: Are repeated occurrences of accidents evidence of a system out of balance? Can one still call events accidents if they are avoidable, foreshadowed, and highly recurrent? After all, accidents are commonly understood as first an unforeseen and unplanned event or circumstance, happening by chance with a lack of intention or necessity; or second, an unfortunate event resulting especially from carelessness or ignorance. In their legal meaning, accidents are understood as an unexpected occurrence causing loss or injury that is not due to any fault or misconduct on the part of the person injured but for which legal relief may be sought (*Merriam-Webster* 2017). The word *accident* itself clouds the question of who is to blame. While it is easily connected with images of injuries, the term still obscures the violence of an event and the agency behind such violence. Workplace injuries or deaths, pollution, and infrastructure failures do not happen intentionally, but they do not happen accidently either. They are incorporated in and a by-product of a capitalist system of extractive industries, which has a certain worldview and set of values.

Nevertheless, the incidents mentioned above are often called accidents.[1] This naming abstracts them from their causes and depicts them as unavoidable, unforeseen, and definitely without someone or something to blame (besides in some circumstances a specific oil well, an individual worker, the weather, or some similar causes). In this chapter, I will investigate work-related accidents that hurt the human body as well as environmental pollution and infrastructure failures—both as accidents and as ongoing and structural issues of extractive industries in a settler colonial state. I argue that querying the term *accident* helps to understand hidden mechanisms of violence. Infrastructure failures that create oil spills and contaminate the surrounding land, air, and water are partly seen as pollution, but they also place bodies of humans, animals, and vegetation at risk in other ways. Therefore, these events are both a cause and a bridge between the two other types of accident: pollution and workplace accidents. I will argue that these three types of accidents can be scrutinized using the concept of wastelanding developed by Traci Voyles (2015). I will then investigate the outcomes of these accidents and argue that accidents in the oil sands industry are evidence of processes that disrespect the land and people and render them pollutable. Last, I will explore how social scientists can use accidents, and how people make sense of them, to discuss power relations, colonial practices, and inequality in northern Alberta, Canada.

This chapter is based on a year of ethnographic fieldwork in the Lac La Biche region of northeastern Alberta during 2013 and 2014, a follow-up visit in the summer of 2015, and continuous engagement with the media discourse surrounding the oil sands since 2010. My research focused on locals who worked in the oil sands industry and their families, most of whom are between the ages of twenty and fifty, and many of whom are of Indigenous background.

## Accidents at Work

Gavin,[2] an Edmonton resident in his early thirties who grew up in northwestern Alberta, told me the following over a beer when I asked him about his experiences working in the oil sands,[3] one hot summer day in the beginning of my fieldwork:

> It was the Wild West out there—only cowboys, it was crazy. There used to be prostitutes in the camps, and everyone was drinking and using lots of drugs. Once there was this guy who fell off his Cat[4] with a bottle of whiskey in his hand. My first job there was when I was twenty. I just got kicked out of music school and I went. The job was six weeks straight; everyone worked six weeks straight. After four weeks, we all were certified insane. It was at Rainbow Lake—as far north as you can go in Alberta—a long piece of pipeline. There wasn't enough space in the camp so they put up an old trailer; that's where I slept and sometimes the heat went away, in the middle of the night. I was lit on fire in the end of the job, but well, I healed. It is not like this anymore, now everything is so disciplined, so organized, it's lost its soul, and it is not memorable anymore. Many workers don't talk about it anymore; there is so much negativity about their work. But the oil industry, you could do what you wanted out there; there

> was a freedom. Now it is all controlled. I was there when they started to talk about safety, and now it is more like prison in the camps, all organized, with guards at the fences, but you get food, and it is warm.

For Gavin, the changes towards more restrictions, more safety procedures, and accountability took away the magic of the experience; he missed the "craziness" (his word) of the old days where only the toughest made it through a whole shift, according to Gavin.[5] Now regulations in theory prevent workers from working more than twenty-one consecutive days, and while drinking and buying sexual services still take place in camps, these practices are more discreet.

Most jobs in the oil sands for people without higher education are of a physical nature and include long shifts, working outside in the cold, and isolation from one's community and family. Accidents and illnesses, mental health issues, and addictions are common. Gavin and other men in their late twenties to mid-forties who worked as labourers in the oil sands industry often stress the endurance they need to do their work well. For working-class men, their bodies—or, more concretely, their bodily strength—becomes the commodity they sell to make a living, and a broken body equals a broken commodity (McDowell 2009, 129). This equation of body and labour adds precariousness to an already often uncertain situation of seasonal, weather-dependent work: the high risk of injuring or wearing out the body, especially in work accidents, brings uncertainty about how long one is capable of working.

Despite Gavin's nostalgia for a less controlled workplace, Alberta job sites are still among the least safe in the country, which reflects inadequate enforcement of occupational health and safety rules, inadequate injury-prevention efforts, and employer-friendly labour law (Barnetson 2015, 225). Also, the unionization rate among oil sector workers is relatively low by Canadian standards.[6] In 2016 Alberta had the lowest unionization rate in Canada at 23.1 percent (Statistics Canada 2017a). Generally, all of Canada experienced a sharp decline in the unionization rate between 1981 and 2014, with the largest decrease by 8 percentage points in the 1990s (Statistics Canada 2017b), which coincides with the start of a boom period in the oil sands industry. The prominence of energy production within Canada's commodity sector nearly doubled during this time, while the previously dominant sectors—namely, agriculture and forestry—dwindled in relative importance (Statistics Canada 2017c). The associated decrease in unionization rates was highest among men, falling from just over 42 percent in 1981 to 27 percent in 2014 (Statistics Canada 2017b). Notably, the oil sands industry has been male-dominated since its beginnings, even though the number of women working in the industry has increased since the early 2000s.

The primary cause of injuries is workplace hazards that exist in part due to employer choices. In addition, there are low levels of state control through workplace inspections, and little threat of penalties for employer noncompliance with provincial safety codes (Barnetson 2015, 229). Bob Barnetson substantiates this point by referring to an official Alberta Works document that states that, on average, workplaces are inspected less than once every fourteen years in Alberta.[7] According to another report, a safety inspector's response to the report of unsafe working conditions can take up to eighteen days (Barnetson 2015, 229). These shortcomings stand in contrast to the lived reality of many of the workers I met, who repeatedly pointed out the strict safety protocols now in place as compared to only a few years earlier. Still, many workers told me about accidents they experienced firsthand, witnessed, or heard of at their workplace. When I asked them to tell me more precisely about safety protocols, they talked about shaving policy, wearing appropriate safety clothes, how they had to call in every couple of hours when working in certain terrain, drug controls before entering the camps, tickets they had to earn, and on-site safety procedures.[8] While these protocols most certainly were intended to increase workers' safety, all the industry measures that these workers discussed were individual and could be used to control the workers as much as to ensure their safety. At the same time, the long working hours and long shifts were usually not addressed by oil companies; neither were the pressures to work quickly when the weather was right, which again compelled workers to take risks. Clearly, there was an imbalance between individual and structural measurements, so that instead of actually increasing site safety, some procedures seemed more to aim at transferring accident liability from the company to the workers.

Interestingly, interlocutors also often placed the cause of the accidents on workers themselves rather than on structural issues, which aligns with the provincial government's call for workers to take ownership of their own safety through various safety-awareness campaigns, again moving responsibility away from the employer and the state and placing it on the individual. Linking this liability transfer with the highly racialized and gendered myth of the "careless worker," which the Government of Alberta, among others, has propagated through its injury-prevention efforts, it becomes clear that the worker is blamed for his or her injury and is seen as disposable, to be replaced with a less careless labourer (Barnetson 2015, 238; Barnetson and Foster 2012). The "careless worker myth," according to Barnetson and Jason Foster, is often embedded in the broader "freedom of choice" narrative, which seeks to explain occupational injury by asserting that some groups of workers are accident-prone, careless, or even reckless, and functions to absolve employers and society of moral responsibility for worker injuries (2012, 136). Historically, the myth is closely linked to male workers of colour, of specific ethnicity (e.g., Indigenous workers), and age (e.g., younger workers) (Barnetson and Foster 2012, 136).

Seeing employers and workers as sharing a joint responsibility for safe workplaces, or even putting the emphasis on the workers' own behaviour, completely ignores the different levels of power they have in the workplace. Workers also do not necessarily have the freedom of choosing a less risky job (Barnetson and Foster 2012, 136). In addition, putting employers in charge of day-to-day workplace safety—employers who then delegate responsibility to the workers, which, in the end, imposes the cost of an accident—i.e., an injury—on the worker—is ultimately a political choice by the state (Barnetson and Foster 2012, 137).

During an interview, Bill, an old union man who had worked as a welder for over thirty years in the oil sands industry in addition to having work experience of over ten years in other sectors, told me that he did not enjoy working with temporary foreign workers (TFWs) or young Indigenous men. When I questioned him further about this comment, which could be construed as rather racist, he argued that these workers took risks, were sloppy with safety precautions, and, in the case of the TFWs, did not always understand instructions because of their poor English language skills. When I asked him who was responsible for accidents caused by communication issues, he said, "This is Canada. Why do they come here if they don't speak English? They put us all at risk." Indeed, the TFW program seems to be designed for accidents. Low-paid workers with fewer legal rights, without connections to the area or local knowledge about climate and wildlife, who live in often marginal conditions, and are almost completely dependent on their employer as their stay in Canada is bound to their contracts—the program looks like a classic set-up for capitalist exploitation, union-busting, and the prevalence of accidents.[9] There is often little solidarity between TFWs and other workers, as the TFW program was seen as a way for employers to pay lower wages and dispense with union members, and foreign workers were perceived as direct competition for local youth or unskilled workers. That being said, I encountered both friendships and romantic relationships between locals and TFWs, so while I often heard a general rejection of TFWs in debates and conversations, relationships between TFWs and non-TFWs looked different in daily life. In particular, the Filipino community of TFWs was highly respected for their work ethic, as well as for their contributions to different church activities on their days off work in Lac La Biche.

When I asked Bill why he specifically pointed out young Indigenous men, besides TFWs, as undesirable colleagues, he just shrugged it off, mentioned his own (possibly Métis) background, and said something about having no statistics but that his experience of forty years of working must be worth something as well. Safety campaigns launched by the Government of Alberta in 2005, 2008, and 2011, for example, have targeted recent immigrants and young workers (Barnetson and Foster 2012, 140). While there is evidence that inexperience correlates with heightened injury rates, it is important to note that, rather than worker carelessness, this correlation reflects the fact that more experienced workers have learned how to mitigate environmental factors better than newcomers (Barnetson and Foster 2012, 140).

Economic booms, particularly in regions with extractive industries, are typically considered a chance to democratize labour opportunities, especially through the discourse of "social inclusion" and "partnership" with Indigenous populations in the contemporary Canadian context (Friedel and Taylor 2011, 29).

The expectation that extractive industries will level out inequality in a given area ignores the fact that this work takes place in a particular political, social, cultural, and historical context. Prejudices and ignorance from both industry and government, in addition to racialized inequalities and structural disadvantages based in historical injustices and colonial power structures, actively hinder or even bar Indigenous people from participating fully in labour opportunities (Friedel and Taylor 2011, 29). In the early 2000s, the unemployment rate for First Nations persons was three times the rate for non-Indigenous Canadians (Taylor and Friedel 2011, 25). Bill's view of the unreliability of young Indigenous men was widespread and shared among many non-Indigenous Canadians. Even though he did not recognize this attitude as a harmful racial stereotype and pointed to his experience in working with Indigenous men to support his belief, it can be safely assumed that his opinion was not only an individual one but one informed by society. High rates of addiction and mental health issues in Indigenous communities could be the cause for higher risk-taking behaviour if his statement were true, but the prevalence of this behaviour also needs to be addressed in the context of unequal access to mental health services (Goraya 2016; Kielland and Simeone 2014; Shimo 2016), unequal education funding (Shimo 2016; Stewart 2006), the legacy of the Indigenous residential school system (Bombay, Matheson, and Anisman 2014; TRC 2015), and structural racism (Comack 2012; Nguyen 2011; Patrick 2014; Piché 2015) that Indigenous Peoples in Canada have endured for centuries.

## Accidents, Spills, and Contamination of the Land and Its Inhabitants

In the following section I paraphrase my field notes from the beginning of 2014. At this point I was quite close with Joey and Cora, the couple mentioned below, and we had spent many days and evenings together. They lived not far from Lac La Biche and regularly invited me to visit them and their family. When this particular conversation took place, I had been spending the weekend at their house and we were sitting in their kitchen having dinner.

> Joey, a Cree heavy equipment operator, shows me his phone. It is actually his partner Cora's phone, but they share it, and he takes it with him when he goes to work in hopes to find reception somewhere and to be able to call her on her landline. I can't really see what he wants to show me; the photo is blurry and of bad quality and the screen is small. "Do you see this?" he asks me. "Do you get it?" He shakes his head in frustration; his voice is elevated by strong emotions. He looks expectantly at me, he wants some reaction. "Is it a bush fire?" I ask hesitantly. I see flames, I see a clearing, but it is winter, and not at all wildfire season, so the whole picture doesn't really make sense to me. "This is what they make me do!" Joey exclaims. His eyes look angry, his movements are hectic, and he steps from one foot to the other. I can't give him whatever he waits for, as I still don't understand.

> "You know, they start bush fires to clear sections," he says. So I guessed right. But why is he then so upset about it, if this is the usual procedure in his job? Joey hasn't struck me as particularly concerned about environmental issues and I know for a fact that he is quite proud of the hard work he is doing and always waiting and hoping for a new gig.
>
> "But here, it was -37 and we didn't manage. So we were told to use diesel to make it burn. It's actually not allowed to use any chemicals, nothing will grow back there for years, and we destroy everything. I didn't want to do this, but we were told we must, it's faster and we weren't successful with the procedure after our official protocol, so in the end I did it. But I filmed it, see! And I took pictures. This is an area where we go berry picking. It used to be a good berry-picking patch. Now, no, I destroyed it. There won't be any berries there next summer."
>
> Cora joins the conversation. She also works in the oil sands whenever she gets a contract. She asks me to get my notebook and to write down what she is saying. So I go to the guestroom and get my book and a pen from my backpack. Cora looks like she has been thinking quite carefully about what she is going to tell me; at the same time I can see that she is also really angry about the incidence.
>
> She says, "It's a catch 22, a Native conundrum, but it's not funny, not at all. We NEED to work. All we First Nations go through this. To be independent, to be us, we need to work. We need to work to live. That's just how it is. And that makes us sell our land and our selves for a dollar an hour. We are hypocrites. We know what's at stake. We can't eat the berries; we KNOW what is in the ground. We were forced to put it there. He [Joey] had to light it. Even though he knew. He knew it would kill everything."

This is not the typical account of an accident; there actually is no accident in it at all. It is about wilful contamination of land. To keep up with the workday schedule, the destruction of a berry patch is accepted. But its destruction plays into the same mindset I saw with workplace accidents. Labour time was valued above land and bodies, and therefore accidents (pollution or destruction) were willingly enacted.

I wondered, how do these berries matter to Indigenous people (see also Baker, this volume)? And what can we learn from this episode when it comes to other examples of destruction, pollution, and contamination of nature? Can we relate this incident to bigger ones such as the ongoing oil spill that occurred during my fieldwork, on the air weapons range outside of Cold Lake (which I discuss below)?

As anthropologist Janelle Baker (2016) points out, the Cree word for contaminate, *piscipowin*, is also used to denote polluting or killing something. What is being killed here? Is it "only" the land and the berry patch? Cora had the answer: respect—respect for the land and its inhabitants and their relations to each other.[10] Tragically, the killing is often unwillingly done by local inhabitants, workers on the ground, who experience such supposedly minor accidents and acts of willing pollution as a quite normal part of their work routine.

For the Cree, as in many North American Indigenous societies, resources should neither be horded nor wasted; they are there to be shared and cared for, and are often seen as a gift. This concept is closely related to the land being understood as part of the first gift the Creator gave the people, a result of their sacred relationship to the Creator. The Creator's second gift included rules and values that help to take care of these relationships. Thus, the land is a sacred gift, and it is a strong, visible link between Creator and the people that shows their relationship (LaBoucane-Benson et al. 2012, 5–6). Keeping the land for future generations is therefore an important and sacred duty. To tolerate contamination and pollution puts the relationship between the (Indigenous) worker, the land, and (if they believe in it) the Creator at risk as well as the relationship between local Indigenous communities and the oil companies.

Contamination and pollution are often considered "slow violence"—that is, "violence that occurs gradually and out of sight, a violence of delayed destruction that is dispersed across time and space, an attritional violence that is typically not viewed as violent at all" (Nixon 2011, 2). Disrespect can be seen as pollution of relations and of the mind, which I argue is at least as harmful as actual ambient pollution, if not more so. It is also important to note the close connection Cora makes between pollution and disrespect; she describes pollution as the direct outcome of disrespect.

In Cora's account, a gift to animals and humans—the berries—is not only rejected but also wasted and destroyed for several generations to come. And what is the reason for this wasting of gifts? The extraction of fossil fuel—namely, bitumen. Bitumen is dead material, from long ago, compressed and transformed into a hydrocarbon that humans can use for energy after intensive refining. Considering bitumen extraction's high carbon footprint, the environmental destruction accompanying its mining and the contamination of air, water, and land associated with the process, it is not only dead material but also deadly material.

## The 2013–2014 Canadian Natural Resources Limited Primrose Incident

Between May and June 2013, Canadian Natural Resources Limited (CNRL) discovered four runaway bitumen leaks at their Primrose and Wolf Lake in situ project. The Alberta Energy Regulator (AER) did not inform the public of the spill before June 24, 2013, but experts suspect that the release started as early as winter 2012–2013 (Timoney and Lee 2014, 4).[11] The uncontrolled releases of bitumen were ongoing throughout 2013 and extended into 2014 with an estimated bitumen release of 1,939 $m^3$ (12,185 barrels) as of January 14, 2013, which makes it the fourth-largest bitumen release on record in Alberta (Timoney and Lee 2014, 3–4). Similar leaks had occurred in 2006 and

2009 at the company's extraction sites (Timoney and Lee 2014, 3). Spills or releases of both bitumen and contaminated water negatively impact not only the environment but also Indigenous relations with governments and companies. In addition, spills evoke uncertainty, fear, and anger, and thus affect the well-being of nearby communities. I will discuss the destructive aftermath of spills below (for further discussion of spills see Gerbrandt 2015; see also Wheatley and Westman, this volume).

The AER and CNRL failed to properly inform the public of the spill and provided delayed, misleading, and incomplete information. Nor did they take earlier incidents in the same area by the same oil company with the same extraction technique into account. And there was no independent committee of researchers to look into the causes of the spill (Timoney and Lee 2014, 4–6). The province, moreover, relied on industry numbers to determine released and recovered volumes of bitumen without verifying these numbers (Timoney and Lee 2014, 5). The cause of the 2013–2014 bitumen releases was unclear, which also was the case for the 2009 incident at CNRL Primrose. In addition, as the releases occurred underground and were not confined to a pipeline conduit, they were difficult to study, quantify, and stop (Timoney and Lee 2014, 6). Still, the company was allowed to continue with their extraction activities in the same area during the first months of the bitumen releases in 2013–2014, as they had been earlier after the 2009 incident.

Following cleanup activities, which included draining an impacted lake (see Westman and Wheatley, this volume) and cutting vegetation, CNRL and the AER reported the following deceased wildlife: 2 beavers, 51 birds, 106 amphibians, and 57 small mammals. This list, of course, reflects only the number of deceased individuals located, not necessarily the actual amount of lost wildlife, and does not indicate the number of otherwise impacted wildlife. Furthermore, they reported the recovery of 1,177.14–1,529 $m^3$ bitumen emulsion and the removal of 1,049.62 metric tonnes of impacted soil (Timoney and Lee 2014, 19–24). These numbers differ from report to report, and it is hard to get more than a general impression of the actual impact of the releases (see also Gerbrandt 2015). While the actual numbers are unavailable, what matters here is that the releases, seen as accidents where infrastructure and extraction procedures fail to contain the bitumen, were of major impact to the ecosystem on a regional scale.

Additionally, CNRL's Primrose site lies in Beaver Lake Cree First Nation territory. When band members wanted to check the extent of the damage, including whether ancestral graves were impacted, CNRL denied them access to the area, quoting health and safety concerns. Cold Lake First Nation members also asked for more information from CRNL and the AER as they were concerned for their drinking water and the flora and fauna in their territory. They were not given any satisfactory answers, which increased their frustration and their concerns for their health. This was not an isolated incidence. In her research, Jennifer Gerbrandt (2015) reports a similar situation and a comparably dismissive initial handling of First Nations' inquiries by representatives of a different oil company, in the territory of the Woodland Cree First Nation. In a lecture on December 9, 2013, at Portage College in Lac La Biche, Beaver Lake Cree First Nation member and Indigenous activist Crystal Lameman called the handling of the CRNL Primrose bitumen releases a "direct violation of First Nations' rights" as access to their traditional territory was denied, and the Treaty Rights of hunting, fishing, and gathering in the area were now effectively obsolete as no one could enter or would like to eat the contaminated objects.

Anthropologist Laura Bear sees accidents as failed acts of labour that reveal incommensurable temporal rhythms and workplace demands (2014, 74). For Bear, accidents are central to practices of capitalism and accepted as inherent to the work process (74–75). This is certainly true in the Albertan oil sands. The expansion of in situ extraction in Alberta, using ever-newer technologies, outpaces the increase in knowledge about the potential sub-surface and surface impacts of these methods (Global Forest Watch 2014). In the Primrose case, the regulators consented for CNRL's bitumen extraction at three of the four release locations to continue throughout the ongoing incidents (Global Forest Watch 2014). In addition, the Cold Lake area has a history of well failures, with more than 250 failed wells as of 2001, where 85–90 percent of these failures were the result of geologic shear stresses generated by steaming operations (Timoney and Lee 2014, 6). The authors of the report about the CNRL's persistent 2013–2014 bitumen releases near Cold Lake conclude, "Given the documented geologic hazards and well failures associated with HPCSS [high-pressure cyclic steam stimulation—one commonly used method to extract bitumen in situ], the demonstrated inability to prevent well failures in areas subjected to high pressure steaming, and previous large and uncontrolled releases of bitumen, the decision by the Alberta Energy Regulator to allow CNRL to continue HPCSS operations in the Cold Lake area illustrates failure of the regulator to protect both the public interest and the environment" (Timoney and Lee 2014, 6). In March 2016 the AER agreed that excessive steaming was one of the reasons behind high-profile leaks at CNRL's Primrose oil sands project. The Pembina Institute, a Canadian non-profit think tank focused on energy, questioned the use of the technology given the huge knowledge gaps both industry and state regulators had when adopting the method (Timoney and Lee 2014, 6). At the point of the AER statement mentioned above, three years after the releases started, the cleanup procedures were not yet finished. Still, the AER insisted that the problem was local to the Cold Lake area and that other oil companies not impacted by the investigation could keep extracting bitumen using the same method (Timoney and Lee 2014, 6). Thus, this accident was also framed as a failure not of the extractive method itself but of the local environment.

Accidents can also be interpreted as crises. David Harvey sees crisis as an inbuilt mode and function of capitalism, and as an enabler of continuity in the socioeconomic order (2005, 69, 162). Therefore, the nature of crisis is not necessarily event-like with a clear onset and end, but rather an ongoing process. Following this argumentation, accidents as crises are likewise processual and structural rather than singular events. In addition, I argue that accidents in the oil sands are more an inbuilt part of the system than a rupture. The high accident rates, low standards of workplace safety, and frequent infrastructure failures leading to air, water, and soil pollution makes it tempting to see bodies and lands as wastelands, as articulated by Voyles (2015).

## Wastelanding and the Background of Settler Colonialism

In her book *Wastelanding*, Voyles articulates the history of uranium mining on Navajo land in the American southwest. She explores how some regions can be defined as pollutable, including all that lives in, on, and under this land. Voyles explains wastelanding as "the mapping of Navajo land and, by extension, other kinds of lands rendered pollutable through discourses of race, gender, class, and/or sexual difference as 'wasteland'…Wastelanding… has been a key and underexplored component of environmental racism. The 'wasteland' is a racial and a spatial signifier that renders an environment and the bodies that inhabit it pollutable" (2015, 8–9). Wastelanding perpetuates a colonial view of the land, erasing its history and meaning, and redefining it as something that can be sacrificed for the greater good, as, for example, energy supply for the nation. Voyles quotes a court decision in which the landscape of northwestern New Mexico is framed as a "coal and uranium region," through which the judge erases entire histories of land uses other than extractive industries (2015, 172). The same happens when northeastern Alberta is referred to as "the oil sands region," a habit I uncritically acquired during the early part of my research. Such discourse naturalizes extractive industrialism as inherent to the landscape itself (Voyles 2015, 8). Indeed, for a long time, oil sands pollution was framed as naturally occurring leakage of bitumen into waterways. This idea of naturally occurring pollution added to the idea of northeastern Alberta as an "oil sands region" and as a natural "wasteland." Water ecologist David Schindler and his team showed that huge parts of the pollution were indeed airborne and caused by industrial oil sands extraction (Kelly et al. 2009).

According to Voyles, wastelanding is a multiscalar process: destroying the environment through extractive activities is not limited to the non-human world and ecosystem (2015, 11). It also deems human bodies as wastable. Worldview, epistemology, ontology, history, spirituality, and cultural practices of the people are similarly deemed as lacking value (Voyles 2015, 11). Aerial photos of northern Alberta show the enormous extent of clearcutting, mining, and linear disturbances on the forest landscape. There is no doubt that both industry's infrastructure and the pollution that comes with it have dire consequences for the whole region's ecosystem. As with uranium mining, oil sands extraction creates wastelands, leaving "dead land" and "dead waters" (Sassen 2014, 2). The Albertan oil sands stand out as they are a set of megaprojects with but few comparable ventures of similar size and environmental impact. They have therefore even been called "the largest industrial project in human history" (Stainsby 2014, 99). Saskia Sassen characterizes the process of transforming natural environments into dead land and dead water as an expulsion of bits of life itself from the biosphere (2014, 2). However, it is not only biological life that gets expelled. Along with goes its meaning, agency, and history.

Being recognized as an Indigenous nation is often linked to attachment to the land and territory, community, language, and the group's capacity for self-government in anthropological and/or social movement literature, but also in Indigenous self-representations (Alfred 2009, 142; Li 2014, 10; Simpson 2014). For Cree, Dene, and Métis nations in Canada, like for many other Indigenous groups around the world, the forest landscape is social, full of relations and oral history. It is therefore a living archive of personal biography and community history (see also Tsing 2005, xi). Community in Dene and Cree understanding includes human and non-human reciprocal relations in a known and cared-for place (Westman 2013, 212). From a Cree perspective, health is not only determined by the individual's physiology but it is also formed and maintained through the individual's social relations to other people, relations to and with the land, his or her spirituality, and cultural identity (Adelson 2000). Therefore, health itself is a relational concept rather than an individual one and has political implications. To contribute with one's work to maintain communal land strengthens one's relation to both the people and the place. It is in a way a performative act of belonging. Strengthening social bounds of belonging is one way of "being alive well" (Adelson 2000). Processes of unearthing the land (Li 2015) for bitumen extraction purposes, or destroying berry patches for a faster work process, are therefore directly connected to harmful behaviour, and place individual and community health at risk. Not only is the oil sands industry connected to pollution of the environment, but also acts of labour in the industry can be seen as polluting. Accidents are merely condensed events or processes that make this structure of pollution and harm more visible.

Indigenous workers in the oil sands have to see their homeland, which is built on reciprocal relations, turned into an uncanny wasteland, an environmental ruin with toxins haunting bodies of humans, animals, and plants. Many Indigenous workers I spoke to related their experience of racism and disrespect while working in the oil sands to the environmental degradation of their homeland and to the high rates of accidents both on workplaces and on the roads leading to and from the worksites. Road accidents are often caused by workers speeding to or from their workplace, not knowing the road and weather conditions well, or by large vehicles transporting material related to the industry under huge time pressure and therefore often driving too fast and with exhausted drivers who sometimes fall asleep or have a hard time focusing while driving. Together with often poor road conditions, these factors lead to a huge number of accidents. It is not coincidental that the Canadian reality TV show *Highway thru Hell* chose Highway 63, which connects Edmonton to Fort McMurray, as its new location at the end of season two; the highway was commonly referred to as the "Highway of Death" by interlocutors during my fieldwork. Such accidents affect community members as much or even more than the workers. Not only are they dependent on the roads to get around (roads are often closed for hours after an accident), they also often are the victims of these accidents. Additionally, they are often first attenders to the incident, are involved in the emergency care or clean up, or have lost family or community members through accidents—all of which can contribute to mental health problems.

Voyles clearly links wastelanding with capitalism through the treadmill of production, in which extraction of raw materials (in our case bitumen) and dumping of material waste (e.g., the wastewater held in tailings ponds, as in Wheatley and Westman, this volume) are expanding with markets, often exponentially (Voyles 2015, 9). Which landscapes of extraction and pollution are excluded from the protection of the state is again closely related to who inhabits those landscapes, rendering race a primary factor (Voyles 2015, 9).

A consideration of race in Canada necessitates a brief discussion of Canada's colonial history (see also Spady, this volume). Settler colonialism "is a form of colonial power that involves the settler making a home in a land that is already home to indigenous people" (Voyles 2015, 7). Settler colonialism is therefore defined by a territorial project, where the acquisition of land, not of labour, was in the foreground (Wolfe 1999, 2006). Labour is still an important concept in settler colonialism, particularly as in relation to John Locke's theory of the connection between labour and property ([1797] 2003). Locke sees the origins of property as intertwined with certain forms of labour—namely, sedentary and fixed labour and thus observable to Europeans (Simpson 2014, 101). Land not mixed with this kind of labour is alienable in this view and not private but common property (Simpson 2014, 101). Locke's understanding of property and social hierarchy, where agrarian-based people rank higher than non-sedentary groups, enabled the moral justification of dispossession in settler states. The argument was that seizing Indigenous land would put it to more intensive and productive use (Ray 2016, 3). In turn, by seeing settler colonialism as a structure not an event (Wolfe 2006, 388), it becomes clear that these structures are still in place and therefore settler colonialism is rather ongoing than finished and in the past. Turning Indigenous land into settler homes involves not only the construction and exploitation of given resources, but "a deeply complex construction of that land as either always already belonging to the settler—his manifest destiny—or as undesirable, unproductive, or unappealing: in short a wasteland" (Voyles 2015, 7).

## Wastelanding the Northern Boreal Forest

So, how does wastelanding happen? Voyles argues for the power of narratives. Through narrating the land as wasteland, it becomes wasteland as people accept the narrative as reality and act upon it. Anna Tsing (2005) provides a similar explanation. She names three features of natural resource management (magnifying the forest, then simplifying, and lastly mischaracterizing it) that lead, in her account, to the destruction of huge parts of the Indonesian rainforest (2005, 15). I argue that a similar process is being enacted in Alberta. First, the wilderness and size of the northern boreal forest is magnified by emphasizing the remoteness of the area, its frontier character, and natural bounty. Therefore, some extractive industry would not harm the ecosystem too much. This idea can also be seen in the national myth of the abundance of Canadian nature, especially forests, reflecting the (settler) Canadian self-understanding as a nation living in a frontier land with a harsh and nearly untouched environment with (too) much of everything wild (see also Spady, this volume).

A common summer job for young Canadians is tree planting, seemingly reversing the visible wounds left by logging while often planting huge areas of monocultures. Consequently, the northern bush is not as untouched as it might have seemed. It was already, in a way, wasteland, impacted by human endeavours. With a long history of logging and agriculture, northern Alberta arguably had lost part of its conservation value prior to the early 2000s energy boom. State representatives have generally argued that part of the forest could easily be sacrificed for the sake of the economy (Pratt and Urquhart, 1994; Urquhart 1998).

Northern Alberta is typically described as a frontier place, a wilderness, with oil sands extraction taking place far away from civilization. Such a reduction does not consider how this area has been home to Indigenous Peoples for centuries and to non-Indigenous Canadians for decades. The common argument paradoxically maintains that the industry cuts into areas that are already touched by people, which are therefore not as worthy of conservation, while it simultaneously represents the northern bush as belonging to the remote sphere of nature and therefore not really of people's concern. Such a mischaracterization is again tightly connected to settler colonialism, erasing Indigenous lives and history in a landscape. The camps and extraction sites for the oil sands in northern Alberta are made possible because of geological and human history and have to be seen in the deep context of settler colonialism.

The blurred line between enabling Indigenous sovereignty through the possibility of escaping the poverty trap and destroying the very base of this sovereignty—namely, the homeland for the local First Nations peoples—is another example of how wastelanding is enabled. It makes it very hard for First Nations and Métis communities in the area to object the industry, since many see it as the only way to become financially independent from the Canadian government. The northern Albertan bush can be seen as a conjuncture where historical capitalist disturbances such as logging and current exploitation meet, and where history enables the current processes.

## Accidents as Evidence and the Refusal of Being Wastelanded

The oil sands industry is a dominating feature of daily life for most northern Alberta residents. Oil sands extraction does not take place in a *terra nullius*, an empty frontier, but in the traditional homeland of several Indigenous groups. Still, the notions of frontier and wilderness attached to the region are absolutely necessary to enable the main narrative used to describe the industry by both its proponents and opponents. In the occurrence of work-related accidents and failure of infrastructure such as pipelines, these notions become particularly clear. Accidents are here understood both as significant and condensed moments, ultimately caused by the acceleration of the production process, by precarious work conditions, and the pressure of the global market, but they are also structural and inherent to capitalist work processes. I described work-related accidents as hurting the human body, as in Gavin's story of the drunken Cat driver; pollution as an ongoing and structural accident demonstrated by the example of the destroyed berry patch; and infrastructure failures creating oil spills or contamination of the surrounding land, air, and water as in the CNRL case. These three types of accidents must be seen in close connection to settler colonialism and can be scrutinized using the concept of wastelanding.

Accidents in the oil sands industry are evidence of disrespect towards the land and the people inhabiting it, and of discourses and institutions that render them pollutable. Examining accidents can shine light not only on how accidents themselves are understood, but also on power relations, colonial practices, and inequality in northern Alberta. It also becomes clear that these so-called accidents are not unavoidable and unforeseen, but are part of a violent system that does not respect certain types of land or the ways of living on and with these forms of nature. These accidents are, as stated above, clearly incorporated in a capitalist system of extractive industries, and are signs of a hidden violence against specific forms of life. In this regard, the word *accident* becomes an emic term of industry and government, and cannot be read in the meaning of the dictionary definition cited above. While I have shown how especially Indigenous Peoples are exposed to accidents (in whichever form they take place) and dependent on the oil sands industry, they are still far from being helpless victims without agency. Actively resisting wastelanding takes many forms, one of which is caring for the land. Caring for the land is in Cree, Dene, and Métis understanding also caring for everything living on it and for the physical, spiritual, and mental well-being of all inhabitants of the land. This interpretation is manifested in ceremonies and practices as well as in the political act of resilience. Through keeping the relationship to the land alive and insisting on ceremonies to heal the land, Indigenous Peoples show their resistance to the process of wastelanding.

## Acknowledgements

I would like to thank my supervisors Thomas Hylland Eriksen, Ingjerd Hoëm, and Keir Martin for their support, as well as Theodoros Rakopoulos and Tuva Beyer Broch for their thoughtful comments on draft versions of my chapter and the book proposal of this volume. Thanks also to Tara Joly and

Janelle Baker for all our discussions and exchanges in our reading group. Caterina Torresani for making my participation at the annual meeting of the American Anthropology Association in November 2016 possible. Clint and Tara, I enjoyed working with you so much. My research leading to these results has received funding from the European Research Council under the European Union's Seventh Framework Programme (FP7/2007–2013)/ERC Grant Agreement n. [295843].

Most of all, I would like to thank everybody who talked to me and shared their lives with me during fieldwork; you know who you are. Without you I would never be where I am now. And Lyra, my love, you have been doing fieldwork with me twice before even starting school, you have been waiting both patiently and impatiently way too often for me to be done with work, and you opened so many doors through your sweetness and openness. Thank you!

## Notes

1 I will therefore also use the term *accident* in this chapter, treating it as the emic term, even though I attempt to deconstruct events described as accidents and show that they are structural rather than accidental.

2 To ensure anonymity I have changed all names and, in some cases, age or background information.

3 Gavin has experience with in situ oil sands extraction and open-pit mining, but he also worked at pipeline construction, as in this example.

4 *Cat* is colloquial term for machinery manufactured by Caterpillar Inc., an American corporation. Gavin did not specify which machine he meant; there are a range of Cats, from tracked tractors to hydraulic excavators, backhoe loaders, motor graders, off-highway trucks, wheel loaders, agricultural tractors, locomotives, and more. In the context of our conversation, I am certain that he was referring to a bulldozer. Also, note that the term *Cat* may be used for any bulldozer, not exclusively the ones produced by Caterpillar Inc.

5 The "old days" Gavin referred to were about ten to fifteen years ago, early in the most recent oil boom.

6 Statistics Canada (2017a) defines the unionization rate as "the number of employed individuals who are union members as a proportion of the total number of employed individuals within a defined framework (enterprise, occupation, economic sector, etc.)."

7 Alberta Works is a provincial government service agency that provides information about Alberta's labour market, work-search support, and career planning.

8 *Tickets* is the industry term for the successful participation in different kinds of training and courses.

9 For a more in-depth discussion on the TFW program, see Foster (2012); Foster and Taylor (2013); Fudge and MacPhail (2009); and Nakache and Kinoshita (2010).

10 For more on respect in Cree ontology, see, for example, Colin Scott's (1996) work on hunting protocols.

11 Here the wording matters. CNRL and AER categorized the incident as "release" rather than "spill" as it occurred underground. This distinction is important both in terms of statistics (since it was not counted in the same way), as well as the impact it has on the public's first impression of the spill, because "release" sounds more controlled and less harmful than "spill," even though the words do not actually denote such a qualitative or quantitative distinction.

## References

Adelson, Naomi. 2000. *"Being Alive Well": Health and the Politics of Cree Well-Being*. Toronto: University of Toronto Press.

Alfred, Taiaiake. 2009. *Wasáse: Indigenous Pathways of Action and Freedom*. Toronto: University of Toronto Press.

Baker, Janelle. 2016. "Do Berries Listen?: Wild Food Contamination and Reciprocity in Alberta's Oil Sands Region." Paper presented at *SOLIDARIT(I)ÉS CASCA and SANA*, Halifax, May 2016.

Barnetson, Bob. 2015. "Worker Safety in Alberta: Trading Health for Profit. In *Alberta Oil and the Decline of Democracy in Canada*, edited by Meenal Shristava and Lorna Stefanick, 225–47. Edmonton, AB: Athabasca University Press.

Barnetson, Bob, and Jason Foster. 2012. "Bloody Lucky: The Careless Worker Myth in Alberta, Canada." *International Journal of Occupational and Environmental Health* 18 (2): 135–46.

Bear, Laura. 2014. "3 For Labour: Ajeet's Accident and the Ethics of Technological Fixes in Time." *Journal of the Royal Anthropological Institute* 20 (51): 71–88. https://doi.org/10.1111/1467-9655.12094.

Bombay, Amy, Kimberly Matheson, and Hymie Anisman. 2014. "The Intergenerational Effects of Indian Residential Schools: Implications for the Concept of Historical Trauma." *Transcultural Psychiatry* 51 (3): 320–38.

Comack, Elizabeth. 2012. *Racialized Policing: Aboriginal People's Encounters with the Police*. Halifax, NS: Fernwood Publishing.

Foster, Jason. 2012. "Making Temporary Permanent: The Silent Transformation of the Temporary Foreign Worker Program." *Just Labour: A Canadian Journal of Work and Society* 19 (Autumn). https://justlabour.journals.yorku.ca/index.php/justlabour/article/view/24/24.

Foster, Jason, and Alison Taylor. 2013. "In the Shadows: Exploring the Notion of 'Community' for Temporary Foreign Workers in a Boomtown." *Canadian Journal of Sociology* [Cahiers canadiens de sociologie] 38 (2): 167–90.

Friedel, Tracy L., and Alison Taylor. 2011. "Digging Beneath the Surface of Aboriginal Labour Market Development: Analyzing Policy Discourse in the Context of Northern Alberta's Oil Sands." *Aboriginal Policy Studies* 1 (3): 29–52.

Fudge, Judy, and Fiona MacPhail. 2009. "The Temporary Foreign Worker Program in Canada: Low-Skilled Workers as an Extreme Form of Flexible Labor." *Immigration and Nationality Law Review* 30 (1): 843–86.

Gerbrandt, Jennifer L. 2015. "Energy Uncertainty: The Effects of Oil Extraction on the Woodland Cree First Nation." MA thesis, University of Saskatchewan.

Global Forest Watch. 2014. "Investigation into CNRL's Uncontrolled Releases of Crude Bitumen in the Primrose Area of Alberta Reveals Failures to Protect the Public Interest." News release, February 6, 2014. http://globalforestwatch.ca/sites/gfwc/files/news_releases/20140206A_CNRL_Release_Media.pdf.

Goraya, Jasjit. 2016. "Access to Health Care on Aboriginal Reserves." *The Public Policy and Governance Review*, April 6, 2016. https://ppgreview.ca/2016/04/06/access-to-health-care-on-aboriginal-reserves-2/.

Harvey, David. 2005. *A Brief History of Neoliberalism*. Oxford: Oxford University Press.

Kelly, Erin N., Jeffrey W. Short, David W. Schindler, Peter V. Hodson, Mingsheng Ma, Alvin K. Kwan, and Barbra L. Fortin. 2009. "Oil Sands Development Contributes

Polycyclic Aromatic Compounds to the Athabasca River and Its Tributaries." *Proceedings of the National Academy of Science of the United States of America* 106 (52): 22346–51. https://doi.org/10.1073/pnas.0912050106.

Kielland, Norah, and Tonina Simeone. 2014. "Current Issues in Mental Health in Canada: The Mental Health of First Nations and Inuit Communities." Library of Parliament Research Publications. https://lop.parl.ca/content/lop/ResearchPublications/2014-02-e.htm.

LaBoucane-Benson, Patti, Ginger Gibson, Allen Benson, and Greg Miller. 2012. "Are We Seeking Pimatisiwin or Creating Pomewin? Implications for Water Policy." *The International Indigenous Policy Journal* 3 (3). http://ir.lib.uwo.ca/iipj/vol3/iss3/10.

Li, Fabiana. 2015. *Unearthing Conflict: Corporate Mining, Activism, and Expertise in Peru*. Durham, NC: Duke University Press.

Li, Tania Murray. 2014. *Land's End: Capitalist Relations on an Indigenous Frontier*. Durham, NC: Duke University Press.

Locke, John. ([1797] 2003). *Two Treatises of Government and a Letter Concerning Toleration*. Edited by Ian Shapiro. New Haven, CT: Yale University Press.

McDowell, Linda. 2009. *Working Bodies: Interactive Service Employment and Workplace Identities*. Hoboken, NJ: Wiley-Blackwell.

*Merriam-Webster*. 2017. s.v. "accident," https://www.merriam-webster.com/dictionary/accident (accessed July 31, 2017).

Nakache, Delphine, and Paula J. Kinoshita. 2010. "The Canadian Temporary Foreign Worker Program: Do Short-Term Economic Needs Prevail over Human Rights Concerns?" *IRPP Study*, No. 5, May 2010. http://irpp.org/wp-content/uploads/assets/research/diversity-immigration-and-integration/new-research-article-3/IRPP-Study-no5.pdf.

Nixon, Rob. 2011. *Slow Violence and the Environmentalism of the Poor*. Cambridge, MA: Harvard University Press.

Nguyen, Mai. 2011. "Closing the Education Gap: A Case for Aboriginal Early Childhood Education in Canada: A Look at the Aboriginal Headstart Program." *Canadian Journal of Education* [Revue canadienne de l′éducation] 34 (3): 229–48.

Patrick, Caryl. 2014. *Aboriginal Homelessness in Canada: A Literature Review*. Toronto: Canadian Homelessness Research Network Press. http://www.homelesshub.ca/sites/default/files/AboriginalLiteratureReview.pdf.

Piché, Allison. 2015. "Imprisonment and Indigenous Masculinity: Contesting Hegemonic Masculinity in a Toxic Environment." In *Indigenous Men and Masculinities: Legacies, Identities, Regeneration*, edited by Robert Alexander Innes and Kim Anderson, 197–2013. Winnipeg: University of Manitoba Press.

Pratt, Larry, and Ian T. Urquhart. 1994. *The Last Great Forest: Japanese Multinationals and Alberta's Northern Forests*. Edmonton, AB: NeWest Press.

Ray, Arthur J. 2016. *Aboriginal Rights Claims and the Making and Remaking of History*. Montreal and Kingston: McGill-Queen's University Press.

Sassen, Saskia. 2014. *Expulsions: Brutality and Complexity in the Global Economy*. Cambridge, MA: Belknap Press.

Scott, Colin. 1996. "Science for the West, Myth for the Rest? The Case of James Bay Cree Knowledge Construction." In *Naked Science: Anthropological Inquiry into Boundaries, Power, and Knowledge*, edited by Laura Nader, 69–86. New York: Routledge.

Shimo, Alexandra. 2016. *Invisible North: The Search for Answers on a Troubled Reserve*. Toronto: Dundurn Press.

Simpson, Audra. 2014. *Mohawk Interruptus: Political Life across the Borders of Settler States*. Durham, NC: Duke University Press.

Stainsby, Macdonald. 2014. "New Beginning: Tar Sands Prospecting Abroad." In *A Line in the Tar Sands: Struggles for Environmental Justice*, edited by Stephen D'Arcy, Toban Black, Tony Weis, and Joshua Kahn Russell, 99–109. Toronto: Between the Lines Books.

Statistics Canada. 2017a. "Chart 4: Unionization Rate, Canada and Provinces, 2016." https://www150.statcan.gc.ca/n1/daily-quotidien/170908/cg-a004-eng.htm (accessed June 3, 2018).

———. 2017b. "Unionization Rates Falling." http://www.statcan.gc.ca/pub/11-630-x/11-630-x2015005-eng.htm (accessed June 3, 2018).

———. 2017c. "Resources: Long-Term Shifts in Commodities." http://www.statcan.gc.ca/pub/11-630-x/11-630-x2014003-eng.htm (accessed June 3, 2018).

Stewart, Sheila Carr. 2006. "First Nations Education: Financial Accountability and Educational Attainment." *Canadian Journal of Education* [Revue canadienne de l'éducation] 29 (4): 998–1018.

Taylor, Alison, and Tracy Friedel. 2011. "Enduring Neoliberalism in Alberta's Oil Sands: The Troubling Effects of Private-Public Partnership for First Nation and Métis Communities." *Citizenship Studies* 15 (6–7): 815–35.

Timoney, Kevin, and Peter Lee. 2014. "CNRL's Persistent 2013–2014 Bitumen Releases near Cold Lake, Alberta: Facts, Unanswered Questions and Implications. Final Report." Research Gate. https://www.researchgate.net/publication/291335003_CNRL%27s_Persistent_2013-2014_Bitumen_Releases_near_Cold_Lake_Alberta_Facts_Unanswered_Questions_and_Implications (accessed September 26, 2018).

Truth and Reconciliation Commission of Canada (TRC). 2015. "TRC Final Report Summary." http://www.trc.ca/websites/trcinstitution/File/2015/Findings/Exec_Summary_2015_05_31_web_o.pdf.

Tsing, Anna Lowenhaupt. 2005. *Friction: An Ethnography of Global Connection*. Princeton, NJ: Princeton University Press.

Urquhart, Ian T., ed. 1998. *Assault on the Rockies: Environmental Controversies in Alberta*. London: Rowan Books.

Voyles, Traci Brynne. 2015. *Wastelanding: Legacies of Uranium Mining in Navajo Country*. Minneapolis: University of Minnesota Press.

Westman, Clinton N. 2013. "Cautionary Tales: Making and Breaking Community in the Oil Sands Region." *Canadian Journal of Sociology* [Cahiers canadiens de sociologie] 38 (2): 211–31.

Wolfe, Patrick. 1999. *Settler Colonialism and the Transformation of Anthropology: The Politics and Poetics of an Ethnographic Event*. London: Cassell.

———. 2006. "Settler Colonialism and the Elimination of the Native." *Journal of Genocide Research* 8 (4): 387–409.

# 5 Wildfire Politics

## The Role of a Natural Disaster in Indigenous–State Relations

*Tarje I. Wanvik*

### Introduction

In May 2016 a massive wildfire, locally named "The Beast," forced the evacuation of close to 90,000 people from Fort McMurray and the surrounding areas. Record heat and tinder-dry conditions contributed to Alberta's most devastating inferno (Alary 2016). In the first week after the fire was ignited, it was considered to be a low-impact event. However, soon the flames had destroyed 2,400 homes, caused the shutdown of two key oil sands facilities (Alary 2016), and burned almost 5,900 square kilometres of forest. While these are all significant impacts, the aftermath of the fire reveals political consequences for local communities in the oil sands that might far outpace the material damages.

Shortly after the wildfire had been contained, regional municipality representatives gathered to take stock and advise on the recovery and rebuilding of the impacted areas of the Regional Municipality of Wood Buffalo (RMWB). The elected officials decided to defer close to one hundred rural development projects to ensure financial support for the recovery. This deferral, especially the Conklin multipurpose activity center, the Conklin Multiplex, was a major blow to local Indigenous communities that are in dire need of improved service infrastructure. It resulted in a massive mobilization among Indigenous Peoples in Wood Buffalo in an act of solidarity. In the weeks and months that followed, Indigenous Peoples saw an opportunity to use the rebuild after the wildfire to reset the relationship between the urban and rural areas. One particular alliance—the Wood Buffalo Métis,[1] consisting of several Métis communities from Fort Chipewyan, Fort McMurray, Fort McKay, and Conklin—was central in the mobilization and played a vital part in the political negotiations in the aftermath of the fire.

There has been considerable scholarly work on the workings of power relations within the "energy–society" nexus. The literature on extractive industry often focuses on conflicts and impacts on Indigenous Peoples' traditional territories, typically focusing on powerful state or industry actors and marginalized local communities (Bebbington 2012; Black, D'Arcy, and Weis 2014; Huseman and Short 2012; Le Billon and Carter 2012; LeClerc and Keeling 2015).

This notion of such permanent power relations is confirmed by the recent global economic downturn, particularly within the energy sector, followed by the 2016 Fort McMurray wildfire: hard-won economic benefits and infrastructure for Indigenous communities are threatened after these devastating events as industrial projects and social investments are cancelled and municipal funds are reallocated to wildfire recovery rather than to urgently needed rural infrastructure investments.

Nevertheless, I will argue that there are no such things as permanent power structures within these contested energy spaces. Instead, they are characterized by rupture, unpredictability, and instability (DeLanda 2016; Haarstad and Wanvik 2017; Wanvik 2014)—in terms of the landscape itself, but also regarding its governance practices and power distribution (Wanvik 2016). To understand these circumstances, I develop a theoretical framework that fuses disaster politics analysis (Pelling and Dill 2009) and assemblage theory (DeLanda 2006; Wanvik 2014). I argue that natural disasters can act as transformative, non-human catalysts, or assemblage converters, as I label them, subsequently creating destabilizing processes within the carbonscape assemblage, where actors within the assemblage renegotiate their relationships.

The chapter proceeds as follows: first, I elaborate on the understanding of the carbonscape of Alberta as prone to change and ruptures. Second, I discuss the unique and hard-won successes of Métis advocacy work in general and in the oil sands region of Alberta more specifically, both through literature review and case findings. Third, I present a case study of an infrastructure project, the Conklin Multiplex, to show how local Métis communities are strategically engaging in disaster politics to enhance their leverage and political impact in the aftermath of the Fort McMurray wildfire. The broader objective of the chapter is to understand how Indigenous groups and communities are working to increase their influence and leverage through what I call wildfire politics—pragmatically exploring and actively creating alliances and collaborations in the wake of the Fort McMurray wildfire to fend for their rights and interests.

## Contextual Framing: Actors and Communities

Contested energy spaces are stretched far beyond the borders of the geographical place where energy extraction takes place, both horizontally, through the networks of energy production and consumption, but also vertically, through the different organizational scales of governments and industry. This implies that the *local* quickly emerges as a set of particular kinds of relationships and networks that link to a much wider set of scale relationships rather than as a singularity focused on a bounded location. Hence, this research has brought me to regional and national head offices of oil companies and interest groups in Calgary and Edmonton and to the traplines of Métis Elders in the RMWB, starting with the particular case of the Conklin-based operations of the Norwegian multinational company Statoil (now called Equinor). However, this focus quickly spread to other actors, areas, and operations as the different networks and scales of the topic revealed themselves through the fieldwork. All this work was interrupted by the outbreak of the Fort McMurray wildfire, and this chapter is an attempt to analyze and understand the political impact of the fire. The research for this chapter is based on fieldwork and data collection from 2014 to 2016 in the contested energy spaces of Alberta, Canada. I have carried out interviews with Métis community leaders and management, Elders, community representatives, government officials, consultants, lawyers, and corporate social responsibility officers and managers.

The three main Métis communities participating in this study are the McMurray Métis, Fort McKay Métis, and Conklin Métis, all of whom represent nodes in a regional Métis grouping spanning northern Alberta (Clark, O'Connor, and Fortna 2015).[2] For this chapter, I draw mainly on these three Métis communities. The McMurray Métis (Local 1935) was founded in 1987. If the province of Alberta recognizes the McMurray Métis as a historical community (like McKay and Conklin: see Joly, this volume; Clark, O'Connor, and Fortna 2015), the members will be eligible not only for the same hunting and trapping rights as other Métis communities but also for mandatory consultation by oil and gas companies (McDermott 2015b). The McMurray Métis community represents a subregional hub within a wider regional Métis grouping that extends from Île-à-la-Crosse, Saskatchewan, north to Fort Chipewyan, east to Fort McMurray, and south to Beaver Lake and Lac La Biche (Clark, O'Connor, and Fortna 2015). The centrality of the waterways to Fort McMurray has led to a strong Métis presence. The river system was the initial means of transport connecting the northeast of Alberta with the historic trail to the west through Saskatchewan, and the Métis played a crucial role in the navigation of the rivers, from scows to steamships. Oral history accounts are clear that the House River–McMurray–La Loche axis along the Clearwater was heavily travelled and inhabited by Métis (Clark, O'Connor, and Fortna 2015).

The Fort McKay Métis community comprises part of the historic Métis grouping who provided labour for the fur trade during the nineteenth and early twentieth centuries in the Athabasca region of what is now northeastern Alberta. Its members have a mixed ancestry that includes French, English, Cree, and Dene heritage with close ties to members of the Fort McKay First Nation. Located in the heart of the mineable oil sands region, its members, along with the neighbouring Fort McKay First Nation,[3] have faced unprecedented change over the past thirty years due to rapid industrial expansion.

The third community is the Conklin Métis, which developed in large measure due to the railway that ran between Lac La Biche and around the hamlet of Fort McMurray. In this area, Métis people have practised trapping, hunting, fishing, and harvesting for over one hundred years, mixed with seasonal wage labour. In recent decades, steam-assisted gravity drainage operations combined with ancillary high-voltage transmission lines and bitumen pipelines have had a great impact on the area. There are currently 337 people living in Conklin, according to the latest census (Regional Municipality of Wood Buffalo 2015). The traditional harvesting territory of the Conklin Métis covers about 10,000 square kilometres, stretching from the Wiau and Grist Lakes in the south to the Algar and Gordon Lakes in the north (Golder Associates 2011).

## Theoretical Framing: Oil Sands Region as Carbonscape

Oil began forming in southern Alberta when tiny marine creatures died and drifted to the sea floor in prehistoric times. Over time, heat and pressure compressed their bodies to form liquid oil—referred to today as petroleum. When tectonic plates shifted to form the Rocky Mountains, the pressure squeezed the oil northwards (Canada's Oil Sands 2017). For centuries, this oil, or bitumen, as it is called, has surfaced and been used by humans, first as a sealing compound for bark canoes, and in recent times, for energy and other petrochemical uses. As in many energy spaces, the traditional lands of Indigenous Peoples encompass the oil sands region.

There is a strong tradition within geography of seeing landscapes as more than material objects, but rather as permeated by, or assembled through, social, political, cultural, and economic relationships (Mitchell 2002). As Sharon Zukin explains, landscapes are "built around dominant social institutions…and ordered by their power" (1992, 221). Such assemblages of actors and materials are characterized by their emergent capacities, contingent on their interaction with other component parts (DeLanda 2016; DeLanda and Harman 2017). Assemblage theory stresses how the interactions between seemingly separate elements produce unstable and contingent entities, revealing the ephemeral character of contested energy spaces, always vulnerable to reconfigurations.

Manuel DeLanda's notion of an assemblage "converter" is helpful in conceptualizing the instability of assemblages (DeLanda 2016; Deleuze and Guattari 1987, 324–25). The idea of assemblage converters highlights the catalytic impact of well-placed component parts in either transforming assemblages or ensuring that relations and parts remain stable (Haarstad and Wanvik 2017; Wanvik 2014). These converters can theoretically ascend from everywhere within or outside of the assemblage. However, component parts of carbonscape assemblages can serve as particularly influential, transformative forces when they happen to be well-placed to create ripple effects. Hence, employing the vocabulary of assemblage theory allows us to better conceptualize change and instability. In what follows, I elaborate on how this instability plays out empirically by scrutinizing landscape, governance, and power instabilities created within the contested energy spaces of Wood Buffalo.

### *Landscape Instability*

Material consequences of resource extraction and the subsequent environmental degradation and limited, non-renewable character of the energy resource are all defining characteristics of contested energy spaces (Le Billon and Carter 2012; Marsden 2010). The disturbing features of the Albertan energy spaces, with their vast tailings ponds, huge open wounds, and crisscrossing seismic lines in the boreal forest landscape, contribute to its vulnerable and unstable characteristics. The boreal forest is the dominant forest region in Canada, making up 35 percent of Canada's landmass and 77 percent of the country's forested land. It is also one of the world's largest ecosystems, comprising 10 percent of global forest cover. The boreal forest plays a vital role in sustaining ecological cycles, including ecological services such as wildlife diversity and carbon storage. It is an essential part of the environment, contributing to healthy air, water, and soil. It provides also a vital economic resource for the region (Flat Top Complex Wildfire Review Committee 2012, 13).

The boreal forest is a dynamic system, subject to highly transformative processes. Among them, wildfires are natural parts of its life cycle; many of the vegetation species are well adapted to large wildfires. Wildfires consume forest canopy and can spread from treetop to treetop, releasing huge quantities of sparks, smoke, and other gases (Flat Top Complex Wildfire Review Committee 2012). Before major wildfire suppression programs, boreal forests historically burned on an average cycle ranging from 50 to 200 years as a result of lightning and human-caused wildfires as part of Indigenous controlled burning practices (Lewis and Ferguson 1988; McCormack 2017). However, due to reduced wildfire activity in the wake of industrial expansion and a history of fire suppression, forests of Alberta are aging, which ultimately changes ecosystems and increases the risk of large and potentially costly catastrophic, unstable wildfires (Flat Top Complex Wildfire Review Committee 2012; McCormack 2017; Baker, this volume).

### *Governance Instability*

Although the landscape of the oil sands region is subject to abrupt changes, the social and political features of the contested energy spaces of Wood Buffalo are equally prone to instability and contestation. The RMWB is located in northeastern Alberta. Formed as a result of the amalgamation of the City of Fort McMurray and Improvement District No. 143 in 1995, it is the second largest municipality in Alberta by area (Regional Municipality of Wood Buffalo 2018). As home to the Athabasca oil sand deposits, the region is one of the fastest-growing industrial areas in Canada. Rural populations of primarily Indigenous Peoples in the RMWB have claimed that they experience most of the negative impacts from industrial extraction (e.g., environmental degradation, influx of foreign specialized labour, increased heavy transport activity), while the urban area of Fort McMurray benefits from most of the tax revenues (McDermott 2016).

Attempting to mend potential conflicts coming out of this inequitable distribution of benefits, and with their traditionally shared interest in smooth operations of extractive industries, government and industry claim to make strong efforts to include and integrate Indigenous communities in the value chain to enable them to benefit from industry (Brownsey and Rayner 2009). These efforts have materialized through consultation processes, environmental impact assessments, and impact benefit agreements. Through these entangled processes, government and industry are trying to manage, maintain, and stabilize contested energy spaces. Most of these stabilizing efforts are delegated to industry and framed as corporate social responsibility and stakeholder management (Wanvik 2016). Turning governance in this way into corporate social responsibility programs, the governance regime within the contested energy spaces of Wood Buffalo is greatly dependent on externalities such as global oil prices (which influence corporate profits and margins) to maintain a certain level of infrastructure and services (Wanvik 2016) provided by industry through such social programs. The drop in *global* oil prices has put tens of thousands out of work in Wood Buffalo, and reduced government revenues substantially (Alberta Energy 2017; Government of Alberta 2017). Hence, a converter in one part of the oil assemblage (fluctuating energy prices) has led to major disruptions within the Wood Buffalo governance regime, and served as an important background for the political negotiations that followed in the wake of the Fort McMurray wildfire.

### *Power Instability*

For decades, the asymmetrical context of the Canadian North, with its economically disadvantaged remote and semi-remote Indigenous communities and explosive economic growth in some urban centres (fuelled by extractive industries), has been a concern for social scientists (Angell and Parkins 2011). Characteristically, the conflicts emerging out of localized energy production are portrayed as skewed in favour of powerful stakeholders such as the state or industry. Several studies portray Indigenous efforts to limit massive exploitation and subsequent destruction of their lands as antagonism, resistance, or subversive activities (Bebbington 2012; Bebbington et al. 2008; Black, D'Arcy, and Weis 2014; Haarstad and Fløysand 2007; Huseman and Short 2012; Le Billon and Carter 2012; LeClerc and Keeling 2015). However, recognizing the limitations of constantly representing Indigenous Peoples in this way as "passive victims," contemporary scholars have advocated a new research perspective—one that is more responsive to the changing milieu of northern Indigenous Peoples and that "recognizes Indigenous peoples as conscious, pragmatic actors in cultural change and adaptation" (Angell and Parkins 2011, 72). The call for a new approach to northern Indigenous research stems from the growing political power among northern peoples

(Hovelsrud and Krupnik 2006) and from attempts to decolonize academia. A better understanding of how Indigenous Peoples are mobilizing to support their own goals and aspirations is required (Alcantara, Lalonde, and Wilson 2017), rather than focusing solely on reactive resistance. Recent literature has also focused on the effectiveness of Indigenous multi-community organizing in the face of oil extraction in Alberta (Longley 2015), adding to understanding Indigenous mobilization of resources.

An analytical framework that breaks from traditional notions of permanent power relations between industry and communities is needed to properly understand and explain recent developments among Métis communities in northern Alberta (Wanvik and Caine 2017). Several Métis communities in this region have mobilized a variety of resources to increase their leverage and expand their rights in the midst of the oil sands frenzy. Such transformative competence is nothing new (Pelling 2011), but it has not been fully elaborated through studies of Indigenous resource politics. (For a comprehensive review of the scholarship on Indigenous communities and disaster management, see Clark 2017.) Hence, I argue that Indigenous communities seize the moment through strategic and pragmatic engagement with an ever-changing environment. As readers will see, the alliance forged among Wood Buffalo Métis communities was instrumental in mobilizing Indigenous and rural people during the Fort McMurray wildfire, and played a vital part in the political negotiations that followed.

## Métis Mobilization of Resources

The Métis have historically been relegated to the status of Canada's forgotten people (Lischke and McNab 2007; Sealey and Lussier 1975). Métis communities were not part of treaty negotiations and land claims agreements in Alberta (see Lee-Jones, Longley, this volume). Subsequently, Alberta provided certain Métis communities with settlement lands, while others were given small private pieces of land through a federal process called scrip (Andersen 2014; Augustus 2005; Chartrand 2008; Isaac 2016; Sawchuk 2001). Without recognition of their collective rights and title, the ability of the Métis to raise revenues from specific extractive projects and to negotiate directly with proponents remains a challenge (Dubois and Saunders 2013; Madden 2016; Weinstein 2007). Industry and government still do not officially recognize a duty to consult Métis communities, apart from eight recognized Metis settlements.[4] Hence, the Métis communities of Fort McMurray, Fort McKay, and Conklin must find other ways of advocating their right to recognition and self-determination.

That the Métis share a sense of nationhood and collective consciousness as a distinct Indigenous people has been well documented (see, for example, Adams, Dahl, and Peach 2013; Andersen 2008; Chartrand 2008; Dubois and Saunders 2017; Madden 2008; Teillet 2013; Weinstein 2007). The term *otipaymishooyahk* translates to the Métis notion of being "people who own themselves," implying an embodied understanding of independence and self-sufficiency (Dubois and Saunders 2017; Gaudry 2014; see Joly, this volume). While formal constitutional recognition of their inherent right to self-government (among other defined rights) remains a goal, in the face of these challenges, the Métis have had to find innovative ways to pursue self-government initiatives on their own (Chartrand 2008; Madden, Graham, and Wilson 2005; Teillet 2013) and make the most out of windows of opportunity.

The Métis communities of Alberta employ a series of strategies to gain leverage and access benefits from industrial intrusion on their traditional territories. (For a critical assessment of the motivation behind these strategies, see Slowey 2009.) Although the Alberta government has not granted consultative status to non-settlement Métis communities in relation to extractive prospecting on their traditional territories (Alberta Consultation Office, email correspondence 2015), several communities have drawn on their close relationship with adjacent First Nations communities to gain leverage in consultation processes. One Métis community leader stated, "For a long time, we piggybacked the First Nation, and they negotiated on our behalf. They were including us in their claims for benefits" (interview, 2015). He added, "Later, we have gained independent negotiation competence, and we are now doing our own claims towards industry, setting up agreements and IBAs [Impact Benefit Agreements]." Although there were challenges related to the joint negotiations and the sharing of benefits, the community gained valuable experience from the process, which enabled them to build capacity from within.

As an outcome of negotiations with industry, several Métis communities have developed traditional land use studies and legal claims (Clark, O'Connor, and Fortna 2015). Industry representatives underscore the importance of these studies: "We know for a fact that our communities use our support to grow negotiating power towards the government" (Statoil Canada, interview 2015). These traditional land use studies contribute to stronger negotiating power and increased legal strength in relation to Métis claims to consultative status and access to traditional territories. Furthermore, there has been a strategic and tactical exchange of consultative capacity and competence between several Métis communities within the carbonscape of Wood Buffalo. Individuals working with one particular Métis community organization have been re-employed several times in other Métis community organizations, transferring experience and working methods from one community to another. This practice, in turn, has led to a closely knit relationship between the three Métis communities of Fort McKay, Fort McMurray, and Conklin, to the extent that they, together with the community of Fort Chipewyan, formed the Wood Buffalo Métis in 2015 (later including the Willow Lake Métis in Anzac, comprising the Athabasca River Métis). As such, the four major Métis communities in the oil sands have signed an agreement that places them under one banner when negotiating with industry and government (McDermott 2015a). This alliance was instrumental when disaster struck and hard-won benefits were taken away from Métis communities during the political aftermath of the fire.

## Disaster and Crisis as Catalytic Assemblage Converter

Some geographers have long theorized a politics of disaster, mainly in relation to development and vulnerability studies (Birkmann 2006; Özerdem and Jacoby 2006). Analyses of disaster politics focus on the interaction of social and political actors and framing institutions in preparing for and responding to extreme natural events, and suggest that the disaster events and their management are part of unfolding political histories (Hewitt 2014). Mark Pelling and Kathleen Dill (2009) approach disasters as both political events in and of themselves and potential producers of secondary political effects, such as new alliances, leadership, and social critiques. According to them, disasters triggered by environmental phenomena can act as catalysts that put into motion potentially provocative social processes at multiple social levels.

Change can be revealed in multiple ways, such as through policy discourse, or material and resource flows. Recent scholarly debate on this question has been influenced by two claims. The first sees disasters producing an "accelerated status quo"; here, change is path dependent on and limited to a concentration or acceleration of pre-disaster trajectories, which remain under the control of powerful elites (Klein 2007). The second viewpoint sees evidence that disasters can catalyze a critical juncture—an irreversible change in the direction or composition of a political regime (or its subsets) (Pelling and Dill 2009). Hence, crisis and disasters might act as assemblage converters, particularly well-placed component parts resulting in transformations across several interlinked assemblages. Thus, although a particular social formation appears strong, it is always dependent upon and embedded within other structures and processes that have their own capacities for change (Haarstad and Wanvik 2017).

## Wildfire Impacts

In 2016 Alberta had a mild, dry winter and spring, attributed to El Niño, as warmer than normal temperatures over the Pacific Ocean influenced weather across North America. Probably caused by human carelessness, the wildfire in and around Fort McMurray had far-reaching effects: 2,400 homes were lost, and the direct and indirect costs skyrocketed, surpassing all former Canadian natural disasters with its cost of an estimated C$9.9 billion (Weber 2017).

Five hundred First Nations and Métis firefighters worked on the Fort McMurray wildfire during the efforts to extinguish the flames and limit their reach and impact on town structures. The Indigenous crews made up half of all fire brigades battling the wildfire and comprised the largest percentage of firefighters working on the blaze. In a video produced by Alberta Wildfire in 2015, wildfire manager Gordon Bisgrove called Indigenous firefighting crews "the backbone" of the forest fire service in Alberta (Pruden 2016). Indigenous communities and groups scrambled to ensure that people were safe. These communities also took in evacuees, as tens of thousands fled the massive wildfire raging through Fort McMurray (Fontaine 2016).

### *Red Hot Politics*

Months later, after Fort McMurray residents returned home to shattered dwellings, scorched woodlands, and a community in disarray, the RMWB was forced to scramble for recovery funds. During an evening municipal council meeting on July 19, 2016, the administration presented recommendations as to whether construction of approximately ninety capital projects should be resumed, deferred, or simply cancelled (Bird 2016a). Halfway through the debate, one of the councillors made an amending motion to defer an additional ten projects that had been scheduled to resume. "Recovery is more than money. It's much more than money. We will need as much money as we can keep our hands on for that," the councillor claimed (Bird 2016a). There was ample need for drastic budget cuts, as the councillor explained in an interview: "The city budget is moving towards a substantial deficit as an effect of the financial downturn, with huge expenditures and a strangled income revenue stream. In the current financial climate, we have to cut. We started out before the fire, cutting flat on all our administration around 10 percent" (urban councillor, interview 2016). This decision effectively reversed previous gains by Indigenous communities.

The single most catalyzing deferral of a proposed capital expenditure was that of a multimillion-dollar facility named the Conklin Multiplex. After significant rallying by Indigenous communities and local councillors over almost six years, a multi-use facility for the people of the predominantly Métis hamlet of Conklin had been discussed more than fifteen times in the Regional Municipal Council (Conklin Resource Development Advisory Committee, interview 2016), and the construction work had finally begun. The project's deferral was to trigger a large mobilization among Indigenous communities across Wood Buffalo.

Three weeks after the council decision to defer the rural development projects, an op-ed by the representative of the Conklin Resource Development Advisory Committee in *Connect Weekly*, a local paper and webpage, ignited the communities. It stated, "The people of the community of Conklin were dealt a major blow on July 19 when RMWB Council voted to defer the completion of the Conklin Multiplex, a project that they have promised the community for over six years—an integral service hub for the community and industry. The hamlet of Conklin had high hopes as this project was finally going to provide a safe place for kids to play, a promising location to house nursing station and policing services, and essential programming for our youth and Elders" (O'Donnell 2016).

The Conklin Resource Development Advisory Committee is a multistakeholder entity facilitating the development of the hamlet of Conklin in the wake of industrial activity. The advisory committee's manager claimed in a 2016 interview that the voice of remote communities is small and often goes unnoticed, and he argued that it was equally the case for the community of Conklin when the funding for the multiplex was halted.

After the massive Indigenous contributions to firefighting, and the vital support given to refugees from the city of Fort McMurray in Conklin, Fort McKay, Anzac, and other outlying communities, the deferral was particularly discouraging. "We stepped up and opened our homes and our wallets for Fort McMurray," said the president of the Fort McKay Métis. The multiplex was the catalyst, concurred the CEO of the same community (interview 2016), and the communities decided that enough was enough (McDermott 2016). On August 16, the communities mobilized massively for the council meeting in downtown Fort McMurray. The council chambers' public seating area was packed with people from all of Wood Buffalo's rural Métis and First Nations communities, as community leaders took turns speaking to council. An overflow area was created in the lobby, where the public watched a live stream of the meeting (Bird 2016b).

The groups present included the Athabasca Tribal Council, the community associations for Conklin and Anzac, and all of Wood Buffalo's Métis Locals. It became clear in the first sentences of Fort McKay Métis president Ron Quintal's presentation that council had awakened a sleeping giant. The group turned the topic of the multiplex from a small issue of poor planning into a massive issue of the overall neglect by the municipality of rural areas since 1995 (King 2016). After the meeting, one of the rural councillors explained to me what happened: "When it came around to the next meeting, one of the councillors, the one that broke the defence line of Conklin the last time, [his First Nation's] chief came along, to the meeting…sitting right in the front row. [The chief] made sure that the councillor in question voted in favour of Conklin. And then there is this other councillor who flip-flops all the time, and he flipped to our side, and so then it was 7–3 in favour [of Conklin]" (interview 2016).

Although the rural councillor described a complex history behind the initial deferral, the massive presence of rural Indigenous communities and their leaders turned the votes and secured the Conklin Multiplex. Once it became clear that construction would continue, delegates and rural residents gave a standing ovation. "It's a huge win, not just for Conklin but for the rural communities," Quintal said (McDermott 2016). The next step, he added, was to continue pushing the minister of municipal affairs, Danielle Larivee, for a review of the entire amalgamation agreement of 1995, thereby calling the very existence and legitimacy of the RMWB, plus the regional primacy of Fort McMurray, into question.

Subsequently, with other grievances ranging from a lack of rural water and sewage services to the polarizing Conklin Multiplex, the RMWB's rural communities petitioned Alberta Municipal Affairs for a review of the 1995 amalgamation to determine if they had been treated fairly under the terms of the negotiations. Representatives from nearly twenty First Nations and Métis groups, as well as the rural hamlets themselves, met with Larivee, arguing that they are increasingly at an economic and social disadvantage compared to Fort McMurray (McDermott 2016). In recent years, rural community leaders had forced quality of life issues into municipal political discourse. Access to piped sewage and running water has been a decades-long fight for some communities, and fresh food is still hours away for others.

Interviewed by local media, Quintal spoke of solidarity: "We have been brought together by the fact that Conklin is a community in crisis and their needs are being ignored" (Heidenreich 2016). He followed up by pointing to the cumulative effects of the grievances faced by the rural communities: "The problems they face have been amplified by the fire and the deferment of the multiplex has damaged the relationship that our communities have with the regional municipality" (Heidenreich 2016). The timing was opportune. There was concern that a political focus on rebuilding Fort McMurray would further direct resources away from rural areas. Yet Quintal noted there was also an opportunity to reset the relationship between urban and rural areas. "At the heart of the issue is the revenue provided by industry sites near our communities to the municipality and what we get in return," said Quintal. "At the end of the day, the rural communities are impacted by oil sands development and if the oil sands developments are what's paying the taxes—the 95 percent of the taxes to the Regional Municipality of Wood Buffalo—why shouldn't the rural communities be able to prosper from that?" (Heidenreich 2016). These statements demonstrate that the consequences of the wildfire had reached their peak. From being a devastating natural disaster, the wildfire had turned into a powerful catalyst of change, pushing the rural, Indigenous communities to lobby for fairer distribution of benefits and tax revenues within the entire regional municipality.

## Conclusion

Disaster politics suggest that disaster events and their management are part of unfolding political histories (Pelling and Dill 2009). The histories of Wood Buffalo carbonscapes and the power relations between the state, corporations, and Indigenous communities influenced the impact and political aftermath of the wildfire disaster of 2016. Métis communities of Wood Buffalo have spent decades seeking recognition as rights-bearing communities among the proliferating industrial developments in the regional municipality (Gaudry 2014; Wanvik and Caine 2017).

Indeed, there is little doubt that Indigenous advocacy has had a substantive impact for Métis communities in Alberta, and on the way multinational companies and provincial and local governments deal with Métis issues. But, when the economic downturn was beginning to have a real impact on municipal revenues in 2015, followed by a devastating wildfire in 2016, political concessions were revoked or deferred. Rural Métis and First Nations communities responded by rising to the occasion and fighting for access to benefits of oil-sands-generated tax dollars. In a disaster politics framing, the council's decision could be considered an attempt to maintain the status quo. On the other hand, the Indigenous mobilization of resources created destabilizing processes that threatened to break with the status quo, first by rescuing the Conklin Multiplex from deferral, and subsequently by attempting to renegotiate the 1995 amalgamation agreement. The renegotiation is currently ongoing. Such events are evidence of a particular mobilization of scarce but potentially effective human and material resources that enable marginalized communities to join forces and fight for their interests as Indigenous Peoples.

The activities of extractive industry have a great impact on the social, cultural, and environmental realities in the carbonscapes of Wood Buffalo. Although there have been benefits for Canadian society, the burden shouldered by local ecosystems and Indigenous communities is substantial, which adds to the prolonged historical conflict between the Crown and Indigenous Peoples in Wood Buffalo over rights and entitlements (Cairns 2000; Veltmeyer and Bowles 2014). Nevertheless, empirical evidence suggests that such a one-dimensional view of power dynamics fails to understand the encounters between industry, the state, and Indigenous communities.

Recent developments among the Métis of Wood Buffalo underscore that their rural coalition, their political impact, and ability to raise their voices in regional, provincial, and even federal issues have grown substantially. Two years after the disaster, rural councillor Jane Stroud of the Regional Municipality—who represents the communities of Anzac, Gregoire Lake Estates, Conklin, and Janvier—told a local newspaper there had been a difference in how the communities are being prioritized from higher levels of government: "I believe the relationship between Fort McMurray and Anzac has certainly changed. I think there's a much better understanding of what the community of Anzac and the rural hamlets have to offer." Quintal underscores the internal strengthening of rural communities in the same article: "The fact that we fought fire hand-in-hand during The Beast strengthened the bond, not just with Fort McMurray, but with all the other communities within the regional fire service" (Beamish 2018). After years of feeling like an afterthought in local and regional politics, leaders in the rural communities surrounding Fort McMurray claim their relationship with the RMWB council is finally improving—much as a consequence of the wildfire.

## Notes

1 During fieldwork in 2014–2016, the Métis communities of the Fort Chipewyan, Fort McKay, Fort McMurray, Anzac, and Conklin were collectively organized as the Wood Buffalo Métis, and, later the Athabasca River Métis (ARM).

2 Métis people are descendants of First Nations and European settlers with their own unique cultural practices and traditions, recognized as Indigenous Peoples under the 1982 Constitution of Canada.

3 The numbers are contested, ranging from forty-four recorded inhabitants of the hamlet of Fort McKay (Regional Municipality of Wood Buffalo 2015) to the "more than three hundred" claimed by local leaders (interview 2015).

4 The Alberta provincial government launched their Metis settlements consultation policy guidelines in April 2016, but these do not include communities outside the settlements by the time of publication. The settlements are Buffalo Lake Metis, East Prairie Metis, Elizabeth Metis, Fishing Lake Metis, Gift Lake Metis, Kikino Metis, Paddle Prairie Metis, and Peavine Metis Settlements.

## References


Adams, Christopher, Gregg Dahl, and Ian Peach. 2013. *Métis in Canada: History, Identity, Law and Politics*. Edmonton: University of Alberta.

Alary, Bryan. 2016. "Fort McMurray Blaze among Most 'Extreme' of Wildfires: Researcher." *Folio* (University of Alberta), May 6, 2016. https://www.folio.ca/fort-mcmurray-blaze-among-most-extreme-of-wildfires-researcher/.

Alberta Energy. 2017. "Resource Revenues Collected." Government of Alberta. http://www.energy.alberta.ca/About_Us/2564.asp (accessed October 20, 2017).

Alcantara, Christopher, Dianne Lalonde, and Gary N. Wilson. 2017. "Indigenous Research and Academic Freedom: A View from Political Scientists." *International Indigenous Policy Journal* 8 (2). doi: 10.18584/iipj.2017.8.2.3.

Andersen, Chris. 2008. "From Nation to Population: The Racialisation of 'Métis' in the Canadian Census." *Nations and Nationalism* 14 (2): 347–68.

———. 2014. *Métis: Race, Recognition, and the Struggle for Indigenous Peoplehood*. Vancouver: University of British Columbia Press.

Angell, Angela C., and John R. Parkins. 2011. "Resource Development and Aboriginal Culture in the Canadian North." *Polar Record* 47 (1): 67–79. doi: 10.1017/S0032247410000124.

Augustus, Camilla. 2005. "The Scrip Solution: The North West Metis Scrip Policy, 1885–1887." MA thesis, University of Calgary.

Beamish, Laura. 2018. "Relationship between McMurray, Rural Areas Continues Growing since Wildfires." *Fort McMurray Today*, May 3, 2018. http://www.fortmcmurraytoday.com/2018/05/03/relationship-between-mcmurray-rural-areas-continues-growing-since-wildfires.

Bebbington, Anthony. 2012. "Underground Political Ecologies: The Second Annual Lecture of the Cultural and Political Ecology Specialty Group of the Association of American Geographers." *Geoforum* 43 (6): 1152–62.

Bebbington, Anthony, Leonith Hinojosa, Denise Humphreys Bebbington, Maria Luisa Burneo, and Ximena Warnaars. 2008. "Contention and Ambiguity: Mining and the Possibilities of Development." *Development and Change* 39 (6): 887–914.

Bird, Cullen. 2016a. "Council Defers Conklin Multiplex Construction, Other Projects." *Fort McMurray Today*, July 20, 2016. http://www.fortmcmurraytoday.com/2016/07/20/council-defers-conklin-multiplex-construction-other-projects.

Bird, Cullen. 2016b. "Rural Coalition Claims a Victory as Conklin Multiplex Construction Resumes." *Fort McMurray Today*, August 16, 2016. http://www.fortmcmurraytoday.com/2016/08/16/rural-coalition-wins-first-victory-at-council.

Birkmann, Jörn. 2006. *Measuring Vulnerability to Natural Hazards: Towards Disaster Resilient Societies*. Tokyo: United Nations University Press.

Black, Toban, Stephen D'Arcy, and Tony Weis. 2014. *A Line in the Tar Sands: Struggles for Environmental Justice*. Toronto: PM Press.

Brownsey, Keith, and Jeremy Rayner. 2009. "Integrated Land Management in Alberta: From Economic to Environmental Integration." *Policy and Society* 28 (2): 125–37.

Cairns, Alan C. 2000. *Citizen Plus: Aboriginal Peoples and the Canadian State*. Vancouver: University of British Columbia Press.

Canada's Oil Sands. 2017. "Oil Sands History and Milestones." Canadian Association of Petroleum Producers. http://www.canadasoilsands.ca/en/what-are-the-oil-sands/oil-sands-history-and-milestones (accessed March 27, 2017).

Chartrand, Larry. 2008. "'We Rise Again': Metis Traditional Governance and the Claim to Metis Self-Government." In *Aboriginal Self-Government in Canada* (3rd ed.), edited by Yale Belanger, 145–57. Saskatoon: Purich Publishing.

Clark, Timothy. 2017. "Natural Disasters, Vulnerability, and Resilience in Indigenous Communities: Literature Review and Conceptual Framework." Technical report. ResearchGate. doi: 10.13140/RG.2.2.15670.60489.

Clark, Timothy David, Dermot O'Connor, and Peter Fortna. 2015. *Fort McMurray: Historic and Contemporary Rights-Bearing Métis Community*. Prepared by Willow Springs Strategic Solutions for McMurray Métis Local Council 1935.

DeLanda, Manuel. 2006. *A New Philosophy of Society: Assemblage Theory and Social Complexity*. London: A&C Black.

———. 2016. *Assemblage Theory*. Edinburgh: Edinburgh University Press.

DeLanda, Manuel, and Graham Harman. 2017. *The Rise of Realism*. Cambridge: Polity Press.

Deleuze, Gilles, and Félix Guattari. 1987. *A Thousand Plateaus: Capitalism and Schizophrenia*. Translated by Brian Massumi. Minnesota: University of Minnesota Press.

Dubois, Janique, and Kelly Saunders. 2013. "'Just Do It!': Carving Out a Space for the Métis in Canadian Federalism." *Canadian Journal of Political Science* [Revue canadienne de science politique] 46 (1): 187–214.

Dubois, Janique, and Kelly Saunders. 2017. "Explaining the Resurgence of Métis Rights: Making the Most of 'Windows of Opportunity'." *Canadian Public Administration* 60 (1): 48–67.

Flat Top Complex Wildfire Review Committee. 2012. *Final Report from the Flat Top Complex Wildfire Review Committee*. Submitted to the Minister of Environment and Sustainable Resource Development, May 2012. https://wildfire.alberta.ca/resources/reviews/documents/FlatTopComplex-WildfireReviewCommittee-A-May18-2012.pdf.

Fontaine, Tim. 2016. "Indigenous communities take in Fort McMurray fire evacuees, scramble to find members." *CBC News*, May 05, 2016, News. http://www.cbc.ca/news/aboriginal/indigenous-communities-fort-mcmurray-evacuees-1.3566938 (accessed August 16, 2016).

Gaudry, Adam James Patrick. 2014. "Kaa-tipeyimishoyaahk – 'We Are Those Who Own Ourselves': A Political History of Métis Self-Determination in the North-West, 1830–1870." PhD dissertation, University of Victoria.

Golder Associates. 2011. *Leismer to Kettle River Crossover Project*. Calgary, AB: TransCanada.

Government of Alberta. 2017. "Unemployment Rate." http://economicdashboard.alberta.ca/Unemployment (accessed October 20.2017).

Heidenreich, Phil. 2016. "Rural and Indigenous Groups near Fort McMurray Call for Major Changes to RMWB, Cite Unfair Tax Structure." *Global News*, August 16, 2016. https://globalnews.ca/news/2884793/rural-and-indigenous-groups-near-fort-mcmurray-call-for-major-changes-to-rmwb-cite-unfair-tax-structure/.

Hewitt, Kenneth. 2014. *Regions of Risk: A Geographical Introduction to Disasters*. 2nd ed. New York: Routledge.

Hovelsrud, Grete K., and Igor Krupnik. 2006. "IPY 2007–08 and Social/Human Sciences: An Update." *Arctic* 59 (3): 341–48.

Huseman, Jennifer, and Damien Short. 2012. "'A Slow Industrial Genocide': Tar Sands and the Indigenous Peoples of Northern Alberta." *International Journal of Human Rights* 16 (1): 216–37.

Haarstad, Håvard, and Arnt Fløysand. 2007. "Globalization and the Power of Rescaled Narratives: A Case of Opposition to Mining in Tambogrande, Peru." *Political Geography* 26 (3): 289–308.

Haarstad, Håvard, and Tarje I. Wanvik. 2017. "Carbonscapes and Beyond: Conceptualizing the Instability of Oil Landscapes." *Progress in Human Geography* 41 (4). doi: 10.1177/0309132516648007.

Isaac, Thomas. 2016. *A Matter of National and Constitutional Import: Report of the Minister's Special Representative on Reconciliation with Métis: Section 35 Métis Rights and the Manitoba Metis Federation Decision*. Ottawa, ON: INAC, Government of Canada. https://www.aadnc-aandc.gc.ca/eng/1467641790303/1467641835266.

King, Tyler. 2016. "A Welcome Flip-Flop." *Fort McMurray Today*, August 21, 2016. http://www.fortmcmurraytoday.com/2016/08/21/a-welcome-flip-flop.

Klein, Naomi. 2007. *The Shock Doctrine: The Rise of Disaster Capitalism*. New York: Macmillan.

Le Billon, Philippe, and Angela Carter. 2012. "Securing Alberta's Tar Sands: Resistance and Criminalization on a New Energy Frontier." In *Natural Resources and Social Conflict: Towards Critical Environmental Security*, edited by Matthew A. Schnurr and Larry A. Swatuk, 170–92. London: Palgrave Macmillan.

LeClerc, Emma, and Arn Keeling. 2015. "From Cutlines to Traplines: Post-Industrial Land Use at the Pine Point Mine." *The Extractive Industries and Society* 2 (1): 7–18. http://dx.doi.org/10.1016/j.exis.2014.09.001.

Lewis, Henry T., and Theresa A. Ferguson. 1988. "Yards, Corridors, and Mosaics: How to Burn a Boreal Forest." *Human Ecology* 16 (1): 57–77.

Lischke, Ute, and David T. McNab. 2007. *The Long Journey of a Forgotten People: Métis Identities and Family Histories*. Waterloo, ON: Wilfrid Laurier University Press.

Longley, Hereward. 2015. "Indigenous Battles for Environmental Protection and Economic Benefits during the Commercialization of the Alberta Oil Sands, 1967–1986." In *Mining and Communities in Northern Canada: History, Politics, and Memory*, edited by Arn Keeling and John Sandlos, 207–32. Calgary, AB: University of Calgary Press.

Madden, Jason. 2008. "The Métis Nation's Self-Government Agenda: Issues and Options for the Future." In *Métis–Crown Relations: Rights, Identity, Jurisdiction, and Governance*, edited by F. Wilson and M. Mallet, 233–90. Toronto: Irwin Law.

Madden, Jason. 2016. "Daniels v. Canada: A Case of Simple Answers with Significant Consequences." *Candian Lawyer*, April 18, 2016. https://www.canadianlawyermag.com/article/daniels-v-canada-a-case-of-simple-answers-with-significant-consequences-3241/.

Madden, Jason, John Graham, and Jake Wilson. 2005. *Exploring Options for Métis Governance in the 21st Century*. Ottawa, ON: Institute on Governance. http://pattersoncreek.ca/wp-content/uploads/2011/02/Exploring-Options-for-Metis-Governance.pdf.

Marsden, William. 2010. *Stupid to the Last Drop: How Alberta Is Bringing Environmental Armageddon to Canada (And Doesn't Seem to Care)*. Toronto: Vintage Canada.

McCormack, Patricia A. 2017. "Walking the Land: Aboriginal Trails, Cultural Landscapes, and Archaeological Studies for Impact Assessment." *Archaeologies* 13 (1): 110–35.

McDermott, Vincent. 2015a. "Local Metis Communities Agree to Fall under One Banner." *Fort McMurray Today*, September 3, 2015. http://www.fortmcmurraytoday.com/2015/09/03/local-metis-communities-agree-to-fall-under-one-banner.

———. 2015b. "McMurray Métis Passes as a Historical, Rights-Based Community, Argues Report." *Fort McMurray Today*, August 17, 2015. http://www.fortmcmurraytoday.com/2015/08/17/report-arguing-mcmurray-metis-passes-as-a-historical-community-would-make-industry-consultation-mandatory.

———. 2016. "Rural Hamlets Asks Province to Examine Amalgamation." *Fort McMurray Today*, August 4, 2016. http://www.fortmcmurraytoday.com/2016/08/04/rural-hamlets-asks-province-to-examine-amalgamation.

Mitchell, Don. 2002. "Cultural Landscapes: The Dialectical Landscape—Recent Landscape Research in Human Geography." *Progress in Human Geography* 26 (3): 381–90.

O'Donnell, Jeffrey. 2016. "Major Blow to Conklin Multiplex." *Connect Weekly*, August 5, 2016. http://www.fortmacconnect.ca/2016/07/major-blow-to-conklin-multiplex/.

Özerdem, Alpaslan, and Tim Jacoby. 2006. *Disaster Management and Civil Society: Earthquake Relief in Japan, Turkey and India*. Vol. 1. New York: I.B. Tauris.

Pelling, Mark. 2011. *Adaptation to Climate Change: From Resilience to Transformation*. New York: Routledge.

Pelling, Mark, and Kathleen Dill. 2009. "Disaster Politics: Tipping Points for Change in the Adaptation of Sociopolitical Regimes." *Progress in Human Geography* 34 (1). https://doi.org/10.1177/0309132509105004.

Pruden, Jana G. 2016. "Indigenous Firefighters Battling Fort McMurray Blaze Follow Long Alberta Tradition." *Globe and Mail*, May 20, 2016. http://www.theglobeandmail.com/news/national/indigenous-firefighters-battling-fort-mcmurray-blaze-follow-long-alberta-tradition/article30110469/.

Regional Municipality of Wood Buffalo. 2015. Census Report. Fort McMurray: Regional Municipality of Wood Buffalo. http://www.rmwb.ca/Assets/Corporate/Census+Reports/Municipal+Census+2015+Report.pdf (accessed May 31, 2017).

Regional Municipality of Wood Buffalo. 2018. *Census Report*. Fort McMurray, AB: Regional Municipality of Wood Buffalo. http://www.rmwb.ca/Assets/Departments/Planning+and+Development/Planning+$!26+Development+Documents/Census+Report+2018.pdf (accessed September 12, 2019).

Sawchuk, Joe. 2001. "Negotiating an Identity: Métis Political Organizations, the Canadian Government, and Competing Concepts of Aboriginality." *American Indian Quarterly* 25 (1): 73–92.

Sealey, D. Bruce, and Antoine S. Lussier. 1975. *The Métis: Canada's Forgotten People*. Winnipeg: Manitoba Métis Federation Press.

Slowey, Gabrielle. 2009. "A Fine Balance? Aboriginal Peoples in the Canadian North and the Dilemma of Development." In *First Nations, First Thoughts: The Impact of Indigenous Thought in Canada*, edited by Annis May Timpson, 229–47. Vancouver: Univeristy of British Columbia.

Teillet, Jean. 2013. *Métis Law in Canada*. Toronto: Pape Salter Teillet.

Veltmeyer, Henry, and Paul Bowles. 2014. "Extractivist Resistance: The Case of the Enbridge Oil Pipeline Project in Northern British Columbia." *The Extractive Industries and Society* 1 (1): 59–68. http://dx.doi.org/10.1016/j.exis.2014.02.002.

Wanvik, Tarje Iversen. 2014. "Encountering a Multidimensional Assemblage: The Case of Norwegian Corporate Social Responsibility Activities in Indonesia." *Norsk Geografisk Tidsskrift – Norwegian Journal of Geography* 68 (5): 282–90. doi: 10.1080/00291951.2014.964761.

———. 2016. "Governance Transformed into Corporate Social Responsibility (CSR): New Governance Innovations in the Canadian Oil Sands." *The Extractive Industries and Society* 3 (2): 517–26.

Wanvik, Tarje Iversen, and Ken Caine. 2017. "Understanding indigenous strategic pragmatism: Métis engagement with extractive industry developments in the Canadian North." *The Extractive Industries and Society* 4 (3): 595–605.

Weber, Bob. 2017. "Fort McMurray Wildfire Financial Impact Reaches Almost $10B, Study Says." *The Star* (Toronto), January 17, 2017. https://www.thestar.com/business/2017/01/17/fort-mcmurray-wildfire-financial-impact-reaches-almost-10b-study-says.html.

Weinstein, John. 2007. *Quiet Revolution West: The Rebirth of Métis Nationalism*. Calgary, AB: Fifth House.

Zukin, Sharon. 1992. "Postmodern Urban Landscapes: Mapping Culture and Power." In *Modernity and Identity*, edited by Scott Lash and Jonathan Friedman, 221–47. Oxford: Blackwell.

# 6 Bear Stories in the Berry Patch

## Caring for Boreal Forest Fire Cycles of Respect

*Janelle Marie Baker*

### Introduction

Learning from First Nations Elders is rarely a straightforward or linear process. Rather, it is continually expanding and shifting, it is circular, and it is personal; it needs to be a humble pursuit, much like berry picking (Michell 2009). This chapter is inspired by the storytelling that people from both Fort McKay First Nation and Bigstone Cree Nation engaged in while in berry patches during the summer of 2016, the year of the massive fires in the Fort McMurray, Alberta, area. Through observations and experiences of monitoring contamination of the wild food supply from oil and gas activity (Baker 2016), these Elders and land users asserted that the fires that summer were not normal. The fires were much larger (see Wanvik, this volume), more out of control and toxic because objects such as housing material and oil and gas infrastructure—not just natural and forest things—were burning. The community-based monitors know from where they speak, as many can cite the exact year, location, path, and size of past fires with remarkable accuracy, those that occurred within their lifetimes and some even going back a hundred years or more. In the berry patch, people will often talk about when a fire last went through the area, relating how long ago it went through to the health and productivity of the berries; the really good berry patches, especially blueberry patches (*Vaccinium myrtilloides*), are ones that have been touched by fire in recent years.

The remarkable thing for me was that during the summer of fires, rather than focusing on fire and berry stories, people shared black bear,[1] or *maskwa*,[2] stories while in the berry patches. Berries are an essential summertime food supply for bears, so bears are always a consideration while we are in the patches, but in 2016, bears were the focal point of my research collaborators' stories. This chapter is a response to these unexpected moments, an exploration of the connections between bears, berries, and fires, and an attempt to make sense of what people were trying to teach me. I rely mostly on *sakâwiyiniwak* (Northern Bush Cree) observations of, and experiences with, a landscape that is central to their identity and survival. I will explain how my research collaborators, in spite of living in an extractive sacrifice zone (Willow 2016), tend to relationships with the boreal forest through fire management, berry picking, and respectful speech, behaviour, hunting, butchering, and ceremonies regarding bears.

Kwagiulth First Nation geographer Sarah Hunt writes, "ontology is, ironically, not a word that comes to mind when I think of Indigenous ontologies. What comes to mind, instead, are stories" (2014, 27). She points to stories and storytelling as "culturally nuanced ways of knowing, produced within networks of relational meaning-making" (27). Many First Nations origin stories serve to remind us that humans were the last species to arrive on earth, and as such, are dependent on the wiser, older beings for their mercy and offerings (Watts 2013, 25).[3] Humans entered already-functioning societies of sentient beings with particular values, cultures, and ethics; humans had to enter into agreements with these societies as relations in order to survive (Reder 2012, 509). As Anna Tsing notes, "The concept of sociality does not distinguish between human and not-human. 'More-than-human sociality' includes both" (2013, 27).

In several Algonquian languages, including *sakâw nehiyawewin* (the Northern Bush Cree language), there is a distinction to be made between the two oral narrative genres (Darnell 1974; Hallowell [1960] 2002; Scott 2018). The first involves "news," including anecdotes and stories describing events that have occurred in the lives of human beings, whether they be everyday occurrences or legendary ones. The second category includes oral traditions or sacred stories that describe events that happen and "are always happening" (Scott 2018) to beings who have existed since the beginning of time. Whether or not one is allowed to tell such sacred stories may be restricted by the season, a ritual, ownership, and these stories are taken very seriously by both teller and listener, as a sort of invocation of ancestors (Hallowell [1960] 2002). These types of oral traditions "depict humans, animals, and other nonhuman beings engaged in an astonishing variety of activities and are committed to mutually sustaining relationships that ensure the continuing well-being of the world" (Cruikshank et al. 1990, xii).

While Elders have shared some oral traditions with me in the berry patch, especially those invoking the trickster, *wīsahkīcāhk*, the majority of the stories I discuss here are of the first sort, and are about events that have happened to humans. Storytellers have an obligation to tell these stories with accuracy, so much so that a storyteller's honesty is never called into question (Darnell 1974). For James Bay Crees, "These stories are events witnessed by humans and are supposed to be passed on with fidelity to those events, whether they happened yesterday or in the time of the great-great-grandparents" (Scott 2018). Bear stories that have been shared with me are not just for the purposes of entertainment or small talk, but rather convey layers of wisdom about the natural world and how to behave appropriately in relation to bears, berries, fire, and the greater world.

## Grandfather Fire

> White people they buy a machine they fill it up with gas and they walk back and forth on their front yards "brrrr brrrr" all day to cut their grass [laughs]. Natives what do we do? What, eh? Burn it. That's right. Spring time. Ohhh the snow is gone hahahahha I'm going to be the first one to do my lawn. Ah, nicimos [lover, hand me the] matches.
>
> —Don Burnstick, Cree comedian from Alexander First Nation, Alberta, "Cuttin' Grass" at Enoch River Cree Casino, 2014

During the Fort McMurray fires of 2016, I was living in Wabasca, Alberta, which is 169 kilometres southwest of Fort McMurray as the crow flies, and 420 kilometres by road. Wabasca is the central hamlet that services several small Bigstone Cree Nation "pocket" reserves. While living in Wabasca, I would drive regularly to Fort McKay (to work with the Fort McKay berry group – about 15 community members who actively check and test berry patches), which is 53 kilometres north of Fort McMurray. Fort McKay was evacuated during the most intense times of the fires, along with the entire city of Fort McMurray. But by berry-picking season in August, the fires no longer posed a direct threat and people were back home. During the evacuation, residents of Fort McKay dispersed all over Alberta and western Canada, and some of the Elders from the Fort McKay berry group came to Wabasca because of familial ties they had there. During that summer, I noticed that while sakâwiyiniwak I knew were concerned about the welfare of people affected by the fire, they were not surprised by it, nor did they seem to view it as the disaster it was being portrayed as in the news. Of course, many in Fort McMurray tragically lost their homes, and people cared deeply about their well-being, but even though this fire was unusually large and toxic, individuals I spoke with calmly observed that fires happen, and have always happened.

Bigstone Cree Nation Elder Albert Yellowknee shared a creation story with me when I asked him about the traditional use of fire in boreal forest management, in which the creator breathes fires into two poplar trees for them to become humans. In this sense, fire is a life-giving force. He reminded me that "everything is interconnected, fire included." Fire, who gives us life, is thus referred to as "grandfather fire" in ceremony (Hallowell [1960] 2002, 21), and is to be respected like a family member and ancestor. Andrew Bouchier from the Fort McKay berry group also referred to fire as a life-giving force, as it is nature's way of "looking after the country." It makes the land fresh. Fire is the creator that cleanses and takes care of the landscape to make it more habitable for all creatures. Rain cleans the landscape on a smaller scale, but after rain, fire comes in and does a major cleaning. Ecologically, traditional burning practices not only clean and invigorate the land, but they increase the availability of light, and release nutrients into the soil that become available to berry plants. While the berry plants burn above ground, fire encourages the sprouting of new shoots from roots, and this reduces the likelihood of disease and insect infestation. The new lushness of vegetation attracts foraging animals like moose and deer. Mechanical forest disturbances, on the other hand, typically have the opposite effect (LeCompte-Mastenbrook 2015, 172).

Handling fire is considered both an honour and a responsibility among First Nations, but sadly many forms of landscape burning have been prohibited. Several Elders in both Fort McKay First Nation and Bigstone Cree Nation have told me that they know their parents or grandparents intentionally burned berry patches in the past, but that the practice was suppressed before the subsequent generation was able to experience it firsthand. Jean L'Hommecourt,[4] a Fort McKay trapper and land user, told me that people traditionally burned in Fort McKay territory. She said her grandmother often used to intentionally set fires in the spring at Poplar Point, down the Athabasca River from Fort McKay, while it was still wet from the melt. They would set a fire one year, and the next year go to pick berries and medicines that were now abundant from the burning. In Wabasca, and many other Indigenous communities in the region, people burn their yards and the grassy areas along the lakes in the spring; it really is much faster than mowing or raking the lawn to clear out old and dead plant growth from the previous year. It helps keep mosquitos and black flies away when they are at their most vicious. Many plants are particularly well-adapted to benefit from fire, especially jack pines (*Pinus banksiana*) and blueberries (which tend to grow together in sandy soils), as pine cones need fire to open and disperse their seeds, and fire acts to prune blueberry plants and prevent fungus and disease. Small, controlled spring fires also help prevent larger, more uncontrollable ones.

Henry Lewis and Theresa Ferguson, anthropologists well-known for their work on Dene burning practices in northern Alberta, describe two patterns of spring burning. "Fire yards," or fields, are comprised of hay meadows and small forest openings including berry patches. "Fire corridors," or lines, are the human-maintained grassy edges of traplines, trails, streams, muskrat sloughs, and lakesides (Lewis and Ferguson 1988). They observe, "the regular firing of trapline corridors and yards was recognized as an integral, necessary feature of a hunting-trapping strategy…the Indians of northern Alberta understood, and many still understand, the complex networks of plant-herbivore-predator relationships" (Lewis and Ferguson 1988, 70). I have had the privilege of visiting some of the remaining hay meadows in Bigstone Cree Nation territory, where friends and colleagues remember burning in the spring, and cutting, drying, and collecting hay in the summer for horses and, occasionally, cattle. They used fire to regenerate these places and bring in fresh green grass that also attracted moose and other ungulates they could hunt. Both fire yards and fire corridors increase the abundance and biodiversity of plants and animals, increase the predictability of animal movements, and improve soil quality (Lewis and Ferguson 1988).

People have practiced cultural or anthropogenic burning in the oil sands region for millennia, and what Europeans thought was wilderness when they first arrived, was, in fact, a mosaic of landscapes managed by controlled burns, harvesting, and natural fires (Lewis and Ferguson 1988). This "constructed landscape" (McCormack 2017, 121) of prairies, parkland, forest-lined rivers, and conifers in muskegs is what settlers thought of as typical boreal forest and was a great deal more open in terms of vegetation than it is today. The names of several locales in northern Alberta attest to the fact that landscapes were shaped by First Nations' burning practices: Grande Prairie, High Prairie, Buffalo Head Prairie, John D'Or Prairie, and Paddle Prairie are all examples of once well-maintained fire yards and corridors, some of which have reverted to forest due to fire suppression.

In 1908 fire suppression was enforced through two-hundred-dollar fine notices prohibiting the practice, which Federal Director of Forestry Robert Campbell had translated into *nehiyawewin* (Cree) and Dene syllabics (Kristensen and Reid 2016, 13). With the introduction of fire suppression, traditional trails, waterways, and fire corridors became choked with vegetation that restricted, or at least altered, the movement of sakâwiyiniwak and Dene in northern Alberta (Kristensen and Reid 2016, 13; McCormack 2017). I hear people regularly lament that their former transportation routes, especially over small rivers and trails through the bush, are now too overgrown to use. This thick regrowth is less biodiverse (Stevenson and Webb 2004) and has increasingly thick and flammable ground layers of litter (Kristensen and Reid 2016). This regrowth also takes over berry patches (Johnson 1999). Since 2012 we have witnessed one of Fort McKay's berry patches become more overgrown and significantly less productive, as the jack pine stand has thickened with young conifers, aspen, and woody shrubs. The Elders often remark that these types of landscapes need to be "cleaned out with fire"—as an act of respect and responsibility towards the plants and animals that provide food for us—in order to continue to be ecologically productive.

Archaeologists working in northern Alberta are currently using sediment cores and optically stimulated luminescence, a technique used to analyze sand grains from dunes for exposure to light, to compare fire history patterns with First Nations' knowledge of forest succession in to optimize controlled burns (Kristensen and Reid 2016). One such archaeologist, Christina Poletto, works in Fort McKay traditional territory to extract mud cores and analyze charcoal and pollen deposits in an effort to provide a baseline of fire history to compare with culturally modified landscapes (see Kristensen and Reid 2016). She ultimately wants to learn about how First Nations managed forests in the past to encourage specific plants to attract specific wildlife. Other research has suggested that restrictions in Indigenous burning practices have caused temporal changes in fire frequency in Wood Buffalo National Park, northeast of Fort McKay, alongside climate change, which is also a likely major factor in the increase in large-scale forest fires in the region (Larsen 1997, 672). Fire suppression has undoubtedly contributed to the large uncontrollable fires frequenting the northern Albertan boreal forest in recent years; the boreal forest is a disturbance forest, meaning that it needs fire for renewal (Urquhart 2016, 10). Since colonization, fires in Alberta have been suppressed to save merchantable timber, but in northern Alberta, oil and gas sites have also motivated protection from burnings. Yet fire suppression, combined with the effects of climate change, mean that when fires take hold in the peat moss and thick black spruce (*Picea mariana*) of the boreal forest, and wildfires now burn much larger tracts of land in Alberta than they did even forty to sixty years ago (Urquhart 2016, 2).

Traditional burning practices for berry management have been well documented by ethnobotanists working in communities on North America's northwest coast. For example, Klamath and Modoc's berry management practices in southern Oregon and northern California are based in burning and land management activities that constitute a "ritualized expression" of the reciprocal obligations between humans and plants (Deur 2009, 317). An increase in berry production indicates that said rituals were successful; that the plants were pleased and so gifted fruit to the grateful humans. Conversely, low berry production is understood to reflect a failure to show the berries proper respect, through insufficient or ineffective rituals or overexploitation. In her dissertation on Coast Salish berry landscapes in Washington State, Joyce LeCompte-Mastenbrook describes fire suppression as a colonizing form of knowledge suppression, alienating people from their traditional homelands (2015, 163–70). She defines Indigenous burning practices as a "cultural keystone process…the absence of which will inevitably have cascading social effects" (167). Coast Salish Elders spoke of how they would burn huckleberry habitat to reinvigorate and cleanse the land and to keep meadows clear from new tree growth. This burning was part of their reciprocal responsibility, to care for the plants just as the berries take care of the people by providing food (170).

The Gitx̱an and Wet'suwet'en First Nation peoples of northern British Columbia used fire to ensure the abundance of the huckleberry and blueberry patches that people depended on for stored winter food sources (Johnson 1999). Like sakâwiyiniwak, Gitx̱an have camps near the berry patches that they return to annually. People would perform burnings in late August and September when the nights were cool and it was likely to rain. This allowed for a light burn that stimulates berry plant sprouting, reducing the hazard of intense uncontrolled fires that limit berry production that consume the organic surface layer of the soil and huckleberry rhizomes (Johnson 1999, 242–43). Now, without regular burning to clear out the undergrowth, berry patches are overgrown with taller shrubs and conifers, and are therefore not as productive, offering fewer and smaller fruits.

Wet'suwet'en Elders also described spring berry patch burning, primarily for lowbush blueberries, but possibly also for black huckleberries (Johnson 1999, 244–45). They spoke of controlled spring burning around villages, on south-facing slopes, and on floodplains, processes I have observed occurring in the Wabasca area today. However, this sort of burning of fire corridors on reserve (Lewis and Ferguson 1988) differs from the intentional burning of fire yards, like berry patches in the forest in size and purpose. In fact, the last berry patch burnings occurred in the 1930s and 1940s, when fire crews were assembled to put out these fires. People today are still very aware that they can be arrested for burning berry patches, due to the rules put in place by the Forestry Service. In spite of the prohibition on burning, Indigenous Peoples across northwestern Canada maintain plant management skills that are often overlooked by government natural resource management research and rules.

Ethnobotanist Nancy Turner (1999) explains how the culturally important plants of the Northwest Coast are mostly perennial species, rather than annuals.[5] Annuals rely on seed production for the gardening and cultivation of their populations, and are typically what people think of in reference to plant management. This has resulted in a lack of recognition of the Indigenous management practices for most plants in this region, and that Indigenous "people actively modified their environment to ensure reliable, predictable and abundant supplies of key resources for food, materials and medicine" (Turner 1999, 145–46). Turner describes multiple peoples' burning practices on the BC Northwest Coast and concludes that controlled burning requires a specialized and in-depth knowledge of ecological systems, especially vegetation characteristics, forest succession, and geographical and climatic landscape features: "This knowledge, acquired through centuries and generations of careful observation and experimentation, seldom has been acknowledged by non-Native people" (201). Instead, settlers, especially foresters, considered Indigenous landscape burning to be acts of carelessness or destruction. Turner notes that, "it is ironic that the landscapes so appreciated by the early explorers and colonists actually were created by the very fires they feared and disliked" (196), as has been the case in northern Alberta.

## Grandmother Bear

During the 2016 Fort McMurray fires, bear sightings and encounters became more frequent, as they had likely been pushed out of the safety of the boreal forest because of the flames. They were now forced to share the remaining berry patches with us, as many of the more private berry patches buried deeper in the forest had burned. We often saw bears as we approached berry patches, bears came into friends' yards more frequently, and when I made my regular 450-kilometre trip from Wabasca to Fort McKay I was astounded by the number of bears I saw on the edge of the highway. Unusually, I saw more bears than deer on those trips.

Fort McKay Elder Bruce Faichney explains that while in the berry patch "we are in his territory; we are stealing his food." Likewise, Fort McKay Elder Harvey Roland says, "the berries are here for him, it's me that's stealing his food" (see also LeCompte-Mastenbrook 2015, 139). As in most of the places where berries grow in northern Alberta, you do not go to a berry patch without considering bears. If you do not meet a bear—who in our case is typically running off as we arrive at a berry patch—there will be signs that a bear has been there. Bushes will be scraped, there will be paw prints in the sandy soil, or the bears will have left behind a jam-like scat. My research collaborators often talk about the bears' eating habits and point out signs in the berry patch that they have been there eating. For example, bears like to pick the larger berries off of the top of the blueberry bushes and, as Celina Harpe, Fort McKay Elder explains, "they leave the little ones for us." We noticed also that the berry bushes in the areas that we protect with electric fences surrounding the air monitoring stations we put up for our studies still have those larger berries on the top because the bears cannot reach past the electric fences to eat them. Though we have put up these small fences, we understand that berry patches are shared spaces; berries are shared resources. Many birds and insects and other animals depend on these "patchy" places (Thornton 1999; Trusler and Johnson 2008), but it is people and, especially, bears who most prefer to spend time in the various types of berry patches to store these small fruits as provisions for winter. And one needs to be observant and punctual to get to the berries, especially blueberries, before the bears.

As I have argued elsewhere (Baker and Fort McKay Berry Group 2019), berries in sakâwiyiniwak territory experience social personhood and can hear what people are saying. People are very careful and conscious about how to speak around, and to, berries, always showing respect and gratitude for the bounty they provide. Bears, who sakâwiyiniwak also relate to as persons, can similarly hear what people are saying. In many Cree communities across Canada, it is observed that bears can understand spoken Cree, even from a seemingly inaudible distance (Brightman 1993; Scott 2006, 2007). Along with powerful medicine people, the bear shares the ability to know what a person is thinking, especially if a hunter's intent is to kill the bear (Scott 2007, 398). I am often advised that a bear will not bother or attack a person if they acknowledge him/her in sakâw nehiyawewin and speak to him/her with respect. Bears are also known to attack if they have been offended by the over-harvesting of any game (especially bears), or if hunters have been wasteful and allowed butchered meat to spoil (Scott 2007).

In many places in the world where humans and bears interact, bears are recognized as having human-like qualities, as they are intelligent, clever, omnivorous, sometimes bipedal, are powerful hunters, make comfortable dwellings with spruce bough floors like humans, and when skinned, they look remarkably like humans (Scott 2007).[6] Moreover, sakâwiyiniwak describe bears as being superior in intelligence and spiritual power to humans, and I have heard people refer to them as "our brothers," or as "grandmother bear." Ethnographic literature across Canada is rich with examples of bears being represented as the most powerful and respected of animals in the broader Cree world (Brightman 1993; Scott 2006, 2007; Tanner 1979). Stories about bears not only teach us how to behave properly and how to function within cycles of reciprocity with the natural world, but they also teach about the spiritual power and agency non-humans possess in the world, and the suffering humans may experience when they do not respect this power (Westman 2015). Anthropologist Colin Scott, who shares his own bear stories, and specifically those of James Bay Crees, notes the importance of teaching and learning through such stories: "What is there in a Cree boy's first encounter with a black bear, compared to his first meeting with a moose, to tell him that it is the bear who carries paramount sacred importance? Both are formidable animals, both are major gifts of food—the moose more so in terms of quantity—yet the boy is pre-equipped by stories and instruction to know that the bear is more significant, before ever meeting one" (2006, 54). As this quotation demonstrates, the importance and spiritual strength of bears is most often taught through stories.

I began to more fully understand the relationship between berries and bears upon asking Elder Albert Yellowknee why people always eat berries at ceremonies. He answered by teaching me for about an hour, through story, about bears and that it was because bears eat berries, and they are considered the most spiritually powerful animal. In ceremonies I have attended, berries have been passed around and each person has eaten some from the same spoon (see Kimmerer 2013). I have recently realized that berries are also often involved in the preparations for the ceremonial lodge, and that berries are served as people come out of the sweat lodge to be the first nourishment they receive in their re-entry to the world outside of the lodge.

I have heard repeatedly that berries nourish the mind, body, and spirit, and act as medicine. Adding to his teaching, Albert explained to me that grandmothers and mothers pick berries to nourish their families, and so in ceremonies berries are eaten and offered to honour the grandmother spirits (see also Westman 2015). You bring the berries for the ancestral grandmother spirit and the grandmother spirit of the bears (both of whom he referred interchangeably). They are eaten and offered to the grandmother bear spirit, who appreciates the gift of berries in reciprocation for sharing knowledge with humans about medicinal plants and the bear's generosity in sharing her meat in times of hunger (Scott 2007, 399). In a similar vein, just as when a human engages in a vision quest, bears fast (hibernate) as a way of seeking knowledge about medicines that can later be shared with humans through dreams or demonstrated use.[7] Bears also come out of hibernation to take pity on humans and respond to their requests—sent through prayer, dreaming, and songs—to hunt and eat the bear (Scott 2007, 397).

Berries are, in part, so special because they are an essential nutritional food source for both bears and humans. For example, bears keep berries in their paws so that they can snack on them during hibernation (Baker and Fort McKay Berry Group 2019). Howard LaCorde and Albert Yellowknee each explained, at different times, this amazing behaviour to me: while bears are in the berry patches feasting, berries get crushed under their feet and dry there. This happens day after day until the bears end up with "felts" made of berries. They make a dried berry fruit leather for snacking on during their fast in the winter, just as women often used to as a way of preserving and storing blueberries for winter (Baker and Fort McKay Berry Group 2019).

I first began to learn about the spiritual connection between humans and bears while working on a traditional land use assessment for Bigstone Cree Nation, concerning a large oil sands development in their territory being proposed by an oil company subsidiary. I was hired as a consultant to record the potential impacts proposed oil and gas developments could have on Bigstone Cree Nation's Treaty Rights to carry out traditional pursuits on Crown lands. The company was in possession of a massive oil sands lease and was proposing a pilot project called the North Field Test site, utilizing in situ bitumen extraction technology (Orenstein et al. 2010); they brag the operations will be ultimately be larger than those of Fort McMurray when fully developed. At the time, their activities were top secret. The lease was held under the name of smaller start-up company as they were extremely paranoid about Chinese spies, and the very trappers the company was consulting were not allowed to know anything about what the company was doing, or where they were doing it.

The oil company was paying for the traditional land use assessment to be completed and integrated into their version of an environmental assessment that they called an "integrated assessment" (Orenstein et al. 2010), which ostensibly was meant to be a new type of assessment that included traditional environmental knowledge throughout. Their project was small enough that it did not trigger a full Environmental Impact Assessment (EIA), as the pilot project fell below the threshold of 12,570 barrels of oil per day (Alberta 2000, 43–44). This is actually a common tactic from companies who, whenever possible, intentionally propose projects and project expansions that will fall under the limits that trigger an EIA, but then continuously expand projects until they are megaprojects. The more recent Environmental Assessment Act (Government of Canada 2012) has further facilitated these kinds of expansions by eliminating the requirement for federal environmental assessment entirely for any in situ projects.

As part of this particular project, in order for the trappers and Elders to be allowed to participate in assessments on their *own* ancestral traplines, they were required to adhere to industry safety standards. This meant they were not allowed to provide their own transportation, carry rifles, or operate chainsaws to clear trails. Rather, they had to use CB radios on the roads, call in from the bush by satellite phone at regular intervals, drive inappropriately large all-terrain company vehicles, and have all of the same health and safety training certificates as are required of contractors, such as first aid, all-terrain vehicle operation, water safety, and bear awareness training. Out of all of the certificates required by the oil company, the latter was the most problematic and insulting. It was a one-day course that took place entirely indoors, in which the company paid an instructor to drive two and a half hours north from Athabasca to teach a group of hunters and trappers—who came from a community 110 kilometres north of Wabasca and did not have road access until very recently—how to be safe in bear habitat. The course "taught" trappers who had grown up on the land how to identify black bears and grizzly bears, how to avoid encounters with bears, and what to do if an encounter did occur.

I attended the various training sessions with the group of hunters and trappers, and while some of the younger trainees joked during the break about how now if they saw a bear they would simply kneel down and display their "bear awareness training card" to avoid an attack, one of the Elders, Dennis Noskiye, an active hunter and trapper, was more deeply troubled and took me aside. He began to explain how sakâwiyiniwak have a completely different understanding of why a bear would attack someone. I assumed his reasoning would include the sharing of some tidbits of wisdom about bear behaviour and habitats, but he surprised me.

Dennis explained that the only reason a bear would attack someone was because a person had put "bear medicine" on them. Bear medicine refers to a type of curse or spiritual power that a person inherits through the generations that, through ritual, gives them the power to compel a bear to attack a particular person. Sometimes this is accomplished by the person in possession of bear medicine transforming into a bear in order to commit the attack themselves (see Hallowell [1960] 2002, 36–37). So for Dennis, unless the course was teaching them how to thwart such medicine, all of the safety precautions they were learning about were useless.

I remembered Dennis's words the following summer when a medicine man and trapper from Calling Lake, which is part of Bigstone Cree Nation, shot a bear on his trapline while I was working on another traditional land use study with a group of their environmental monitors. The hunter explained that the event meant that he had broken free from a curse. The fact that he was able to shoot the bear meant he had successfully broken the cycle of negative reciprocity he had with bears (see Scott 2006). Apparently, in his past this man had offended someone who possessed bear medicine, and that person had placed a curse so that rendered him unable to hunt bears. Such cycles of negative reciprocity may also be sparked when a hunter has not shown an animal proper respect during hunting or butchering practices. The animal's spirit is offended and so does not come back to the hunter—through the process of reincarnation—to offer itself again as it would normally. The environmental monitors who were with the hunter when he shot the bear spoke of how the bear cried and climbed a tree and how it took many shots to finally kill it, which they interpreted as it having been a particularly difficult curse to break (see also Scott 2007, 391–92). Once the bear was being butchered in a respectful fashion, they were excited for the smoked ribs and highly valued bear "grease" (the rendered fat), which is used in medicine making and ceremonies (Westman 2015, 307), and as for use as a protective layer in the hair.[8]

I have since heard many stories about how bears will not attack you if you are respectful to them, speak sakâw nehiyawewin to them, and as long as no one has placed a curse on you. Many people wear special protective medicine that they keep with them to help shield themselves from curses, but I am often advised that simply refraining from speaking rudely to people will ward off bad medicine, like bear curses. Albert Yellowknee often laughs about my questions regarding negative acts—about things like someone putting a malicious curse on another—and reminds me that good medicine is much more common than bad medicine. Several people have told me that cursing often only happens between powerful medicine people, but still, certain friends of mine in Wabasca check with me regularly to see if I have had dreams about bears, and if so, whether or not I was afraid of the bears or if they were attacking me, as these are signs someone is trying to put medicine on me. I have also heard people refer to those who practice traditional medicine, or spiritual leaders, as individuals who "worship the bear." The idea that these people worship the bear is partly due to important ceremonies regularly practiced in the region, including a bear sweat lodge or a night lodge, during which participants cover themselves in a paste of red ochre mixed with bear grease (fat) to transform themselves into bears.

While collecting medicinal plants for contaminants testing, Albert Yellowknee explained to me that bears seek out special landscape features in the muskeg called "bear holes," for cleansing and healing. These holes are very deep places in the muskeg that are a creamy red in colour, and bubble with ochre-rich soils. I have asked other friends and collaborators about them and have been told that sometimes they are springs with caves underneath the surface, that they are infinitely deep or bottomless, and that some might even be gateways to other worlds or "dimensions." In general, the muskeg acts as a filter to clean water and air, but bear holes are particularly cleansing and healing for wounded animals, and the water in them acts as medicine to them. There are many stories about hunters wounding a moose and tracking it over many kilometres to see its footprints go into a bear hole and not come out the other side. A wounded animal will go into a bear hole and stay there until they are healed. If a bear finds this red ochre, they will "make a mess in there" by covering themselves in the reddish mud and bedding down to treat their wounds, much like humans do in the bear sweat, by covering their body parts that need healing in red ochre. A bear sweat lodge is also very much like a bear den, and during these ceremonies it is said that a bear will reach out and tap participants on the shoulder.

Fort McKay Elder Howard LaCorde frequently describes just such an encounter just after the Fort McMurray massive fires; it is one we always laugh at when he recounts it to others as we pick berries. Howard had been at his cabin at Moose Lake, a sacred "cultural keystone place" (Cuerrier et al. 2015) and important berry-picking area (Baker and Fort McKay Elders 2019). He was sitting outside alone by the campfire during the day while his companions were out checking rabbit snares. He saw a bear by the edge of the lake and had been keeping a careful eye on it—but the bear left without confrontation. Then, suddenly, Howard felt someone tap on his shoulder, and it was the bear, who had come around from behind. Howard jumped up and asked him, "What are you doing here?" and the bear bounced back, just as startled as he was, before running off into the bushes. I asked Howard if he was scared and what he thought the bear was doing. He replied laughing, but with a seriousness in his eyes, "Yes, I was scared, but he had just come to say hello."

Barbara Faichney has also told me stories that illustrate the human-like behaviour of bears and the various dimensions of their social personhood. She spoke of how she found a bear cub when she was a child, thinking it was a puppy, and so was carrying it with her as she and her siblings were following along behind their family's hay wagon. When Barbara's mother saw that she had picked up a bear cub, she sternly told her to drop it. When she did, the cub went running back with other cubs to their mother, who was now nearby, and who grumbled and growled at her cubs. The funny thing is that Barbara compared how the mother bear "gave the cubs heck for going too close to humans," just as her own mother had chastised her for coming into too close a contact with bears. During the same conversation, I mentioned to Barbara, who has familial ties and a history in Bigstone Cree Nation, that I had heard stories about a woman in Chipewyan Lake who had breastfed a bear cub because his or her mother had been killed by hunters, and so the woman had an obligation to care for it. Barbara then spoke of a woman at nearby Moose Lake who had also breastfed a bear cub. The bear would go under her house and hibernate in the winter as it got older, and it never bit her. At about two years old the bear started getting restless "to go breeding," so prior to its departure the lady tied a red scarf around the bear's neck. Years later someone shot the bear and found the scarf had grown into his or her neck. Both of Barbara's bear stories—she has since shared several versions of each—demonstrate the personhood and intentionality of bears, and how sakâwiyiniwak treat them as persons (Hallowell [1960] 2002).

Similarly, Colin Scott explains that "root metaphors in Cree hunting serve both to humanize animals and to animalize humans, such that humans are construed as one of many species of 'persons' in the world whose interactions are mutual and reciprocal rather than hierarchical" (2007, 388). Bears are also sometimes used as a metaphor for a woman's vagina, or for menstruating woman (Brightman 1993, 129). "Hunting bears"—just like hunting in general—is occasionally used as a metaphor for pursuing women sexually; I remember well the riotous laughter when one of my friends while berry picking went to relieve herself and yelled out to one of the males present, asking if he "wanted to see a bear."

Humans also mimic, or borrow from, bear paws. If you have ever used a human-made berry picking device, or simply a "berry picker," you will notice that it looks like you have bear paws while you are using it, and the device functions like a bear's claws to scrape the berries and some of the leaves free from the bush. Both a bear's paw and a berry picker leave the bush in a particularly scraggly state. The Elders from Fort McKay with whom I have worked mostly prefer not to use berry pickers even though they do the job quickly. They prefer to "pick the berries clean," meaning that they have been taught by their mothers and grandmothers to pick just the berries, without leaves, twigs, or insects falling into the pail (Baker and Fort McKay Berry Group 2019). However, it appears that bears help to increase berry production and overall population by pruning berry bushes with their claws, as well as through the warming of the seeds through digestion and through their scat, both of which help to distribute those seeds and spread and diversify berry populations (Auger, Meyer, and Black 2002). Bears prune high bush cranberries (*Viburnum edule*), a fruit highly valued by sakâwiyiniwak, called "*môsomina*" in their language, which means "moose berries." The bears enjoy these juicy berries and prune their tall, shrubby bushes by breaking off the outer branches, which stimulates new growth and berry production.

In the same vein, there is an interesting conservation effort ongoing in southern Alberta to preserve grizzly bear habitat by identifying berry patches with multiple berry species that are a distance away from roads, and marking these places specifically for protection (Braid and Nielson 2015). There is no doubt that the communities I work for, and with, in northern Alberta would love to protect their berry patches in any way they can, including as bear habitat. Those I work with can easily list the number of berry patches that have been lost in order to erect oil sands extraction infrastructures and dig open-pit mines. I have been out on a few adventures with people in an effort to record these lost places (Baker 2017). Unfortunately, governments and resource extraction companies do not acknowledge the loss of berry patches as having dispossessed First Nations of their familial sacred places, traditional livelihoods, or treaty rights (Baker and Westman 2018). Instead, they consider berry patches to be plentiful forest types that are interchangeable with any other. Some companies even claim they have created spaces through deforestation for new berries to grow.

The Fort McKay community-based berry monitors have selected some of their remaining accessible berry patches to study. However, access to berry patches, as well as finding ones near communities that are free from polluting industries, are both becoming increasingly difficult endeavours. Monitors do not trust the berries from most of these patches because of their proximity to oil sands extraction and processing sites. We see a serious decline in "safe" berry patches as communities struggle to protect the remaining few places that people know to be "clean" (Baker and Fort McKay Berry Group 2019). We also observe that berry habitat is in decline due to changing weather patterns, fire suppression, loss of pollinators, and the literal loss of berry patches. Sakâwiyiniwak will tell you that berries are also in decline due to loss of pollinators and being unpicked due to fears of contamination; because if people are not tending to their relationships with bears, berries, and the forest, the various species will stop producing the gift of fruit for humans. If berries are not picked and shared, they will not continue to produce berries for humans to find and consume (Baker forthcoming).

There can be little doubt that bears feel the same pressure as humans to find safe, reliable berry patches. An increase in roads and human activity near berry patches means that there has been an increase in bear encounters (Gross 2016), which can easily lead to the unfair and wasteful extermination of bears. Sakâwiyiniwak are very aware of bear habits of consumption and movement, and share bear sightings with one another. Fort McKay members look for bears to hunt in late summer by floating down the Athabasca River where the white "bear berries" (Red-osier Dogwood; *Cornus sericea*) are ripe, as bears go along the river banks to eat them. When this happens, the bears are fat and good to eat. However, members from the Fort McKay berry group now say that you cannot really eat the bears because you do not know where they have been. They often go to the dump, work camps, and people's yards to eat garbage, rendering them inedible to humans, because animals taste like what they eat. Bears who eat garbage taste like garbage and could be full of all sorts of pollution and toxic substances inherited from people's waste. Sakâwiyiniwak used to live all along the Athabasca River, hunting and trapping from Fort McKay to Fort Chipewyan. However, bear habits are now changing; the berry group members said they never used to see bears while they were picking in blueberry patches when they were younger. The bears used to stay near the river eating bear berries and only came inland to the other types of berry patches in October. But berry production is now less reliable, precipitation and the seasons increasingly unpredictable, and bears are disrupted by the increases in human activity. Also, while regular cycles of respect endure, people are no longer able to set fires to clean and balance the patches in the boreal forest, breaking an ancient cycle, and having far-reaching ramifications.

## Cycles of Respect

An Elder recently gave me the advice to "always follow the bear—he knows where the good berries are," and I have attempted to follow the bear to find the good berries in my research (Michell 2009), and in this chapter. For the sakâwiyiniwak Elders and land users who patiently try to teach me, humans are obliged to tend to the forests as a part of their responsibility to the plants and animals who provide food for them. Tending means collecting, hunting, trapping, and, in the past, it also meant starting fires under the right conditions. When people do not tend to their responsibilities and cycles of respect, imbalances occur, and massive uncontrollable fires ignite, or bears attack (Gross 2016). Sometimes those imbalances are more subtle: bears eat garbage instead of berries because it is simply easy and pleasant to find, or the bears change their habits and spend more time during the summer in inland berry patches rather than along the river. Living creatures, humans included, adjust and adapt, but when do imbalances become chaos, and a threat to food security and sovereignty?

While perhaps not surprising, the fact that people are sharing bear stories more frequently when we are in the berry patch—particularly during the year of massive fires in the region—demonstrates that they are trying to convey particular wisdom about spiritually significant beings in the context of specific environmental conditions. When there are large out of control forest fires, people look to the bears for wisdom and signs while in the bear's "grocery store." After all, bears, who, as persons, behave with intent and awareness, are the boss of the berry patches. "If we think of oral tradition as a social activity rather than some reified product, we come to view it as part of the equipment for living rather than a set of meanings embedded within texts and waiting to be discovered" (Cruikshank 1998, 41). Bear stories remind us of our responsibilities to live in social relations with the beings that make up the sentient landscape.

## Notes

1 While I have heard stories about grizzlies in the region, people are referring to black and brown/cinnamon bears (*Ursus americanus*).
2 *Maskwa* is the sakâw nehiyawewin (Northern Bush Cree language) word for black bears.
3 See Brightman (2007) for several versions of the Manitoba Rock Cree oral tradition "Bear's Eye Medicine" in which the trickster *wīsahkīcāhk* uses cranberry juice to blind bear so he is easy to kill and eat. Scott (2007, 391–92) also describes an Eastern Cree story that explains how it came to be that the black bear is not *too* easy to kill. The story starts in a berry patch.
4 Jean is also the Fort McKay Sustainability Department's Traditional Land Use Research Co-coordinator.
5 I would extend this observation into the boreal forest and prairies.
6 Sakâwiyiniwak still use spruce bough floors in ceremonial lodges and while camping in the bush. Both structures resemble a bear den.
7 I have been told in other communities about bears using a plant medicine in front of a person as a way of demonstrating or gifting them that knowledge.
8 See Brightman (1993, 145–46) for a description of how bear grease is used as protection against the feared cannibal, *wîhtikow*.

## References

Alberta, Government of. 2000. Environmental Protection and Enhancement Act. Edited by Province of Alberta: Alberta Queen's Printer.

ARC Winnipeg. 2014. "Don Burnstick - 'Cuttin' Grass.'" YouTube, November 24, 2014. https://www.youtube.com/watch?v=iWaGmq78-IY.

Auger, Janene, Susan E. Meyer, and Hal L. Black. 2002. "Are American Black Bears (*Ursus americanus*) Legitimate Seed Dispersers for Fleshy-Fruited Shrubs?" *The American Midland Naturalist* 147 (2): 352–67.

Baker, Janelle Marie. 2016. "Research as Reciprocity: Northern Cree Community-Based and Community-Engaged Research on Wild Food Contamination in Alberta's Oil Sands Region." *Engaged Scholar Journal: Community-Engaged Research, Teaching, and Learning* 2 (1): 109–23.

———. 2017. "In Search of the Toxic Berry Patch." *Engagement* (blog), December 12, 2017. https://aesengagement.wordpress.com/2017/12/12/in-search-of-the-toxic-berry-patch/.

———. Forthcoming. "Do Berries Listen? Berries as Indicators, Ancestors, and Agents in Canada's Oil Sands Region." In "*Phytocommunicability and Plant–Human Sociality*," edited by Becky Schulthies, special issue, *Ethnos*.

Baker, Janelle Marie, and Clinton N. Westman. 2018. "Extracting Knowledge: Social Science, Environmental Impact Assessment, and Indigenous Consultation in the Oil Sands of Alberta, Canada." *The Extractive Industries and Society* 5 (1): 144–53.

Baker, Janelle Marie, and Fort McKay Berry Group. 2019. "Cranberries Are Medicine: Monitoring, Sharing, and Consuming Cranberries in Fort McKay." In *Wisdom Engaged: Traditional Knowledge for Northern Community Well-Being*, edited by L.M. Johnson, 117–42. Edmonton: University of Alberta Press.

Braid, Andrew C.R., and Scott E. Nielson. 2015. "Prioritizing Sites for Protection and Restoration for Grizzly Bears (*Ursus arctos*) in Southwestern Alberta, Canada." *PloS One* 10 (7):1–15.

Brightman, Robert. 1993. *Grateful Prey: Rock Cree Human–Animal Relationships*. Berkeley: University of California Press.

Brightman, Robert. 2007. *Ācaðōhkīwina and ācimōwina : traditional narratives of the Rock Cree Indians*. Regina: University of Regina, Canadian Plains Research Centre.

Cruikshank, Julie. 1998. *The Social Life of Stories: Narrative and Knowledge in the Yukon Territory*. Lincoln: University of Nebraska Press.

Cruikshank, Julie, Angela Sidney, Kitty Smith, and Annie Ned. 1990. *Life Lived Like a Story*. Vancouver: University of British Columbia Press.

Cuerrier, A., N.J. Turner, T.C. Gomes, A. Garibaldi, and A. Downing. 2015. "Cultural Keystone Places: Conservation and Restoration in Cultural Landscapes." *Journal of Ethnobiology* 35 (3): 427–48.

Darnell, Regna. 1974. "Correlates of Cree Narrative Performance." In *Explorations in the Ethnography of Speaking*, edited by Richard Bauman and Joel Sherzer, 315–36. Cambridge: Cambridge University Press.

Deur, Douglas. 2009. "'A Caretaker Responsibility': Revisiting Klamath and Modoc Traditions of Plant Community Management." *Journal of Ethnobiology* 29 (2): 296–322.

Government of Canada. 2012. *Canadian Environmental Assessment Act*. S.C. 2012, c. 19, s. 52. http://laws-lois.justice.gc.ca/eng/acts/C-15.21/.

Gross, Lena. 2016. "(Uncomfortable) Solidarities: Doubtable Belongings and Human and Non-Human Relations in Alberta's Tar/Oil Sands Region." Paper presented at *the SOLIDARIT(I)ÉS, Canadian Anthropology Association Conference*, Halifax, June 2016.

Hallowell, Irving A. ([1960] 2002). "Ojibwa Ontology, Behavior, and World View." In *Readings in Indigenous Religions*, edited by Graham Harvey, 18–49. New York: Bloomsbury.

Hunt, Sarah. 2014. "Ontologies of Indigeneity: The Politics of Embodying a Concept." *Cultural Geographies* 21 (1): 27–32.

Johnson, Leslie Main. 1999. "Aboriginal Burning for Vegetation Management in Northwest British Columbia." *Human Ecology* 22 (2): 171–88.

Kimmerer, Robin Wall. 2013. *Braiding Sweetgrass: Indigenous Wisdom, Scientific Knowledge, and the Teachings of Plants*. Minneapolis, MN: Milkweed Editions.

Kristensen, Todd, and Ashley Reid. 2016. "Alberta on Fire: A History of Cultural Burning." *Wildlands Advocate: The Alberta Wilderness Association Journal* 24 (2): 11–13.

Larsen, Chris P.S. 1997. "Spatial and Temporal Variations in Boreal Forest Fire Frequency in Northern Alberta." *Journal of Biogeography* 24: 663–73.

LeCompte-Mastenbrook, Joyce Kelly. 2015. "Restoring Coast Salish Foods and Landscapes: A More-than-Human Politics of Place, History and Becoming." PhD diss., University of Washington.

Lewis, Henry T., and Theresa A. Ferguson. 1988. "Yards, Corridors, and Mosaics: How to Burn a Forest." *Human Ecology* 16 (1): 57–77.

McCormack, Patricia A. 2017. "Walking the Land: Aboriginal Trails, Cultural Landscapes, and Archaeological Studies for Impact Assessment." *Archaeologies: Journal of the World Archaeological Congress* 13 (1): 110–35.

Michell, Herman J. 2009. "Gathering Berries in Northern Contexts: A Woodlands Cree Metaphor for Community-Based Research." *Pimatisiwin: A Journal of Aboriginal and Indigenous Community Health* 7 (1): 65–73.

Orenstein, Marla, Titus Fossgard-Moser, Trevor Hindmarch, Susan Dowse, Jordon Kuschminder, Pádraig McCloskey, and Robert K. Mugo. 2010. "Case Study of an Integrated Assessment: Shell's North Field Test in Alberta, Canada." *Impact Assessment and Project Appraisal* 28 (2): 147–57.

Reder, Deanna. 2012. "A Complex Web of Relations That Extends beyond the Human." *Journal of Chinese Philosophy* 39 (4): 507–17.

Scott, Colin. 2006. "Spirit and Practical Knowledge in the Person of the Bear among Wemindji Cree Hunters." *Ethnos* 7 (1): 51–66.

———. 2007. "Bear Metaphor: Spirit, Ethics and Ecology in Wemindji Cree Hunting." In *Nature des esprits dans les cosmologies autochtones* [Nature of Spirits in Aboriginal Cosmologies], edited by Frédéric B. Laugrand and Jarich G. Oosten, 387–99. Québec: Les Presses de l'Université Laval.

———. 2018. Personal communication (email).

Stevenson, Marc G., and Jim Webb. 2004. First Nations: Measures and Monitors of Boreal Forest Biodiversity. *Ecological Bulletins* 51: 83–92.

Tanner, Adrian. 1979. *Bringing Home Animals: Religious Ideology and Mode of Production of the Mistassini Cree Hunters*. St. John's, NF: Institute of Social and Economic Research, Memorial University of Newfoundland.

Thornton, Thomas F. 1999. "*Tleik̲w aaní*, the 'Berried' Landscape: The Structure of Tlingit Edible Fruit Resources at Glacier Bay, Alaska." *Journal of Ethnobiology* 19 (1): 27–48.

Trusler, Scott, and Leslie Main Johnson. 2008. "'Berry Patch' as a Kind of Place: The Ethnoecology of Black Huckleberry in Northwestern Canada." *Human Ecology* 36 (4): 553–68.

Tsing, Anna. 2013. "More-than-Human Sociality: A Call for Critical Description." In *Anthropology and Nature*, edited by Kristen Hastrup, 27–42. New York: Routledge.

Turner, Nancy J. 1999. "'Time to Burn': Traditional Use of Fire to Enhance Resource Production by Aboriginal Peoples in British Columbia." In *Indians, Fire, and the Land in the Pacific Northwest*, edited by Robert Boyd, 185–218. Corvallis: Oregon State University Press.

Urquhart, Ian. 2016. "Wildfire: Nature, Government, Choice." *Wildlands Advocate: The Alberta Wilderness Association Journal* 24 (2): 4–10.

Watts, Vanessa. 2013. "Indigenous Place-Thought and Agency amongst Humans and Non-Humans (First Woman and Sky Woman Go on a European World Tour!)." *Decolonization: Indigeneity, Education & Society* 2 (1): 20–34.
Westman, Clint. 2015. "The Wihkohtowin: Ritual Feasting among Cree and Métis Peoples in Northern Alberta." *Anthropologica* 57 (2): 299–314.
Willow, Anna J. 2016. "Indigenous ExtrACTIVISM in Boreal Canada: Colonial Legacies, Contemporary Struggles and Sovereign Futures." *Humanities* 5 (55): 1–15.

# 7 Urban Buffalo

## Métis–Bison Relations and Oil Sands Extraction in Northeastern Alberta

*Tara L. Joly*

This chapter describes competing ways of relating to northern Alberta's wood bison (*Bison bison athabasca*), as Indigenous governance comes up against industrial and state management systems.[1] I discuss wood bison as significant actors—animals with their own agency—in extraction and management regimes, which often diminish opportunities to engage with bison. Wood bison are distinguished from the plains bison (*B. bison bison*) by their larger size, heavier build, and pronounced shoulder hump (Sandlos 2007, 26).[2] Historically, the species ranged across the Canadian northwest, including in northern Alberta's boreal forest. This bison territory is also inhabited by Métis, Dene, and Cree peoples, who have lived with and hunted wood bison for generations. Today, northern Alberta is also an area of extensive oil sands extraction that threatens bison habitats. In this chapter I show how oil companies use bison as a spectacle of corporate social responsibility in oil sands reclamation. For Métis people, however, these corporate bison are "urban buffalos," as one Métis trapper stated. Urban buffalo are distinct from free-roaming bison due to community concerns about contamination, lack of access to the fenced-in herd, the separation of bison from the greater landscape, and the framing of human–bison relationships as a spectacle. Common themes across these four qualities are a lack of autonomy or agency provided to the bison, alongside a disruption of the ability of Métis people to relate to bison in their own ways. In other words, urban buffalo erase and obfuscate Métis legal orders that focus on autonomy and relationality in human–animal engagements.[3]

The accounts of bison in this chapter primarily focus on Métis–bison relations, drawing on ethnographic fieldwork from 2013 to 2014 and my ongoing research partnership with the Fort McMurray Métis (Baker 2017; Chartier 2015).[4] The McMurray Métis is a local government of the Métis Nation of Alberta representing members who have historic and contemporary ties to a settlement in the town of Fort McMurray; however, members of the McMurray Métis are also related to a wider regional community of Métis people throughout northeastern Alberta connected by the Athabasca and Clearwater Rivers (Clark, O'Connor, and Fortna 2015). McMurray Métis members maintain complex and, often, familial relationships with other

Indigenous nations in the region (including pre-existing Cree and Dene communities). Beyond the human, Métis people also maintain relations—social, political, material, and spiritual—with animal and plant inhabitants of their territory (Dene and Cree inhabitants of northern Alberta often share similar relationships; see Baker, this volume). As Métis scholars explain, Métis relationships with the land, including its animal populations, are fundamental to articulating Métis collective identity, histories, and governance relationships (Todd 2016, 49–50; MacDougall 2010). In particular, as bison hunts shaped Métis governance historically (especially on the plains) and continue to influence political imagination today, bison play a vital role in articulating western Métis legal orders.

Wood bison are currently listed as a threatened species under the Species at Risk Act (SARA) and integrated into land management processes. As part of a species recovery strategy, wood bison in Alberta are protected from hunting within Wood Buffalo National Park (WBNP) and in designated areas under SARA and the provincial Wildlife Act (Wildlife Regulation, Alberta Regulation 143/97). Further, while First Nations people are able to harvest bison outside WBNP (Ronald Campbell, personal communication, January 2018), these laws still interfere with hunting bison outside of WBNP in some areas, such as in the northwestern Alberta bison management area. Under Treaty 8, First Nations individuals may hunt wood bison within Alberta. Métis individuals in Alberta, in contrast, are relatively limited in their harvesting rights and range: individuals must be registered as a "Métis harvester" and associated with a "historic Métis community" in order to harvest animals within a 160 kilometre range, or in a government-recognized traditional territory (Government of Alberta 2010, 2–3). Despite overwhelming evidence of being a historic community (Clark, O'Connor, and Fortna 2015), the Government of Alberta does not recognize the McMurray Métis as such a community, which restricts their (federal) constitutionally protected rights to harvest animals, including bison (see Thurton 2017a). Wood bison are therefore entangled in a complex web of government-defined harvesting rights and species protections, which come up against Indigenous legal orders and territorial authority.

Wood bison in northeastern Alberta are also caught between the threat of ongoing oil sands extraction and the promise of land reclamation. Leases on mineable oil sands deposits extend northwards from Fort McMurray towards the boundary of WBNP and thus are encroaching upon and threatening wood bison ranges as the land is increasingly fragmented with roads, forestry operations, and open-pit mines (see Figure 7.1). As a mitigation strategy, impact assessments include reclaiming (re-establishing) an ecologically productive boreal ecosystem, such as creating habitat for wood bison and lands that can be used by Indigenous Peoples. However, impact assessments and mitigation measures often do not consider Indigenous legal orders or definitions of land use (see Joly 2017; McCormack 2016; Westman 2013).

In this chapter I contend that northeastern Alberta's wood bison are significant actors in extraction and management regimes, which often disrupt

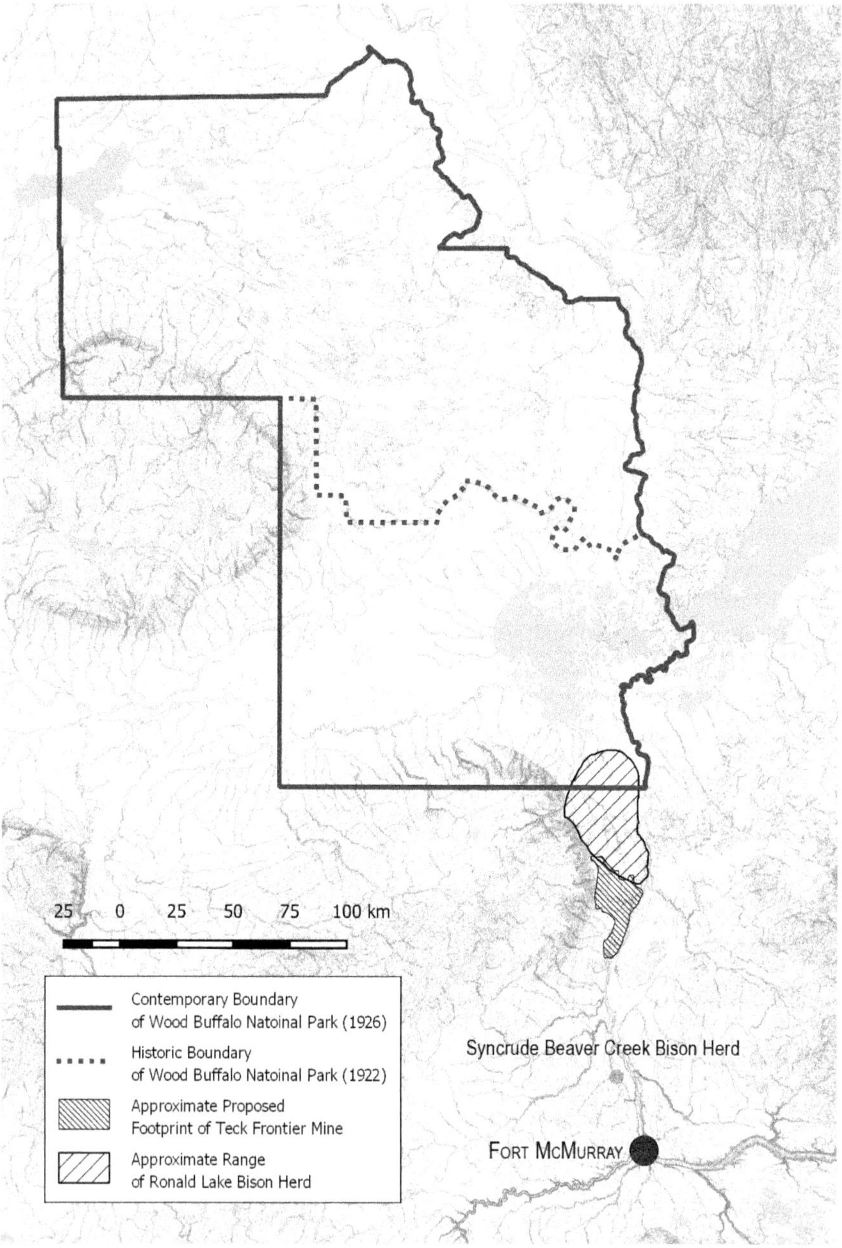


*Figure 7.1* Map of northeastern Alberta, including Wood Buffalo National Park, the Ronald Lake bison range, a proposed oil sands mine, Syncrude's Beaver Creek bison. Map by Alessandro Pasquini.

Indigenous governance systems and relations to bison. In the first section, I describe the concept of Métis space and three other principles that inform Métis legal orders: *mekiachahkwewin* (spirit gifting) (Ghostkeeper 2007), *wahkootowin* (a concept of relatedness or family) (MacDougall 2010), and *kaa-tipeyimishoyaahk* (translated as "we are those who own ourselves" by Gaudry 2014). To explore relations to bison in northern Alberta, the sections that follow present three ethnographic accounts of state management of and Métis engagements with three bison populations to demonstrate how state-centred resource management misinterprets Métis land use and has the potential to proliferate the creation of urban buffalo. I open the second section with a discussion of the Beaver Creek bison on a reclaimed area of one of the major oil sands companies, Syncrude Canada, Ltd. Métis narratives of the Beaver Creek bison depict Métis perceptions of contemporary industrial management regimes. Drawing from a focus group with Métis Elders, I argue that the Syncrude bison are, as one trapper remarked, "urban buffalo": they lack autonomy, are separate from the landscape's ecology, are perceived as contaminated, and present a spectacle. In the third section, archival documents and secondary literature on the WBNP bison illuminate the histories of colonial management in a national park founded in 1922. The history of the park shows how Indigenous harvesting was regulated and restricted, limiting opportunities for movement and practising hunting protocols. The fourth section articulates Métis versus corporate narratives of the free-roaming Ronald Lake bison (RLB), whose territory intersects the footprint of a proposed open-pit mine and therefore provide an example of a uniquely healthy bison population at risk of becoming urban buffalo. I show how large-scale landscape changes are justified through industrial narratives of removing muskeg and reclaiming uplands to "improve" bison habitat. I conclude the chapter by reflecting on this ethnographic material to call for the inclusion of Métis legal orders and reconciliation in wildlife management processes.

## Métis Space and Legal Orders

Métis relationships with animals and their environments are fundamental parts of articulating Métis culture and legal orders (Todd 2016)—which includes place-specific norms, practices, and governance. Accordingly, it is important to understand how Métis people describe cultural landscapes and their connections to place. In a community-based cultural impact assessment, McMurray Métis members describe how their culture is deeply interconnected with place using a concept termed "Métis space" (Clark 2015, 57). By providing a place where Métis people feel at home, Métis spaces make "the existence, adaptation, and transmission of McMurray Métis culture possible" (Clark 2015, 57). Métis space represents places in the community's traditional territory where members feel they can comfortably and freely practice a Métis way of life. In these places, components of Métis culture as identified by McMurray Métis members can flourish, including traditional land use, family and community, values and spirituality, identity, autonomy, and self-determination. McMurray Métis members note that these places that sustain Métis culture have diminished over time in their traditional territory, due to encroaching settlement and the expansion of the oil sands and other industries such as forestry (Clark 2015, 57). Métis relations to animals such as bison must be understood within the context of Métis space; in other words, Métis–bison relations require physical places for their reproduction.

Métis legal orders can be described in part through three concepts documented in broader Métis literature: *mekiachahkwewin*, *wahkootowin*, and *kaa-tipeyimishoyaahk*. First, McMurray Métis members describe good relationships to each other and the land through the value of "respect" (Clark 2015, 109). In my work with community members I have also heard that this respect goes hand in hand with spiritual reciprocity. With the land and its inhabitants, reciprocity takes the form of exchanging respect through different practices and ceremonies, such as offering tobacco before harvesting medicinal plants (see Joly 2017, 189–90). In northwestern Alberta, Paddle Prairie Métis Elder Elmer Ghostkeeper (2007) notes that Métis relations to the land are embodied in reciprocal relationships called *mekiachahkwewin* in Cree, translated as "spirit gifting." He explains that "gifts are considered by the Metis to be the intangible and tangible forms of the aspects of mind, emotion, spirit, and body exchanged in a relationship between donor and recipient. A gift without the spiritual aspect of its donor is not considered a gift by its recipient" (11). *Mekiachahkwewin* for Ghostkeeper is embodied in a gift exchanging ceremony that strengthens spiritual relations with the land. For example, animals may give themselves as gifts to hunters, and (some) hunters give to the animal by providing an offering of tobacco, a prayer, or respectfully butchering and sharing the meat amongst community members (see Nadasdy 2007). Spiritual reciprocity is thus a key principle to articulating Métis legal orders.

Second, McMurray Métis members have also noted that family is a key component of their culture and identity, expressing another aspect of a Métis legal order. Clark notes that family and community are "not simply mechanisms of internal social organization and cohesion; they are also the mechanisms by which autonomy is asserted against external forces" (2015, 133). Echoing these sentiments, Métis scholar Brenda MacDougall describes how, in nineteenth-century Île-à-la-Crosse, Saskatchewan, Métis governance was informed by the Cree concept of *wahkootowin*, or familial relations. MacDougall clarifies that "*wahkootowin* is predicated upon a specific Aboriginal notion and definition of family as a broadly conceived sense of relatedness with all beings, human and non-human, living and dead, physical and spiritual" (2010, 3). Here kin relations and responsibilities of care towards them are not only extended to humans but also to other-than-human beings such as bison.

Finally, McMurray Métis members describe Métis space as places where Métis people feel free to practice self-determination and autonomy.

In describing Métis governance in nineteenth-century Red River, Manitoba, Métis scholar Adam Gaudry similarly defines Métis governance as stemming in part from the principle of *kaa-tipeyimishoyaahk*, translated as "we are those who own ourselves," and defined as a state of political autonomy and independence (2014, 77–78). From conversations with McMurray Métis members, Clark elaborates this concept using the term *self-determination*, which includes the individual and collective ability to make political decisions that will affect a community's shared future (2015, 136). Taking these concepts together, Métis legal orders and connection to place can be described, at least in part, as predicated on these principles of Métis space, spirit gifting, family, and self-determination.

## "Urban Buffalo": Syncrude's Beaver Creek Wood Bison Ranch

My larger research project revolves around understanding how Métis individuals, scientists, industrial proponents, and government officials relate to reclaimed landscapes. Reclamation is a process of reconstructing landforms and ecological functions on oil sands leases after oil sands extraction is complete. The overall aim of reclamation is to create a useful, ecologically repaired landscape: a self-sustaining boreal forest.[5] Government policy defines the reclamation process according to a utilitarian philosophy: it requires the reconstruction of ecological criteria that will support certain land uses (Government of Alberta 2016). In the early decades of oil sands reclamation from the 1960s to 1990s, government and industry focused primarily on improving the landscape's economic uses, rather than ecological integrity (Joly 2017; Powter et al. 2012). This utilitarian focus translated into plans and construction of ecologies that could support commercial forests, agricultural activities, or cattle ranches (Joly 2017; Powter et al. 2012).

In 1993, to help test the sustainability and economic productivity of its reclaimed lands, Syncrude opened the Beaver Creek Bison Ranch on its oil sands lease (see Figure 7.1). At the time of writing, Syncrude's wood bison herd consists of about 300 animals grown from the original thirty animals relocated from Elk Island National Park near Edmonton (Thurton 2018). The herd is co-managed by Fort McKay First Nation and Syncrude; the former have access to a bison harvest each year. The bison live in a fenced ranch on 300 hectares of reclaimed land on Syncrude's oil sands lease, next to an oil sands upgrading plant, tailings ponds, and an open-pit mine, where they consume local grasses and sedges but also hay from outside the region, and are not afforded freedom of movement in the greater landscape. The bison ranch itself represents a massive public relations success for Syncrude, as it not only exemplifies the re-establishment of a culturally important, threatened species, but also demonstrates that post-extractive landscapes can support wildlife. The herd is symbolic for Syncrude representatives, as an example of "responsible oil sands operations" that puts a "positive light on what [operators] can do," as Syncrude Vice President Greg Fuhr noted in a recent interview with the Canadian Broadcasting Corporation (Thurton 2018). However, as I argue elsewhere (Joly 2017) and return to later in this chapter, reclamation initiatives such as bison ranching can act as a spectacle of corporate social responsibility that do not afford opportunities for Métis peoples to recreate a cultural landscape.

During a focus group in November 2013 with nine McMurray Métis members, I inquired about their perceptions of oil sands reclamation efforts. Citing the bison ranch as an example, focus group participants agreed that while governments attempt to make reclaimed land useful again, reclaimed areas are, as Elder Harvey Sykes put it, "no good" for Métis peoples' use, such as for gathering food plants or hunting (Joly 2017, 171).[6] Another Elder clarified further, using the example of the bison herd: "It is not the way our buffalo grew up." A trapper added that the fenced, ranched herd resemble "urban buffalos" (focus group transcript, 72–75). The nine focus group participants chuckled at this new term, and continued to reference it throughout the meeting.

Through the remainder of the conversation about bison, participants outlined four reasons why Syncrude's urban buffalo are not useful for Métis people and convey a disruption of opportunities for relating to bison in their own ways. First, they spoke about limited access to the land upon which the bison are housed, and restricted access to the bison themselves. One Elder joked that, like in the bush, anyone can go in to the reclamation area and take one of the bison. After laughter subsided from the group, she added, "You know they can't" (focus group transcript, 72). The herd is not free roaming and does not fall under Métis constitutionally protected harvesting rights. Instead, the Beaver Creek herd is co-managed exclusively by Fort McKay First Nation and Syncrude, meaning that other Indigenous communities whose territory overlaps Fort McKay's cannot gain access to the bison meat as easily. Unlike in the past, harvested meat is not shared equally within and beyond Indigenous communities. Communities such as the Métis lack autonomy to hunt bison, and thus cannot enact *mekiachahkwewin* (ceremonies of spirit gifting) by harvesting or sharing meat.

Yet, even if the herd were accessible to the Métis, members noted (in our focus group and other interviews) concern about the health of the herd. The second characteristic of urban buffalo, then, is contamination and lack of trust. Syncrude upholds that the herd is not contaminated, evidenced by consistent awards won for the health of the herd from the Alberta Bison Association. However, concern expressed by McMurray Métis members about the health of the herd speaks to a larger issue in the region about contamination. Concern about pollution stems from a lack of involvement in the life of the herd, and a mistrust of government and industry research findings on environmental health of the region (see Baker 2017; Checker 2007).

Third, Métis participants in our focus group noted that urban buffalo are characterized by a separation from the region's ecology. Urban buffalo on Syncrude's ranch are enclosed in a relatively small area compared to their free-roaming relatives. They are fed imported hay, rather than solely consuming wild-growing grasses and sedges. The bison are further held in separate areas to breed and provided veterinary treatment throughout their life to ensure herd health. Treated as ranch animals, Syncrude's urban buffalo are not provided the autonomy granted to free-roaming species. Instead, their health and sustenance are highly regulated by humans.

Fourth, the Syncrude bison are considered urban buffalo for their emplacement in a reclamation politic of visual spectacles. McMurray Métis members often noted during my fieldwork that reclamation processes do not seek to create a landscape that is useful for Indigenous Peoples to re-establish relations to place, but rather seek to create the *appearance* of a "green" landscape (see also Wheatley and Westman, this volume). Reclamation, then, is a type of spectacle that separates humans from their environments—the land becomes something to look at from a distance, rather than a spiritual entity to be engaged with (Joly 2017). Indeed, public visitors (including the Métis) to the Syncrude bison ranch can view the buffalo from the roadside, behind a fence carefully marked with warning signs denying entry. Rather than being engaged with in ceremony, the bison have become a public symbol of reclamation for Syncrude, and emblematic of their claims to sustainability and corporate social responsibility (see Spady, this volume).

Urban buffalo are thus defined through four characteristics: access, contamination, separation from the region's ecology, and visual spectacle. A lack of autonomy or agency provided to the bison is a common theme across these four qualities. Contained within fences, rather than free roaming, the Beaver Creek herd is not autonomous—not capable of freedom of movement, social and familial association (with humans and non-humans), work, or play. Relying on external subsistence and medical resources, such as hay transported into the region from the south, the herd is also disconnected from the ecology of northeastern Alberta's boreal forest. The agency of the bison is denied in this colonial management framework, separating humans from animals and impacting relationships between Métis peoples and bison. Thus, Métis principles of *wahkootowin*, *kaa-tipeyimishoyaahk*, and *mekiachahkwewin* are disrupted by industrial management frameworks that create urban buffalo.

The characteristics of urban buffalo highlight the fact that Syncrude's bison have lost emplaced relationships with their human companions through state-driven wildlife management and industrial reclamation practices. Instead, the bison on Syncrude's ranch are urban buffalo in that they are the imposition of a settler colonial management regime, rendering the animals inaccessible, perceived as contaminated, lacking autonomy, and separate from humans. The following two sections show, first, the histories of bison management in a national park and entangled management of Indigenous harvesting and, second, how the logic of urban buffalo serves as a cautionary tale for a population at risk of oil extraction impacts.

## Managing Bison and People in WBNP

This section describes the establishment of WBNP and the related histories of state management and Indigenous harvesting rights in the park. In the 1880s the decline of the wood bison population began to alarm naturalists and governments in Canada. A combination of natural disasters, wolf predation, and overhunting rendered the wood bison nearly extinct by the turn of the twentieth century (Isenberg 2001, 197–98). The bison decline was erroneously blamed by some wildlife officials, such as Major A.M. Jarvis, on Indigenous overhunting. To protect and revive the species, in 1894 the federal government first responded by placing a general ban on the hunting of wood bison. Then, in 1922, the government formed Wood Buffalo Park (now WBNP) in northern Alberta, bound to the south by the Peace River and extending north into the Northwest Territories, to protect the approximately 1,500 remaining wood bison (McCormack 2010, 234–46). While no one was allowed to harvest bison in the park and white trappers were excluded from the park immediately, for the first year of the park's existence, Treaty and Métis individuals continued to hunt and trap in the park (McCormack 1984, 127). After the first year, Métis were excluded from the park. The Indian agent at the time saw the issue "as a way to get more Métis into the labor force and change their culture" (McCormack 1984, 131). Maxwell Graham, the chief of the federal government's Animal Division, argued that "it is notorious that half-breeds are among the worst offenders against our game law" and allowing them to harvest in the park would mean similar privileges would have to be made for "other classes" in the park (McCormack 1984, 131). The exclusion of Métis from the park may have led some to elect to become treaty signatories.

Further south and at the turn of the century, in 1909, the Canadian government established a plains bison park at Buffalo National Park near Wainwright, Alberta, where a herd of bison were relocated from Montana, after being purchased from Michel Pablo, a Métis man.[7] The bison flourished and overpopulated Buffalo National Park, eventually leading to disease and starvation. Because slaughter of these excess bison was immensely unpopular among the public, by the 1920s some government officials argued for their relocation to Wood Buffalo Park, which was "already equipped for bison protection, seemingly half-empty and waiting" (Ogilvie 1979, 41, quoted in McCormack 1984, 139). Amidst controversy, between 1925 and 1928, 6,673 plains bison were taken by rail to Waterways, Alberta then barged down the Athabasca and Slave Rivers to Wood Buffalo Park in the vicinity of what is now Hay Camp (ECCC 2016, 4; McCormack 1984, 140). In the winter of 1925–1926, the plains bison migrated beyond park boundaries south of Peace River and into the Lake Claire region (McCormack 1984, 140). As a response, in 1926, the federal government expanded the southern boundary of Wood Buffalo Park, annexing an additional 17,600 square kilometres for the bison (Wetherell and Kmet 2000, 369; see Figure 7.1).

The expansion of the park boundaries was met with opposition from Indigenous peoples living near and using the lands to be annexed, who expressed concern over the potential loss of the use of their traditional lands for harvesting to non-Indigenous trappers and hunters. Treaty holders who had previously hunted and trapped in the "Old Park" and the annexed area "were to be granted access to the park, and 'any persons' who had hunted and trapped south of the Peace River prior to its inclusion within the park would be granted access in the annexed area" (Order-in-Council P.C. 1444, Sept. 24, 1926, in McCormack 1984, 144). In 1926 a formal permit system was introduced for hunting and trapping in the park, and the park expanded its warden service to protect the bison from Indigenous land users, who were also monitored by the Royal Canadian Mounted Police (McCormack 1984, 149). As a result of increased surveillance and control of Cree, Dene, and Métis hunters, Indigenous ways of life, including relating to animals through harvesting, were redefined as criminal activities (Sandlos 2007, 236). In the years that followed Wood Buffalo Park's creation, numerous Cree, Dene, and Métis hunters were charged for harvesting bison in the park (Wetherell and Kmet 2000, 370). Around 1928 the park began cancelling permits of those who violated game regulations, which Treaty 8 holders viewed as a violation of their Treaty Rights (McCormack 1984, 150).

However, some harvesting of bison within the park continued. In the 1920s bison were hunted in a small-scale seasonal slaughter program to retain dried bison meat for use by the residential schools in Fort Chipewyan and Fort Resolution (McCormack 1984, 152). McCormack notes that "although the park had been established to protect the bison from Indian subsistence hunting, the bison could be hunted when it would save the government money, a factor which may have been important in the 1930s" (153). The park administration controlled the hunting of bison and distribution of meat, channelling it through missions and Indian agents.

Conversely, Métis, Dene, and Cree individuals near Fort Chipewyan relate to bison as active agents in their shared environments. At the time of the plains bison transfer, Dene and Cree individuals had long followed bison trails as they were often "the easiest and shortest way through forest and muskeg and between heads of rivers" (Graham 1923, 9, quoted in McCormack 2010, 154). Shared human–bison trails, and bison habitats of grasslands and parklands, were also likely maintained by controlled burning (McCormack 2010, 155; McCormack 2017). In turn, bison reciprocate the creation of grazing areas through their willingness to be killed by Indigenous hunters. After a hunt, bison meat is distributed amongst Indigenous communities in an act of sharing. These actions of interacting with the landscape and creating a shared home with people and animals are not reflected in the state management systems in the early years of the park.

While subsistence and recreational hunting in the park were restricted, park authorities harvested bison for other economic purposes in the post–Second World War era. Although the 1920s bison transfer program primarily aimed to alleviate overcrowding in Wainwright in the short term, the transfer also generated interest in the commercial potential for bison ranching in the North. One of the strongest supporters of the transfer program, Graham, argued that "a reserve stock of pure blood bison of the highest potency should be kept in reserve" to protect its hardiness and "first-class beef qualities" (Graham 1923, 12). As a commercial product, the value of protecting both plains and wood bison lay in their potential for ranching.

A commercial slaughter program was eventually introduced in 1950, marking the most intensive period of manipulation and exploitation of the bison population in the park (McCormack 1992, 368). The commercial program stemmed from the postwar desire of federal biologists and northern bureaucrats to increase the Subarctic's resource potential. From 1950 to 1967, 1.75 million pounds of bison meat was made available for sale from the park, including to churches, the Hudson's Bay Company, and Indian Affairs for Indigenous people across the country (Loo 2006, 141). The bison corral and slaughter program also involved a component of testing for disease and gathering data on bison pathology. After the Second World War, biologist William Fuller (1962) discovered that a quarter of the Wood Buffalo bison population was infected with tuberculosis—a result of interbreeding and contact with plains bison imported from Wainwright that were diseased. Tuberculosis and later discovered brucellosis were considered problematic because the diseases required pathology testing and resulted in wasted meat, thus increasing the cost of slaughtering for commercial purposes. Diseases thus compromised market value and necessitated intensive management in what was already a high level of intervention required to transform the bison into a marketable product. Here, bison were conceptualized as productive units rather than autonomous, spiritual actors in a shared environment, and thus responded to the interests of southern markets, governments, and scientists, rather than needs and interests of local Indigenous Peoples or Treaty Rights (McCormack 1992, 373).

Since 1967 management of bison in WBNP has been characterized as one of non-intervention (McCormack 1992). Contemporary park bison are influenced by a complex array of historically contingent anthropogenic and natural factors, including the construction of the W.A.C. Bennett Dam along the Peace River, ongoing tuberculosis and brucellosis infections, hybridization from plains-wood bison interbreeding, and wolf predation (Government of Alberta 2011; McCormack 1992, 373). Government management has shifted its efforts towards preventing the diseased, hybrid populations from mixing with healthy, genetically purer wood bison: the Wabasca-Mikkwa population in north-central Alberta and the RLB immediately south of the park (Government of Alberta 2011). Neither Indigenous nor non-Indigenous peoples may harvest bison within the park, yet First Nations members are able to harvest bison beyond park boundaries in Treaty 8 territory. McMurray Métis members remain restricted in their ability to hunt bison both within and outside of the park. The current harvesting policy in Alberta allows Métis individuals to hunt, trap, and fish for food 160 kilometres or within the government-recognized traditional territory from the harvesting community in which they are registered (Government of Alberta 2010). The McMurray Métis is not considered a harvesting community by Alberta, forcing members to register as harvesters outside their home communities or not harvest at all. Compared to Treaty First Nations, whose Treaty Rights allow members to harvest relatively freely, McMurray Métis members are restricted in their ability to harvest throughout their territories (Clark 2015, 72–73). McMurray Métis members have described these harvesting constraints as impacting their ability not only to obtain meat for themselves, but also to share the harvest with their Elders and families, pass on Métis knowledge to youth, and practice self-determination, or freely practice a Métis way of life (Clark 2015, 72–73).

The history of wildlife management, as seen in the park case study, challenged the ability of Métis and other Indigenous Peoples to maintain relationships with bison on their own terms. The park surveillance and larger context of harvesting rights is exemplary of a history of (threats of) evictions from traditional territory and limitations of Indigenous harvesting. Protocols of sharing bison meat were redefined by government entities as bison became a commercialized product. While the WBNP bison cannot strictly be defined as urban buffalo, there are echoes of concerns shared by McMurray Métis members, such as the reduction in access to territory, freedom of movement, and Indigenous harvesting rights. This brief history suggests that a state management framework supplanted and criminalized Indigenous legal orders predicated, in the case of the Métis, on concepts of reciprocity, sharing, and self-determination. Indigenous people are still contending with regulations that restrict harvesting today, and the historic concerns documented by McCormack about access to territory to practice these rights remain among Métis people with whom I work, especially in the context of ongoing expansions of oil sands industry.

## "It's Only A Buffalo": The RLB and Oil Sands Extraction

In this section I describe a bison population threatened by a proposed oil sands mine and describe how these bison are at risk of becoming urban buffalo.[8] In February 2014 I joined five Métis Elders and McMurray Métis consultation office staff on a tour of the Teck Resources Inc.'s (Teck) Frontier Oil Sands lease, the boundary of which is approximately 110 kilometres north of Fort McMurray. The tour was part of Teck's Indigenous engagement process and intended to familiarize McMurray Métis members and staff with the company's Corehole Drilling Program, which analyzes the oil deposits and geotechnical makeup of the lease to inform the oil company's environmental assessment (EA) and open-pit mine planning. The drilling program operates only in winter as the lease area is predominated by muskeg, a local term for boreal peatlands or wetlands, which pose difficulty for heavy machinery in the summer. As we travelled in a hired van through the lease area, over an ice road cut through a forest of birch, spruce, jackpine, and muskeg, an applied ecologist employed by the McMurray Métis asked, "Do you think we will we see the [Ronald Lake] bison?" An Elder on the tour, Harvey Sykes, responded simply, "No." They are scarce, skittish, and, besides, it was too early for their migration through this area.

The RLB consists of approximately 200 animals that range from the southern edge of WBNP to the northern parts of Teck Frontier project lease. At the time of the tour, despite lack of rigorous research, the government assumed that the RLB interacted with the WBNP bison and was also diseased (see ECCC 2016, 6). During my fieldwork in 2013–2014, because of this assumed disease status, the population was categorized and managed by the provincial government as "feral livestock," not "wildlife," and therefore was not protected under the Alberta Wildlife Regulation (Alberta Regulation 143/97) or the federal SARA (2002). In September 2016 the Government of Alberta recognized the Ronald Lake population as disease-free, placing it under provincial protection under the Wildlife Regulation, and which closes general hunting for the bison but allows Indigenous hunting. The Métis, however, are still governed by Alberta's restricting harvesting policy (Government of Alberta 2010), limiting their access to the herd.

Because of its "non-wildlife" status, the RLB is the only population in the Regional Municipality of Wood Buffalo that is available to Métis and First Nations individuals for harvesting. Further, it is known amongst Indigenous communities, and now federal and provincial managers, as the only disease-free population of bison in northeastern Alberta (ECCC 2016). Protecting the RLB's habitat is therefore of utmost importance. In land use study interviews, Métis trappers expressed concern over Teck's proposed mine and its infrastructure, including roads and work camps, for clearing habitat and opening access for recreational hunters. A Métis trapper, Leonard Hansen Sr., who has hunted bison from the RLB in the past, explained that the Métis practice is to consume and share your entire hunt out of respect for the gift of the animal (see Nadasdy 2007) and to only hunt when the animal populations are healthy, abundant, and not threatened. However, many recreational hunters do not follow this protocol and overkill animals for the sake of killing.[9] Hansen and other McMurray Métis members have noted a decline in the population of the RLB since the early 2000s, due to overharvesting by non-Indigenous hunters as the landscape becomes more accessible after construction of oil sands and forestry infrastructure. Consultation with Indigenous land users throughout the life of the mine will thus be essential, along with the continued enforcement of a hunting ban that does not interfere with Indigenous harvesting rights.

However, while significant strides have been made by joint efforts of Indigenous communities and government researchers to increase knowledge and recovery and protection strategies for the Ronald Lake population (ECCC 2016), Teck's oil sands mine remains a threat to the integrity of the bison. There is a concern that the mine will impact the bisons' health and push them towards diseased populations or outside of harvesting range, as described by Métis Elders John Grant and Mary Sykes. Grant, an Elder whose trapline is near the RLB range, explained,

> Well then again, how does oil companies impact with all the other animals? Well then, you know, they say, "It's only a buffalo." But, I just finished saying, animals are smarter than people. A buffalo's got a big head…So, what they're going to do if they get the smell of this [oil sands] plant? What if they get this odour? What if they hear a noise? Eventually, they're going to get down that far [into the park]. Like I say, the oil companies are going to be greedy and go a little bit further north, a little bit further north. Next thing you know there'll be nothing…Thirty years from today, there'll be nothing…So, eventually, they'll just, maybe they'll move back into the park.[10]

Grant and Sykes describe buffalo (a more common term locally for wood bison) as autonomous agents who respond to environmental damage by moving away from extraction areas. Grant notes that oil companies do not create an environment in which humans or animals can live well and survive. Echoing other sentiments I heard during my fieldwork, the planned construction of an open-pit mine in the RLB's range is interpreted as yet another inevitability in a long line of government approvals for oil sands projects despite impacts to wildlife.

Another concern regarding the Teck Frontier project is the removal of muskeg and alteration of the watershed in the project area. The Ronald Lake population and proposed Frontier project are located in the foothills of the Birch Mountains, where water flows through muskegs towards the Athabasca River. On the whole, scientists note that, even with reclamation of disturbed land, oil sands mining results in a significant loss of peatlands due to company focus on and the relative success of reclaiming uplands (Rooney et al. 2012). While wetlands covered nearly half of the mineable oil sands landscape prior to extraction, after reclamation, the landscape will undergo desertification as water is removed for mining and mine pits are filled with water to become lakes (Wheatley and Westman, this volume). On the tour of Teck's lease area, I asked Teck employees about their mine reclamation plans and whether the wetlands that will be lost during the mine's lifetime would be reconstructed. The company representatives replied that their reclamation activities focus on building uplands, lakes, and riparian areas, but not peatlands. Indeed, while Syncrude and Suncor Energy (the latter being another major player in the oil sands region) have self-proclaimed successfully reclaimed peatlands, the ability for companies to reclaim this landform on a large scale remains uncertain.

The removal of muskeg and impacts to the bison are justified in part through Teck's argument that the reclaimed high ground will be beneficial for bison. During Teck's regulatory approval process, the company upheld that final reclamation would "support sedges and grasses and would potentially enhance the quality of habitat available to bison" (Alberta Energy

Regulator 2013, 13). In Teck's Environmental Impact Assessment supplemental information request, the company states,

> As designed, the reclaimed landscape will result in an increase in preferred wood bison habitat on the closure landscape (e.g. shrubby swamps, marsh and wet meadows)...Therefore, while the Project may cause displacement of wood bison from the Ronald Lake herd into WBNP, where they may come into contact with the infected herds, it is assumed that this may already be happening naturally and therefore the Project's effect would be considered negligible...[and] the effects on wood bison mortality risk will be reversible with reclamation.
>
> Teck Resources (2012, 1–21)

Reclamation is here treated as a mitigation strategy with the ability to reverse and, at best, improve the landscape post-extraction. Further, Teck provides no evidence to support its statements, a common practice in environmental impact assessment writing (see McCormack 2016; Westman 2013).

More recently, in its *Draft Ronald Lake Bison Mitigation, Monitoring and Adaptive Management Plan*, Teck proposed programs to manage impacts to wood bison. Reclamation is one of several key mitigations proposed to address potential project impacts, including change in habitat availability, change in landscape connectivity, and change in mortality risk (Teck Resources 2017, 11–12). Teck rightfully notes that reclamation success is in fact uncertain, and, while reclamation aims to increase habitat for wood bison, the decades needed to reclaim an ecosystem that may support wildlife may negate the net benefit to bison (14). The ways that wildlife will use reclaimed land is also unknown and has been scantily researched, yet Teck notes Syncrude's Beaver Creek ranch demonstrates that wood bison may use reclaimed land.

Despite being upheld as a mitigation strategy in regulatory processes, reclamation is largely documented in the wider literature as inadequate for reinstating Indigenous Peoples' land use, due in part to the dramatic alteration of a cultural landscape and material landscape in the extraction process, including the removal of naturally occurring landforms such as muskeg (Buffalo et al. 2011; Joly 2017). Wood bison, being migratory and historically associated with boreal forest parklands and grasslands, must rely to some extent on the relationship between boreal uplands and muskeg. Boreal peatlands are often dominated by sedges (NWWG 1997, 27), a key food source for bison in the winter (Strong and Gates 2009). In summer months, bison graze upon meadows in uplands (Rubec 1997, 49); yet these meadows are uncommon in the Athabasca region today due to fire suppression (McCormack 2010, 2016; Strong and Gates 2009), increasing the need for sedge-dominated muskeg as a bison food supply.

When I asked what he thought about this rhetoric of improvement of bison habitat post-reclamation, including the change of a muskeg landscape to one with uplands and lakes, Métis Elder and trapper David Waniandy told me, "What industry doesn't know is that the bison were living in muskeg areas long before any industry started—they don't need industry to make them habitat" (paraphrased, author field notes, May 8, 2014). Waniandy elaborated that the RLB eat sedges in the muskeg areas when they are frozen in the winter. The RLB, he told me, are the healthiest population in all of Alberta because of its ability to move around a healthy landscape; impacts to the landscape or any enclosure of the bison, conversely, would lead to their disease and death (personal communication, April 9, 2018). Yet by focusing on the ability of reclaimed land to support bison as an indicator for successful mitigation, oil companies and regulators silence the complexities of the greater landscape's ecology, including the bison's interactions with a healthy regional landscape. The fragmented representation of the land (e.g., fencing areas or neglecting reclamation of peatlands) that informs the conservation of wood bison habitat in mine planning then, at worst, provides an opportunity for oil companies to justify landscape changes.

The RLB are therefore entangled in systems that manage bison as "urban buffalo." In this case, bison can be used to rationalize industry's large-scale landscape changes through a rhetoric of improvement. With the predictive power of EAs (Westman 2013), which outline plans for reclaimed areas and potential offset reserves, government and oil company management can construct a future that may perpetuate Métis alienation from wood bison. Importantly, while I am critical of reclamation goals and the co-existence of bison and oil sands extraction, Teck has been forthcoming in engagement with Indigenous communities about the RLB and their proposed project plans, setting the company apart from others in the region. The McMurray Métis and other Indigenous communities in northeastern Alberta have signed long-term agreements with Teck (Thurton 2017b). These agreements secure funding for the needs of McMurray Métis members as well as a foundation for a long-term industry partnership that will hopefully allow for Métis input into the planning and reclamation of the mine throughout its operation (see also Zalik 2016). Due to Teck's willingness to work with Indigenous communities, there is an opportunity for the company to incorporate the development priorities of communities, who are not diametrically opposed to extractive industries, but are continuing to fight for benefits (see Wanvik, this volume) and for their legal orders to be taken seriously in oil sands decision-making processes.

## Discussion

In the examples above—Syncrude's ranch, the national park history, and reclamation planning regarding the RLB—concerns about urban buffalo and competing harvesting protocols are apparent. In histories of state management, wood bison are entangled in state-imposed harvesting regulations and limitations. Contemporary reclamation practices further propagate a separation of Métis people from wood bison through limiting access, contamination, separation from the landscape, and perpetuating a visual spectacle. These urban buffalo are seen as "no good" for many Métis individuals with whom I work (Joly 2017, 171), in part because Métis individuals' ways of relating to bison and the land are disrupted. Métis accounts of bison as spiritual kin, active agents, and mobile beings who respond to environmental disturbance and relocation are informed by related Métis principles of *wahkootowin* (relatedness), *kaa-tipeyimishoyaahk* (self-determination), and *mekiachahkwewin* (spirit gifting). Instead, the state often manages bison according to a regime that serves to disrupt Métis legal orders, restricting access to bison and the ability for Métis people to access Métis space and maintain their way of life. Due to state harvesting regulations paired with expanding extraction zones, the remaining healthy wood bison in Alberta are at risk of becoming incorporated into the spectacle of urban buffalo.

The stories of the three bison populations and the principles of Métis space, *wahkootowin*, *kaa-tipeyimishoyaahk*, and *mekiachahkwewin* have not only aided my understanding of wildlife management and Métis knowledge, but also inspired me to consider my role as a researcher studying sociocultural aspects of environmental change with Métis individuals. As a Euro-Canadian scholar, I am learning from concepts of kinship, spirit gifting, and self-determination in order to uphold ethical relations with my research partners. For example, I strive to place Métis thought at the forefront of my writing (including concepts like urban buffalo, but also by reaching out to McMurray Métis members through the writing process) to honour stories with which I am acquainted, and to act in good relations with my research partners (see Baker 2017; Chartier 2015)—tasks I attempted to take up in crafting this chapter.

Put simply, the exploitation of natural resources is fundamental to settler colonial control, predicated upon the material and discursive transformation of the land as not belonging to, or erased of, Indigenous Peoples (Wolfe 2006; see Lee-Jones, Longley, this volume). In this chapter I attempted to show how Métis spaces (Clark 2015) for engaging with bison are diminished as wildlife management systems are implemented, and Métis self-determination is often excluded from planning the future of disturbed landscapes in reclamation. Industrial proponents and governments often treat wood bison as urban buffalo rather than mutually autonomous agents in a shared landscape, or a home. While the disruptions to Métis–bison relations and exclusion of Métis legal orders in management decisions I described in this chapter have impacted Métis space and well-being, it is important to note that bison continue to play a fundamental role in articulating western Métis legal orders—a resiliency which warrants further attention than I have provided here.

Beyond academic work, there is a related need to implicate Métis and other Indigenous thought and legal orders in wildlife management arenas more fully. I do not mean to vilify contemporary wildlife management officials or company representatives in this chapter. However, many Indigenous individuals are still facing structural injustices based on long-term impacts of poor historical wildlife management practices and oil sands expansion. I therefore encourage government representatives, industrial proponents, and those who work in the wildlife sector in Alberta and beyond, to consider how they could better foreground Métis and other Indigenous communities' thought into their everyday work and policies. A starting point might be to consider, in ongoing consultation and dialogue with local Indigenous communities, how characteristics of urban buffalo might appear in their work and how principles including *wahkootowin*, *kaa-tipeyimishoyaahk*, and *mekiachahkwewin* could be incorporated into practice. In an era of reconciliation (TRC 2015) (a term federal and provincial governments in Canada are quick to endorse), industry and wildlife management processes must make more efforts to partner with Métis and other Indigenous Peoples to avoid the proliferation of urban buffalo and the suppression of Indigenous legal orders. It remains to be seen whether industrial proponents and the state will live up to the opportunity at present to reconcile relations with Indigenous Peoples and to attend to a renewal of relations to Alberta's wood bison.

## Acknowledgements

I am grateful to conversations with members and staff of the McMurray Métis who provided the conceptual framework for this chapter and who continue to teach me about the land. Appreciation is especially extended to John Grant, Len Hansen, Bill Loutitt, Sara Loutitt, Harvey Sykes, Mary Sykes-Cardinal, David Waniandy, and Carmen Wells from Fort McMurray, and Ronald Campbell from Fort Chipewyan. Conversations with Gillian Donald, Kim Dertien-Loubert, and Peter Fortna provided key insights for this chapter. Thank you to readers for their thoughtful and detailed comments, including Clinton Westman, Lena Gross, Katherine Wheatley, Rob Wishart, Patricia McCormack, and Hereward Longley. This research was supported by the Social Sciences and Humanities Research Council of Canada (Partnership Development Grant, University of Saskatchewan), the Justice Bertha Wilson Scholarship (University of Aberdeen), and Angus Pelham Burn Fieldwork Grant (University of Aberdeen).

## Notes

1 I sparingly use the term *Indigenous* in this chapter to refer broadly to rights-holding communities in Canada, opting to otherwise use more specific terms delineating nations and peoples. For example, *Métis* is a term used to describe those self-identified people who formed a distinct cultural group through ethnogenesis of European and Cree, Dene, and Iroquois ancestors. Specific names of individuals are included where permission is granted or if names are already published elsewhere.

2 Yet the division of the two subspecies is not well-supported genetically and can be challenged (Patricia McCormack, personal communication, July 10, 2018).

3 There is a growing body of scholarship on Indigenous legal orders in Canada (e.g., Borrows 2010, Todd 2016). I follow Val Napoleon, who writes, "I use the term 'legal system' to describe state-centred legal systems in which law is managed by legal professionals in legal institutions that are separate from other social and political institutions. For example, Canada and other nation states have such central legal systems. In contrast, I use the term 'legal order' to describe law that is embedded in social, political, economic, and spiritual institutions. For example, Gitksan, Cree, and Dunnezah peoples had legal orders. Indigenous law is a part of and derives from an Indigenous legal order. In distinguishing between legal systems and legal orders, I hope to avoid imposing western legal ideas onto Indigenous societies" (2013, 2).

4 This chapter reflects conversations with McMurray Métis members since 2013, including focus groups and informal discussion with members and specific meetings with individuals named in the chapter (e.g., in 2018). However, in this chapter I am not speaking *for* the Métis community in any official capacity, nor am I attempting to represent them. Instead, my goal is to document stories that I have been granted permission to share by individuals, and to contribute to a literature that may be of use for Métis and others in rights pursuits and environmental management. The analysis and any errors are my own.

5 For a description of oil sands mine reclamation methods for wetlands and forests, see Wylynko and Hrynyshyn (2014) and Harris (2006), respectively. See Simmons (2010) and Klein et al. (2015) for an Indigenous methodology for oil sands reclamation.

6 In this chapter, I attribute participants' names to quotes where permission was granted at the time of the interview. At least one phone call has been made to the participants or their descendants to glean permission regarding the use of their names in this publication.

7 Here I focus on Métis people of western Canada, but Métis territory also extends into the western United States. While Métis people reside in the United States as well as Canada, the term *Métis* is official in Canada only.

8 The mine described in this section was proposed at the time of writing and has since been approved by a Joint Review Panel.

9 This quote is from a Traditional Land Use interview with Leonard Hansen Sr. (McMurray Métis internal database interview code TECTLU2014-01, HLA05-23).

10 This quote is from a Traditional Land Use interview with John Grant (McMurray Métis internal database interview code TECTLU2014-02, HLA11-18).

## References

Alberta Energy Regulator (AER). 2013. *Teck Resources Limited Application for Oil Sands Evaluation Well Licences, October 21, 2013*. Decision 2013 ABAER 017. Calgary: AER.

Baker, Janelle. 2017. "Research as Reciprocity: Northern Cree Community-Based and Community-Engaged Research on Wild Food Contamination in Alberta's Oil Sands Region." *Engaged Scholar Journal: Community-Engaged Research, Teaching, and Learning* 2 (1): 109–24.

Borrows, John. 2010. *Canada's Indigenous Constitution*. Toronto: University of Toronto Press.

Buffalo, K., C.E. Jones, J.C. Errington, and M.I.A. MacLean. 2011. "Fort McKay First Nation's Involvement in Reclamation of Alberta's Oil Sands Development." In *35th Annual British Columbia Mine Reclamation Symposium Proceedings*. University of British Columbia Library, Vancouver.

Chartier, Clément. 2015. "Partnerships between Aboriginal Organizations and Academics." *The International Indigenous Policy Journal* 6 (2): 1–11.

Clark, Timothy David. 2015. *McMurray Métis Cultural Impact Assessment of the Teck Frontier Oil Sands Mine Project*. Prepared by Willow Springs Strategic Solutions for Fort McMurray Métis Local 1935.

Clark, Timothy David, Dermot O'Connor, and Peter Fortna. 2015. *Fort McMurray: Historic and Contemporary Rights-Bearing Métis Community*. Prepared by Willow Springs Strategic Solutions for McMurray Métis Local Council 1935.

Checker, Melissa. 2007. "'But I Know It's True': Environmental Risk Assessment, Justice, and Anthropology." *Human Organization* 66 (2): 112–24.

Environment and Climate Change Canada (ECCC). 2016. "Recovery Strategy for the Wood Bison (*Bison bison athabascae*) in Canada [Proposed]." Species at Risk Act Recovery Strategy Series. Environment and Climate Change Canada, Ottawa, ON.

Gaudry, Adam. 2014. "Kaa-tipeyimishoyaahk—We Are Those Who Own Ourselves: A Political History of Métis Self-Determination in the North-West, 1830–1870." PhD diss., University of Victoria, BC.

Ghostkeeper, Elmer. 2007. *Spirit Gifting: The Concept of Spiritual Exchange*. Raymond, AB: Writing on Stone Press.

Government of Alberta. 2010. "Métis Harvesting in Alberta – July 5, 2007 – Updated June 2010." Alberta Environment and Parks. http://aep.alberta.ca/fish-wildlife/fishing-hunting-trapping/documents/MetisHarvestingAlberta-Jun2010.pdf (accessed August 30, 2017).

———. 2011. "Managing Disease Risk in Alberta's Wood Bison with Special Focus on Bison to the West of Wood Buffalo National Park." February 2011. http://www.wildlifecollisions.ca/docs/managingdiseasewoodbisonwoodbuffnatpark-feb2011.pdf (accessed March 25, 2014).

———. 2016. *Conservation and Reclamation Regulation*. Environmental Protection and Enhancement Act. Alberta Regulation 115/1993 with amendments up to and including Alberta Regulation 103/2016. Edmonton, AB: Queen's Printer.

Graham, Maxwell. 1923. *Canada's Wild Buffalo: Observation in the Wood Buffalo Park*. Ottawa, ON: Department of the Interior.

Fuller, William A. 1962. *The Biology and Management of the Bison of Wood Buffalo National Park*. Wildlife Management Bulletin Series 1, Number 16. Ottawa, ON: Canadian Wildlife Service National Parks Branch, Department of Northern Affairs and National Resources.

Harris, Megan. 2006. *Guidelines for Reclamation to Forest Vegetation in the Athabasca Oil Sands Region*. Fort McMurray, AB: Cumulative Environmental Management Association.

Isenberg, Andrew. 2001. *The Destruction of the Bison: An Environmental History, 1750–1920*. Cambridge: Cambridge University Press.

Joly, Tara. 2017. "Making Productive Land: Utility, Encounter, and Oil Sands Reclamation in Northeastern Alberta, Canada." PhD diss., University of Aberdeen.

Klein, Heidi, Trieneke Gastmeier, Allice Legat, and Kim Poole. 2015. *Traditional Knowledge Wildlife Habitat Reclamation Guidance: Final Report*. Fort McMurray, AB: Cumulative Environmental Management Association.

Loo, Tina. 2006. *States of Nature: Conserving Canada's Wildlife in the Twentieth Century*. Vancouver: University of British Columbia Press.

MacDougall, Brenda. 2010. *One of the Family: Metis Culture in Nineteenth-Century Northwestern Saskatchewan*. Vancouver: University of British Columbia Press.

McCormack, Patricia A. 1984. "How the (North) West Was Won: Development and Underdevelopment in the Fort Chipewyan Region." PhD diss., University of Alberta.

———. 1992. "The Political Economy of Wood Bison Management in Wood Buffalo National Park." *Arctic* 45 (4): 367–80.

———. 2010. *Fort Chipewyan and the Shaping of Canadian History, 1788–1920s: "We Like to Be Free in This Country"*. Vancouver: University of British Columbia Press.

———. 2016. "Doing Credible Cultural Assessment: Applied Social Science." *Environmental Practice* 18: 148–56.

———. 2017. "Walking the Land: Aboriginal Trails, Cultural Landscapes, and Archaeological Studies for Impact Assessment." *Archaeologies* 13 (1): 110–35.

Nadasdy, Paul. 2007. "The Gift in the Animal: The Ontology of Hunting and Human–Animal Sociality." *American Ethnologist* 34 (1): 25–43.

Napoleon, Val. 2013. "Thinking about Indigenous Legal Orders." In *Dialogues on Human Rights and Legal Pluralism*, edited by René Provost and Colleen Sheppard, 229–45. Dordrecht: Springer Netherlands.

National Wetlands Working Group (NWWG). 1997. *The Canadian Wetland Classification System*. 2nd ed. Waterloo, ON: Wetlands Research Centre, University of Waterloo.

Ogilvie, Sheilagh C. 1979. *The Park Buffalo*. Calgary, AB: Calgary-Banff Chapter, National and Provincial Parks Association of Canada.

Powter, Chris, Neil Chymko, Gordon Dinwoodie, Darlene Howat, Arnold Janz, Ryan Puhlmann, Tanya Richens, Don Watson, Heather Sinton, Kevin Ball, Andy Etmanski, Bruce Patterson, Larry Brocke, and Ralph Dyer. 2012. "Regulatory History of Alberta's Industrial Land Conservation and Reclamation Program." *Canadian Journal of Soil Science* 92 (1): 39–51.

Rooney, Rebecca C., Suzanne E. Bayley, and David W. Schindler. 2012. "Oil Sands Mining and Reclamation Cause Massive Loss of Peatland and Stored Carbon." *Proceedings of the National Academy of Sciences* 109 (13): 4933–37.

Rubec, C.D.A. 1997. "Policy for Conservation of the Functions and Values of Forested Wetlands." In *Northern Forested Wetlands: Ecology and Management*, edited by C.C. Trettin, M.F. Jurgensen, D.F. Grigal, M.R. Gale, and J.K. Jeglum, 45–60. New York: CRC Press.

Sandlos, John. 2007. *Hunters at the Margin: Native People and Wildlife Conservation in the Northwest Territories*. Vancouver: University of British Columbia Press.

Simmons, Deborah. 2010. *Renewing the Health of Our Forests: An Aboriginal Road to Reclamation*. Fort McMurray, AB: Cumulative Environmental Management Association.

Strong, W.L., and C.C. Gates. 2009. "Wood Bison Population Recovery and Forage Availability in Northwestern Canada." *Journal of Environmental Management* 90: 434–40.

Teck Resources. 2012. "Appendix 219c.1: Supplemental Wildlife Species Assessment – Ronald Lake Bison Herd." Frontier Oil Sands Mine Project Integrated Application, Supplemental Information Request. ESRD and CEAA Responses.

———. 2017. *Draft Ronald Lake Bison Mitigation, Monitoring and Adaptive Management Plan*. Frontier Oil Sands Mine Project, May 2017. http://www.ceaa-acee.gc.ca/050/documents/p65505/119189E.pdf.

Thurton, David. 2017a. "Fort McMurray Métis Hunter Claims Victory after Province Returns Confiscated Bear Skin." *CBC News*, November 1, 2017. https://www.cbc.ca/news/canada/edmonton/fort-mcmurray-m%C3%A9tis-bear-skin-1.4381275.

———. 2017b. "Proposed Oilsands Mine gets Support from Fort McMurray Métis, Four Other Indigenous Groups." *CBC News*, September 6, 2017. http://www.cbc.ca/news/canada/edmonton/mcmurray-metis-frontier-project-oilsands-open-pit-mine-1.4275573.

———. 2018. "25 Years Later, Syncrude's Bison Herd Thriving on Reclaimed Oilsands Lands." *CBC News*, February 16, 2018. http://www.cbc.ca/news/canada/edmonton/25-years-bison-reclaimed-syncrude-oilsands-lease-1.4538030.

Todd, Zoe. 2016. "From a Fishy Place: Examining Canadian State Law Applied in the Daniels Decision from the Perspective of Métis Legal Orders." *TOPIA: Canadian Journal of Cultural Studies* 36 (Fall): 43–57.

Truth and Reconciliation Commission of Canada (TRC). 2015. Honouring the Truth, Reconciling for the Future: Summary of the Final Report of the Truth and Reconciliation Commission of Canada. Winnipeg, MB: Truth and Reconciliation Commission of Canada.

Westman, Clinton N. 2013. "Social Impact Assessment and the Anthropology of the Future in Canada's Tar Sands." *Human Organization* 72 (2): 111–20.

Wetherell, Donald G., and Irene R.A. Kmet. 2000. *Alberta's North: A History, 1890–1950*. Edmonton: University of Alberta Press.

Wolfe, Patrick. 2006. "Settler Colonialism and the Elimination of the Native." *Journal of Genocide Research* 8 (4): 387–409.

Wylynko, David, and James Hrynyshyn. 2014. *Guidelines for Wetlands Establishment on Reclaimed Oil Sands Leases*. 3rd ed. Fort McMurray, AB: Cumulative Environmental Management Association.

Zalik, Anna. 2016. "'Duty to Consult' or 'License to Operate'? Corporate Social Practice and Industrial Conflict in the Alberta Tar Sands and the Nigerian Niger Delta." In *First World Petro-Politics: The Political Ecology and Governance of Alberta*, edited by Laurie Adkin, 356–84. Toronto: University of Toronto Press.

# 8 Reclaiming Nature?

## Watery Transformations and Mitigation Landscapes in the Oil Sands Region

*Katherine Wheatley and Clinton N. Westman*

This chapter focuses on understanding and theorizing current and proposed future watery transformations in northern Alberta. In the oil sands region, water is both evidence of and a vehicle for pollution and landscape transformation. Water bodies are the object of much public attention, as well as government regulation, divided between federal and provincial governments. Oil sands mining relies upon the withdrawal of large volumes of water; for instance, up to 3 percent of the Athabasca River flow is taken up annually (Natural Resources Canada 2015). Water thus provides a window into a future characterized by altered relations between humans and other beings in a transformed Anthropocene nature. As well as examining industrial pollution in existing water bodies and in liquid tailings disposal systems—tailings ponds—we consider future hydrological transformations, specifically the new lakes that are proposed as part of the reclamation of large industrial sites.

Open water—in the form of rivers and lakes—does not make up a significant portion of landscape cover in the oil sands region (Rooney, Bayley, and Schindler 2012). Instead, northern Alberta predominantly consists of a variety of wetlands, although aquifers underlie much of the region's landscape. Indeed, wetlands constitute 64 percent of the vegetation cover of the surface of mineable oil sands area, while open water represents only 2 percent of the landscape cover (Rooney, Bayley, and Schindler 2012, 4935). Yet industrial plans for reclaiming the land following energy extraction will leave much of the region in altered forms. Waterscapes, and specifically anthropogenic lakes, play a pivotal role in proposals for redesigning natural spaces.

When walking in Alberta's boreal forest, what seems like solid ground is often ice (or, if one is unlucky, water). Bogs and fens (different kinds of wetlands but both known locally as muskegs) abound. Thus, in order to "ground" our discussion of landscape change, we are primarily considering lakes and wetlands. The liminality of these wetlands is also fitting for a discussion of bitumen, which has characteristics of both a liquid and a solid. So, future human-made lakes and similar anthropogenic water bodies become a pivotal ground for representation and dispute.

Members of northern Alberta Indigenous communities, among other groups, generally perceive reclamation activities, such as the treatment of tailings, as contentious. Reclamation plans for aquatic spaces such as tailings ponds affected by industrial development are presented in highly techno-bureaucratic fashions that are typically at odds with local values and worldviews. Indeed, waterscapes are fertile ground for competing representations and futures.

By assessing anthropogenic aquatic spaces of interest, predominantly tailings ponds and end pit lakes, this chapter reviews the attempts by industrial actors to reshape the region's aquatic landscape. The chapter is based on our ethnographic research among Indigenous communities in both the Athabasca and Peace River oil sands zones, and on our research in public policy. One of us—Wheatley—is a recent MA graduate in environmental anthropology at the University of Saskatchewan. Her multi-sited ethnographic fieldwork with the Mikisew Cree First Nation has enabled her to engage with a variety of review committees and groups that assess tailings management and other industrial processes (Wheatley 2018). The co-author, Westman, has been conducting ethnographic fieldwork and working with Indigenous communities in northern Alberta since 1996. In this chapter, we largely focus our methods and analysis on media and policy documents as well as secondary studies, while also drawing on Indigenous perspectives about future landscapes.

## Second Nature and the Mitigation Landscape: Water in Anthropocene Futures

Historian Liza Piper (2009) documents the "industrial transformation of Subarctic Canada," which was well established prior to Alberta's post–Second World War oil booms. Significantly, Piper draws on examples from fisheries and related watershed management efforts to illustrate this transformation. Elaborating the nature of this industrial transformation, and also working in the context of western North America, William Cronon (1991) develops the concept of "second nature," whereby anthropogenic landscape change becomes so ubiquitous that it fundamentally alters the character of the previous ecosystem. Human life persists in these spaces, and people may even come to regard the changed landscape as natural and, perhaps, beautiful. In this way, people simply lose their awareness of the scope of changes that have occurred. We draw on the insights of second nature in our reflections on future lives in degraded and mitigated landscapes in our discussion of the oil sands region's transforming hydrology. Many social science scholars have considered the problems of human–nature interactions in similar critical terms (e.g., Castree 2014). Relatedly, in the wake of the ontological turn in anthropology, a focus on human–nature interactions is blossoming. Posthuman anthropology recentres and reconfigures humankind's relations with the non-human. The realities of anthropogenic climate change necessitate a long-term exploration of changing human relationships with landscapes and the world at large (Cruikshank 2005). Future landscapes, such as those of the reconstructed oil sands region, lend themselves to such an analysis.

Water itself provides and creates its own entry points into theoretical debates about the relationship between human and non-human worlds (Cruikshank 2005). Powerful on both symbolic and material levels, water seeps through boundaries separating nature from culture and science from social science. It crystallizes into new conceptual forms, drips into multiple frames of analysis, and erodes distinctions between human and non-human as it forms the very core of our bodies and our ecosystems. Indeed, water is at the centre of several influential anthropological analyses of contemporary environmental issues. Veronica Strang (1997, 2014), in particular, reviews how water is good to think with, given how its many properties create "affordances" (Ingold 2000) that function in tandem with other human and non-human ecosystem components to create very real, but culturally variable, worlds.

Fabiana Li (2015) has focused on contested equivalencies and related negotiation processes that place knowledge sources at odds. She also touches upon the conflicting social dimensions of water. Li explains that planners and proponents embrace the logic of equivalence, in that they assume the commensurability of landscapes, provided material benefits appear to be equivalent. Li condemns this tendency, arguing that landscapes are in fact incommensurable, especially in the eyes of land users. As Tara Joly (2017) argues, Métis community members' reactions to waterscape alterations in northern Alberta suggest that the same dynamic of contested equivalences and commensurabilities is at play in reclamation in the oil sands region.

In turn, water has taken centre stage as a contested analytic field in debates over oil sands extraction. Both physical scientists (Gosselin et al. 2010; Kelly et al. 2009; Schindler 2010; Timoney 2015) and social scientists (Candler et al. 2010; Ervin 2012) have focused on water quality and quantity, which in turn have become key issues in oil sands politics, so much so that advocacy groups (e.g., Keepers of the Athabasca) and Indigenous communities have made central use of water's power in their own communications and strategies. In part, the prominence of water in such debates reflects the politics of Canada as a federal state, in which matters such as fisheries and navigation have become fulcrums for federal action on environmental management, as well as pressure points that stakeholders may use to push or force federal action and oversight through advocacy and litigation. Since 2010 both federal and provincial governments and agencies have commissioned reports that are critical of existing water monitoring (among other management practices) in the oil sands region (e.g., Commissioner of the Environment and Sustainable Development 2014; Hopke et al. 2016). Governments have struggled in subsequent attempts to revamp monitoring systems, while arguing that a world-class monitoring system is being developed nevertheless.

Even as water has become high profile in the region's environmental politics, much of the regional literature on environmental issues neglects the ontological character of water that is reflected in Cree, Métis, and Dene worldviews. To take Cree and Métis examples, lakes may have "something of the *manitow*" about them (Westman and Joly 2017); that is, they resemble or allow access to the power of a non-human person or persons. Lakes, shores, and wetlands—and creatures who move between these zones—may fall into a liminal or transformative category. Such places enable relations between different classes of beings, including *manitowak* and other non-human persons.

Anthropological studies of landscape have shown that landscapes create or afford particular cultural meanings and practices (Basso 1996; Ingold 2000; see McLeod 2007; Westman and Joly 2017 for relevant examples from the Prairie provinces). For Indigenous people, aquatic spaces were and are habitation sites and productive milieus, as well as places where relations with non-human persons are honoured and envisioned. These relationships reinforce the sense of an immanent spiritual character to the land and particularly the waters of the region (Buffalo et al. 2011). The loss of such sites puts those particular transfers of knowledge and cultural practice at risk. Cree and Métis people might also say that that is not the only risk, given that one purpose of ceremonies such as the *wihkohtowin*—a commensal feast invoking animals and the dead (Westman 2015)—is to maintain natural cycles and relations, including blessing and invoking the creatures of the water to continue their relationship with humans. Such pre-existing social and ecological obligations are generally neglected in industrial remediation planning. Moreover, Indigenous people are rarely willing to discuss such concerns with outsiders or in meetings or hearings.

At risk is the future of the landscapes and waterscapes of northern Alberta, including the relationships that these places entail. Westman's (2013b) research indicates that defining future landscapes is precisely what is at stake in oil sands planning documents and impact assessment studies. The function of the documents is to inscribe particular landscape futures and preclude others, notably those land uses and spaces based on hunting, trapping, fishing, gathering, and especially spiritual uses of the land. Moreover, such processes are a good example of hubris on the part of industrial planners. Given the ontological issues at stake for Indigenous people, they may trigger mythological or cosmological consequences associated with greed and carelessness, neglecting relational principles. In one such myth, the trickster protagonist is nearly swept away in a river of his own excrement after overconsumption. So, the interpretive leap from discussing the trickster to discussing liquid tailings disposal is not as large as it may seem at first (Westman 2013a). When industrial proponents dismiss Indigenous perspectives about the land's power and its known and unknown creatures, they are making the mistake of misrepresenting the ontological character of the land, and particularly the relations of Indigenous inhabitants with the land.

Water is an ambiguous substance or agent within the region's hydroecology and political ecology. Just as what appears solid may sometimes turn out to be liquid (or at least too soft to walk on), what appears to be pure water may turn out to be contaminated, or at least unsafe to those who regularly consume the water or its watery creatures. While the idea of industrial processes contaminating or consuming potable water supplies is familiar to most people, what is equally striking in the oil sands is the creation of process-affected water, which often becomes the most pressing concern as a potential contaminant. This water comes from heating and pressurizing water to extract bitumen from earth, a process used in diverse oil sands technologies across the region. Jennifer Gerbrandt (2015) has ethnographically documented the concerns in the Peace River oil sands zone created by a 2013 pipeline break that spilled highly saline and otherwise contaminated "produced water," and subsequently contaminated the wetlands. The spill exposed problems in the region's environmental governance, monitoring, and consultation regimes. Water in this and in other instances became a killing, rather than a nurturing, power. Industrial activity had "produced" and "processed" water that ultimately had toxic consequences for relationships in the region.

The culturally inflected politics of water monitoring in the region dictate that its inhabitants—particularly Indigenous land users—will increasingly live in "mitigation landscapes" (Little 2014), dwelling permanently with the structures and features designed to cleanse their environment to a level deemed livable by outsiders. The term *mitigation landscape* here applies not only to acute incident (spill) cleanups and everyday technologies monitoring chronic exposure, such as those documented by Gerbrandt, but also to vast tailings ponds as well as the cyborg (see Haraway 1991) lakes of the future. The latter will be created from the pits and ponds but will require technological assistance to "live" within the regional hydrological ecosystem. The term further applies to those who must assess and report dusty berries (see Baker, this volume) and deformed or cancerous fish and wildlife, and who must live with the fear that the creatures they eat are killing them and their families. In the new mitigation landscape, a sacrifice zone, or wasteland (see Gross, this volume), people who once cherished the opportunity to dip a cup in the lake for a quiet, contemplative drink as the essence of traditional land use, frequently may no longer feel able to do so. Nevertheless, people continue to take steps to exercise their rights to use and harvest from these damaged lands (Westman 2017).

In Cree mythology, lakes are membranes that allow passage by powerful beings from different levels of reality. In the history of bitumen discovery, similar transformations and passages are apparent, though of a different kind. Early European visitors to what became the mineable oil sands zone described bitumen oozing out of the sands near the Athabasca River, which suggested a messy solution of water and oil at the core of the region's promise. While the image is a powerful one, such free-flowing surface oil was historically confined to a small geographic area. Today, through industrial processes, lakes and other water bodies may become similarly liminal, in the sense that their earthy and watery membranes no longer function to exclude oily contamination. Consider the case of a small lake (usually said to be nameless) leaking oil from high-pressure extraction techniques, which appears to exemplify such concerns (see Gross, this volume). In this lake, located in the boreal forests of northeastern Alberta's Cold Lake Air Weapons Range, efforts to pressurize and fracture oil-bearing geological formations with steam have resulted in persistent anthropogenic leaking of oil from the lake bottom, specifically through older, previously capped drilling holes from earlier conventional resource plays.[1] There have been four such leaks on the lease areas, totalling thousands of barrels of oil into the lake since leaking was discovered in 2013. The company, Canadian Natural Resources Limited (CNRL), has been ordered to drain the lake and store both its water and its watery creatures (CNRL claims that the lake does not include any fish) offsite, separately, until the situation can be remediated. To borrow a phrase from the US–Vietnam conflict, CNRL had to destroy the lake in order to save it! There is thus ample evidence that in situ production methods, documented in these examples from the Peace River and Cold Lake oil sands zones, also result in long-term landscape-scale disturbance and surface water quality concerns, just as in the better-known mineable zone. So, the drained, relocated lake, bereft of its watery inhabitants, as well as the saline, contaminated wetland, become features of the remediation landscape.

Lakes that are actually toxic ponds visible from space; lakes that do not exist yet, but that will soon take the place of existing terrestrial, wetland, and riparian environments used by hunters, gatherers, and ceremonialists; lakes that leak oil and thus have to be removed and stored elsewhere; bodies of water that are contaminated by process-affected or produced water (which, itself, was previously pumped from the region's surface waters or aquifers, then mixed with chemicals, pressurized, shot into the earth, and then piped back up to be spilt when a pipe broke): each of these scenarios sets the stage for discussing the liminal and transformative nature of water in contemporary and future mitigation landscapes. For the remainder of the chapter, we turn to the most pressing cases of aquatic transformation in the mineable region of the Athabasca oil sands zone, those of end pit lakes and tailings ponds. This discussion first requires an examination of processes of reclamation, operationalizing the creation of second natures in the region.

## Reclamation in the Oil Sands

Alberta's Environmental Protection and Enhancement Act (2000) requires that resource extraction firms active in the oil sands region invest rigorously in the development and implementation of reclamation strategies, which must be planned prior to project approval. According to the Act, reclamation can consist of removing equipment and physical infrastructure, decontaminating structures and the surrounding natural environment, and maintaining and conditioning or reconstructing the land surface. The aim, fundamentally, is to reclaim oil sands developments to a condition that is "functionally equivalent to the natural conditions" (CEMA 2012, 7). This common interpretation becomes problematic in light of the competing ontological claims, aesthetics, and land uses among regional populations. The Environmental Protection and Enhancement Act outlines operators' reclamation duties, setting forth that an operator must reclaim and conserve specified land and obtain a certificate to this effect. Surface leases and right of entry orders cannot be surrendered or terminated without reclamation certificates.

In cases where oil sands process-affected water is too toxic to be released into surrounding waterways, zero-discharge water management is needed (Miller 2012). Thus, governments have allowed companies to construct large tailings ponds to collect and store tailings. The first such effluent pond opened in the oil sands in 1967. However, in the last fifty years, industry has failed to develop possible treatment options for these ponds.

The commitments made by operators thus far, which include tailings ponds and end pit lakes, are insufficient. It is our opinion that this calls into question the viability of Alberta's future waterscapes. Through reclamation, corporate actors are in the business of constructing new landscapes (Joly 2017), and government regulators are in the business of approving them. In the oil sands region, reclamation will take many decades, if not centuries.

## Tailings Ponds: Reclamation and Risk

One major form of emergent aquatic space in the oil sands is the tailings pond, many of which are very old. Tailings ponds are designed to contain oil sands process-affected water. These anthropogenic landscape features are built on bare ground, using materials excavated from bitumen-mining processes. As of 2018, tailings ponds cover over 250 square kilometres of northern Alberta and are visible from space. Tailings ponds are not lined with impermeable sheets separating their toxic materials from nearby watersheds and ecosystems (Price 2008). The toxic materials contained within the tailings ponds include lead, mercury, arsenic, and benzene, some of which are known carcinogens, and all of which have deleterious effects on human development (McNeill and Lothian 2017). Given the array of problems presented by tailings ponds, many see them as a temporary solution to the industry's waste problems (Hutchins 2013), though they seem to have a somewhat indefinite timescale. Indeed, operators themselves admit that tailings, formally referred to as mature fine tailings, "do not settle into a material suitable for reclamation for many decades" (COSIA 2018). A plethora of remediation technologies and engineering options have emerged in attempts to get tailings ready for reclamation. These technologies, such as water-capping, thin lift drying, centrifuging, and end pit lakes, attempt to de-water mature fine tailings—that is, maximize their solidity.[2] Water-capping, for instance, involves sealing off mature fine tailings that settle beneath freshwater in hopes that the ponds will eventually metamorphose into functional aquatic ecosystems. Yet these technologies are largely unproven and remain experimental; the conundrums posed by tailings ponds lack viable long-term solutions.

Tailings ponds constitute a dilemma of colossal magnitude. The Pembina Institute, a non-partisan environmental think tank, reports that by 2015, fluid tailings totalled 1.18 trillion litres (McNeill and Lothian 2017). The National

Energy Board (2004) acknowledges that Alberta's tailings ponds pose a number of environmental threats, chief among them being the groundwater-based diffusion of pollutants, and the rise of leaks into soil and surface water. Contaminants will leach from settled tailings for decades, if not centuries (Miller 2012). Leakage of toxic chemicals from the tailings ponds is a major and growing concern. Environmental Defence Canada compiled industry reports to find that by 2008 the ponds were already leaking over eleven million litres of contaminated water into the environment every day (Price 2008). Moreover, a major breach of a tailings pond would have permanent consequences on the local area. If the breach were sizeable enough, it could endanger the ecological integrity of northern watersheds.

During the twenty-first century, environmental organizations have been sounding alarms about the fiscal management of tailings ponds. To date, $1.4 billion has been secured from industry through cash reserves. Yet, as of late 2016, the potential taxpayer liability had risen to $44.5 billion for tailings cleanup (Environmental Defence Canada 2017). According to Environmental Defence Canada and the Natural Resources Defense Council, the potential taxpayer liability of the tailings ponds now surpasses the total royalties obtained by Alberta over the past fifty years of extraction (Environmental Defence Canada 2017).

The Alberta government has established a number of policies and regulatory frameworks on tailings ponds. The Tailings Management Framework for Mineable Athabasca Oil Sands is one of five major environmental management frameworks legislated under the Lower Athabasca Regional Plan. The Alberta Energy Regulator (AER), the corporation that oversees all energy resources in the province, administers the framework. Released in March 2015, the Tailings Management Framework aims to minimize fluid tailings accumulation through mandating the reclamation and treatment of tailings during a project's lifecycle (AER 2016). The Tailings Management Framework resulted in the suspension of Directive 074, which the AER previously utilized to outline tailings performance criteria and related mining requirements. Industrial actors complained that 074 (AER 2009) was not feasible, as it required tailings volumes to be reduced and landscape reclamation to occur within five years of mine closure. No oil sands operators met their own guidelines under Directive 074. Instead, the more flexible Directive 085 was developed to facilitate the implementation of the Tailings Management Framework (AER 2016, 3). First released in July 2016, Directive 085 is said to hold "operators accountable for their fluid tailings as opposed to instituting universal requirements." Directive 085 obtained cabinet approval in October 2017, following minor amendments. Although AER CEO Jim Ellis celebrated the directive for having "the broadest consultation in [the regulator's] history" (Mertz 2016), while Wheatley was in the field, informants lamented that engagement was limited to a single multi-stakeholder technical advisory committee. (See Wheatley 2018 for a fuller discussion of the implementation of these directives as an example of regulatory capture in the oil sands.)

Corporations have developed tailings management plans that aim to comply with Directive 085 and the Tailings Management Framework. All active operators submitted tailings management plans to the AER by fall 2016. Suncor's plan was the first to be reviewed. In March 2017, Suncor was informed that its proposed plan did not adequately fulfill the requirements of either the Tailings Management Framework or Directive 085 (AER 2017). The main issues identified with Suncor's tailings management plan by the AER centred upon water-capping, which is an "unproven technology" (AER 2017, 2) that involves setting a layer of water over fine tailings; terrestrial alternatives to water-capping, which are underused and do not constitute a timely reclamation option; and the plan's overall lack of details and timeliness. Inadequate information prompted the AER to reject Suncor's initial plan (Canadian Press 2017a), yet at Suncor's objections, the AER agreed to reconsider. Ultimately, the AER accepted Suncor's plan despite outstanding concerns about its use of unproven technologies (Canadian Press 2017b). This case raises further critical concerns about the power of industry and its influence on energy regulators.

Technical reviews of the tailings management plans by independent consultants have flagged three main categories of concerns with the plans. First, all of the plans incorporate water-capped tailings or end pit lakes. Yet the efficacy and reliability of these technologies are subject to debate. Second, tailings ponds and end pit lakes are questionable at best in terms of their compatibility with traditional land uses. The plans do not account for community preferences regarding end land use. Third, the industry's responses may require permanent upkeep and never become self-sustaining spaces. Some firms' cleanup strategies will take seventy years once mining operations have been completed, as the Pembina Institute reports (McNeill and Lothian 2017).

The Alberta government hails the Tailings Management Framework as a purportedly holistic approach to tailings management. According to the AER, Directive 085 "provides sufficient flexibility to support site-specific optimization of tailings management planning and mine operation to maximize the opportunities for responsible and sustainable resource development" (2016, 7). Yet flexibility lessens the directive's enforceability. As they have been written, the Tailings Management Framework and Directive 085 lack the rigorous standards needed to ensure adequate reclamation post-extraction.

Tailings ponds are emblematic of a wider array of issues entangled in northern Alberta's waterways and their management. Among these is the reality that technical solutions to problems of water management are not informed by local worldviews or perspectives. The deep-seated regulatory shortcomings in Alberta are apparent. The regulatory system is sanctioning leakage and mismanagement of toxic fluid tailings. Mitigating the impacts of tailings ponds entails reducing these fluid tailings and ultimately reclaiming the land. The sheer magnitude of this task demands binding regulations and community-informed solutions. One mechanism for reclaiming the landscape is to consolidate tailings into an end pit lake, which we examine next.

## End Pit Lakes: A Grand Experiment

Companies are heralding end pit lakes as a permanent solution to tailings ponds, as well as the final land use for many of the mine pits themselves. The Cumulative Environmental Management Association (CEMA) defined an oil sands end pit lake as "an engineered water body, located below grade in an oil sands post-mining pit. It may contain oil sands by-product material and will receive surface and groundwater from surrounding reclaimed and undisturbed landscapes" (2012, 17).[3] Planning for the oil sands' first end pit lake began in 2013. Situated mostly within abandoned mines, end pit lakes may or may not store tailings beneath their lakebeds. Project proponents hope to fully integrate these water bodies into the local environment.

According to CEMA, end pit lakes serve five aims:

1 Manage water flow
2 Maintain acceptable water quality
3 Bioremediate process-affected waters and store tailings
4 Operate as a "sustainable aquatic ecosystem"
5 Support other uses—be they ecological, economic or social (2012, 13).

Such an ambitious array of end-use goals is central to the industry's championing of this remediation technique. In 2005 Alberta's Ministry of Sustainable Resource Development required that end pit lakes be designed for use by all, as well as supporting fish and wildlife populations (Barker 2005). This goal is paradoxical given that end pit lakes will cover tailings and pits containing hydrocarbons, salts, and napthenic acids too toxic for release directly into rivers and wetlands.

Currently, plans exist to construct a full lake district spanning across the mineable area. It is projected that the mineable oil sands region north of Fort McMurray will host up to some thirty large end pit lakes, totalling over one hundred square kilometres, on at least seven former mining leases (Vanderklippe 2012). In the long run, industrial proponents have argued that end pit lakes will improve sport and subsistence fishing in the area, and even make up for loss of fishing habitat due to disturbances, rerouting, removal, and pollution of many other previously existing waterways and water bodies (Westman 2013b). Such arguments are critical to project approval, as the federal Fisheries Act requires protection for, and no net loss of, certain fish habitats. Nevertheless, at this point, we regard such plans as wishful thinking, and we suggest that the region stands to become an anthropogenic "second nature" wasteland, par excellence. Indeed, we wonder who will use these landscapes in the future, and under what circumstances. Indigenous Peoples have said that they will not.

Syncrude Canada commissioned the first commercial-scale end pit lake in the area, named Base Mine Lake, in 2012. Base Mine Lake has been the subject of much media attention, largely due to its tremendous scale. Base Mine Lake constitutes a demonstration lake and test wetlands. It is the earliest established commercial-scale adoption of pit lake technology in the oil sands. Creating the lake has entailed pumping water over accumulated mine effluent forty metres deep. Smaller, experimental lakes also exist on Syncrude's and Suncor's (the most established bitumen-mining companies) lease lands. Prior to the mid-1990s, Syncrude's impact assessment documents and project proposals asserted that the end pit lakes would offer pollution-free fishing and recreation (including photography) and would be a net benefit to fish habitat. These highly optimistic and largely unsupported claims rest on a Western landscape aesthetic and devalue muskegs and other wetlands in favour of large lakes (Westman 2012).

A more recent proposal, that of the CNRL Horizon project, includes a plan for "Horizon Lake" (the current mine pit). Unlike Syncrude, CNRL acknowledged that it is uncertain whether Horizon Lake will ever support fish. Horizon Lake replaces a productive, moose- and beaver-hunting, wetland habitat (Westman 2012).

While end pit lakes have had mixed results in other types of mine reclamations, they have never been used to reclaim an oil sands mine. Suncor's experimental "sustainability ponds" have had problems with the supposedly inert tailings at lake bottom periodically creating surface oil slicks even after years of clean water conditions. It seems that there is no clear evidence that the lakes will result in a safe aquatic environment, let alone a fish habitat of equal value to what existed before. Indeed, the new lakes could function as a vector for spreading contamination through cyborg watersheds. In some cases, corporations admit, permanent ongoing water treatment will be necessary to maintain safety and cleanliness in this proposed lake district. This renders questionable the prospect of people living and harvesting food in a hypothetical, technologically mediated, mitigation landscape. Indeed, local people have consistently expressed skepticism about the physical and spiritual aspects of such reclamation plans.

As reported by the Canadian Press (2012), prior to public hearings on the proposed expansion of Shell's Jackpine oil sands mine, the federal departments of Environment and Fisheries each expressed concern about the uncertain science around end pit lakes proposed as a reclamation measure for this and other mines, and particularly Shell's ability to predict and control water quality in the lakes and their watersheds. Yet regulators still gave their approval to the project. The safety and productivity of the end pit lakes as fish habitat became especially critical given that Shell had committed to no net loss of fish habitat. Many land users now avoid the formerly productive fisheries of the Athabasca River due to concerns about water quantity and quality. This puts extra pressure on the tributaries and lakes in the watershed. Indeed, given that increasing levels of extraction from the river and dumping of effluent into the Athabasca are forecast, in conjunction with changing water levels, to pose the likelihood of major contamination, and given that Shell has mined out and rerouted twenty-three kilometres of the Muskeg River, a tributary to the Athabasca, end pit lakes constituted an essential part of the "no net loss to fishing habitat" equation. Instead, the proposed mine has wiped out a number of small lakes, streams, and muskegs, which will likely be reclaimed (if at all) as an upland environment or end pit lake.

End pit lakes represent only one major landscape change proposed by corporate entities, who argue that they will not only fix any environmental problems but also make the landscape better than it is now. Incredibly, corporate and government spokespeople have claimed repeatedly that reclaimed landscapes may even increase use values for recreationalists and Indigenous traditional users alike (Westman 2013b). Such assumptions pose special problems for spiritual and subsistence uses of the land by the latter group in particular. The land will have changed, and Indigenous people at Fort McKay believe that the spirit of the land will not return (Buffalo et al. 2012). The end pit lakes would constitute a major change from the existing muskeg and jack pine landscapes, and a poor substitute for lakes such as Kearl Lake. A sacred place, ceremonial location, and habitation site that had especially good moose hunting in its adjoining wetlands, Kearl Lake is or will be bermed and diked at the nexus of multiple oil sands leases (Westman 2013b).

Regulators and operators have stated that the end pit lakes for oil sands projects will approximate those already established within parallel mining industries for metals, coal, and quarries (CEMA 2012). The Sphinx Lake system is commonly cited as a key model. Located near Sparwood, British Columbia, the Sphinx Lake system was established to remediate an open-pit coal mine. Curtis Brinker and colleagues conducted a comprehensive review of the system five years following its establishment, with a particular eye to the state of biological diversity (Brinker, Symbaluk, and Boorman 2011). It appears the Sphinx Lake system meets all necessary hydrological, physical, and chemical criteria set out by the End Pit Lake Working Group (2003) as guidelines to indicate the success of an end pit lake. The evaluation also found that the system now supports a substantial rainbow trout population and could host a regulated sport fishery (Brinker, Symbaluk, and Boorman 2011). However, while the Sphinx Lake system has received numerous accolades, they note, many challenges and uncertainties remain. For instance, fish movement upstream has been limited. Continued intensive monitoring is required.

Such case studies demonstrate that end pit lakes may provide an opportunity to restore fisheries and various ecological functions of the disturbed landscape. However, for every success story emerging from parallel mining industries, there seems to be a number of failures. Many of these examples point to difficulties in understanding and predicting end pit lakes' long-term outcomes (e.g., Wilton and Lawrence 1998). Indeed, parallel industries that have implemented end pit lakes also lack long-term data on end pit lake behaviour. Fashioning lakes from abandoned industrial sites is no simple task. This is likely even more the case given the characteristics of bitumen, tailings, and process-affected water.

Research findings thus far have presented leaseholders with a number of challenges, including the flaws inherent in modelling end pit lakes and the continued presence of major contaminants. Glenn Miller (2012), an environmental chemist, emphasizes that modelling the contaminants in end pit lakes is difficult, especially given the variability in lake dynamics (in particular, seasonally) and in levels of contaminants being released. End pit lakes contain an array of contaminants such as salts, naphthenic acids, polycyclic aromatic hydrocarbons, as well as diverse metals such as mercury, cadmium, aluminum, iron, and possibly radioactive materials.

A number of additional major concerns emerge when considering the adoption of end pit lakes for remediation. For instance, designing end pit lakes necessitates that particular attention is paid to seasonal fluctuations in lake level (CEMA 2012). As Ellen Petticrew et al. (2015) document in British Columbia, changing isothermal conditions and overturn—the cycling of surface and bottom water that often accompanies temperature changes in the fall and spring—can remobilize settled tailings seasonally, with deleterious impacts to surrounding aquatic systems.

The continued presence of major contaminants within end pit lakes results in ecological uncertainty. As Miller (2012) explains, methane and hydrogen sulphide may be produced within settled tailings, which could compromise the ability of sensitive species to survive in the new ecosystem. Moreover, given the proposed integration of end pit lakes in the wider aquatic landscape, if tailings were to leech from the capped lakes, they could have wide-spanning reverberations on northern Alberta's environment as well as downstream, as end pit lakes will be part of regional cyborg watersheds.

A cutaway depiction of a conceptual end pit lake, seen in one technical document (CEMA 2012, 19), illustrates the speculative art of modelling end pit lakes. The figure illustrates how, in relation to end pit lakes from other mining sectors, these human-made landscape features will be rather shallow (6–55 metres deep), yet with large surface area (0.6–13 square kilometres). The figure is worth describing further, for it underscores the extent to which this exercise of making up landscapes is profoundly conjectural and abstract. The foreground depicts an active mine pit, while in the middle of the picture the pit is transformed to a lake with boats and greenery. Thus, in a kind of magical realism, the projection created is one in which the (mining) present and the (lake) future are together in the same frame. We would, in turn, highlight the quasi-fantastical nature of such predictions and exercises, in contrast to the serious and demonstrable risks that such proposals entail. Similarly, if more scientifically, Miller concludes that the modelling of end pit lakes is insufficient, calling them "a grand experiment that is highly uncertain and problematic" (2012, 15). Altering the waterscapes of northern Alberta produces consequences that may seep far beyond the boundaries of the oil sands.

End pit lakes are intended to be permanent landscape features. Leaseholders, we are told, will fully integrate these anthropogenic lakes into the watercourses of northern Alberta. Yet no large-scale oil sands reclamation project has undergone independent evaluation. As such, the ultimate success of closure plans remains uncertain (Rooney, Bayley, and Schindler 2012, 4935).

The need for continued monitoring and government oversight into an unspecified future poses a tremendous, ongoing burden. In sum, end pit lakes are largely unverified models; companies should be required to research alternative remediative strategies to properly treat drainage water (Miller 2012). The legacy that end pit lakes will leave is unknown and worrisome.

## Planning for Post-Industrial Landscapes

Primary hurdles to adequate and effective reclamation and waterscape planning centre upon issues of feasibility, as well as public engagement. Scientists have raised doubts about the possibility of engaging in the thorough reclamation of northern Alberta's landscapes, and they continue to do so. Rooney, Bayley, and Schindler (2012) have conducted an evaluation of the open-pit oil sands mines' transformations of the boreal landscape. Their study is the first quantitative evaluation of the landscape's large-scale alteration, assessing the closing plans of four major mines. Rooney, Bayley, and Schindler paid particular attention to the relative abundance of vegetation cover in pre- versus post-mining landscapes. Their research findings suggest that wetlands (bogs and fens) destroyed by oil sands mining will not be restored. In fact, no one knows how to restore the various wetlands that are being destroyed in the region. At present, wetlands are slated to be replaced by tailings storage strategies, including end pit lakes, as well as upland forest (Rooney, Bayley, and Schindler 2012). The region's natural affordances will be severely reduced in the wake of oil sands mining. Habitat destruction and capacity for carbon offset are among the chief concerns (Rooney, Bayley, and Schindler 2012). Further research is required to ensure the generalizability of research into vegetation and landscape composition changes and their multitude of impacts—whether they may be aesthetic, cultural, and/or ecological. Additional research is particularly needed when taking the relational ecology inherent in Indigenous ontologies and worldviews into account.

During Wheatley's fieldwork in 2017, Indigenous community members spoke skeptically of reclamation promises. There is fundamental disbelief among Mikisew Cree First Nation members and those of other Indigenous communities that corporate reclamation is a viable plan fitting for local landscapes. One Mikisew Cree leader reflected, "Industry will take over our land, and, they say they're going to reclaim it and stuff like that, but who really lays down a seed better than the Creator? Bends the rivers like he's done, or raised a tree up?" (interview, June 27, 2017). Such discord between the views of corporate representatives and presumably of government officials and those of local Indigenous perspectives is profound. (See Westman 2013b and Joly, this volume, for other examples of Indigenous people's perspectives on present and future reclaimed landscapes.)

Disputes over watery spaces and their futures are of paramount concern in this context. Moreover, there is evidence of a lack of attention to community priorities and local needs regarding end land uses in the oil sands region, despite ongoing engagement processes that the provincial government deems sufficient. The models and procedures for water treatment and impact mitigation that we document here are centred around industry and government needs and preferences, with an eye on the financial viability of the relevant corporate players and anticipated revenues for government. As the *Globe and Mail* reports, "local residents aren't convinced end pit lakes are a good choice for anyone but the companies involved" (Vanderklippe 2012). At present, landscape planning lacks meaningful consultation and input, while reclamation is uncritically heralded as a go-to remediation strategy by proponents and governments alike (Westman 2013b).

Tailings ponds and end pit lakes are complex approaches to oil sands remediation, novel in terms of their scale and their application in the oil sands sector, but evidence of a blinkered outlook on the part of industrial proponents and state regulators. Thus, it is likely—perhaps certain—that some of the more optimistic projections about end pit lakes will not come to pass. While reclamation will be "a century-long process," as CEMA (2012, 5) underscores, we question whether large-scale reclamation in this context will ever result in more than a catastrophic second nature wasteland, particularly for Indigenous people attempting to exercise their rights to traditional land use in a radically changed, spiritually deadened, and likely contaminated locale.

Indigenous voices and perspectives are markedly absent from these planning exercises. As Wheatley observed, the engagement of corporate representatives with Indigenous communities on reclamation plans suffers the same major flaw. In interviews, corporate representatives spoke of taking Elders out on the land to see the spaces they were beginning to reclaim, occasionally even accepting input on the variety of plants to be prioritized. Indigenous input is not solicited in the decision-making phases, but after the fact.

Energy extraction in northern Alberta is leaving an indelible footprint on the environment and its inhabitants. CEMA warns, "perpetual water treatment systems may be required to meet closure criterion" (2012, 88). This future remediation landscape is also tacitly acknowledged in the major players' own proposals and assessment documents (Westman 2013b). The mitigation landscape, with its inherent insults to the spirit of the land, will in all likelihood be perpetual, no matter what the companies say.

## Conclusion

The future of vast expanses of land in northern Alberta is being planned by industry and accepted by government representatives. Oil sands development has already caused significant aquatic transformations and will continue to do so. The existing sprawl of tailings ponds can be seen from space. In the future, the set of artificial watersheds currently being planned would spread over a larger area of some 2,500 square kilometres (Vanderklippe 2012). The long-term impacts of such wide-ranging landscape alteration are uncertain, but there is little room for optimism.

The future of waterscapes is a pivotal ground for dispute and representation. One First Nations consultation officer and community member referred to wetlands as "local rainforests," comparing them with the tropical rainforests, to reflect the value that local people put on their northern resource (Wheatley, interview, June 27, 2017). This is an apt comparison. Equating the humble bogs and fens of the boreal forest with the globally valued rainforest reminds us that local aesthetics and values also reflect the global importance of a huge ecosystem that functions as one of the earth's lungs but is now being systematically altered. The toxic tailings ponds, proposed end pit lakes, and disappearing wetlands and other water bodies associated with oil sands mining are thus of more than theoretical interest.

The planning of post-industrial spaces is riddled with complexities. In particular, the large-scale redesign of waterscapes in northern Alberta following energy extraction is a hubristic act of speculative futurism. At this point, reviewing the plans for landscape reclamation into a completely new ecotype poses more questions than answers. The idea that a claim of functional equivalence is at play in addressing the divergences between pre- and post-mining landscapes is remarkable. It is hard to see how large-scale reclamation that depends heavily on end pit lakes and tailings ponds can make a credible claim at commensurability when it results in the eradication of pre-industrial landscape forms. Indeed, it appears unlikely that current reclamation strategies will even meet the requirement for productive equivalence. How local land users and communities will perceive and respond to these remarkable shifts in land composition over the long term is also unknown.

It is our opinion, and that of local Indigenous people, that policy and regulatory frameworks must be strengthened to demand reclamation plans and waterscape management strategies that are evidence-based, adaptable, and responsive to the needs and wishes of nearby communities. Indeed, civil society actors, stakeholders, and Indigenous communities are pushing for a moratorium on new tailings ponds—and for some, a moratorium on all new oil sands development—until the consequences of resource extraction in this region are fully recognized and addressed.

The above exploration of tailings ponds, end pit lakes, and other aquatic controversies demonstrates that industry actors cannot be left to engage independently in the speculative act of redesigning northern waterscapes. Without prescriptive policies and regulations, existing management plans are highly abstract and thus insufficient. Moreover, the post-industrial project of reclaiming nature (and creating second natures) is all for naught unless the needs and values of local land users are prioritized. This consideration compels ontological pluralism and thorough collaboration, especially given the pre-existing webs of social and ecological obligations that span across northern Alberta. Redesigning human/non-human coexistence necessitates integrative, holistic policy-making and collaborative land use planning. Opening up space for public dialogue on the future of boreal forest landscapes is critical.

We are convinced that the lens provided by seeing from underwater, so to speak, is an informative one for considering ethnographically how a transformed post-industrial second nature will appear to its future inhabitants and what it will afford them, materially, aesthetically, and spiritually. We document a non-existent, highly speculative, almost fantastically scientistic ontology, in which futures already exist alongside the present. Such aquatic futures are modelled in a manner that takes little regard for cultural difference, or for the limitations inherent in water management and containment technologies, not to mention the multiple and manifest existing problems with the region's water bodies. Importantly, industry actors' failure in these landscape changes to adequately consider Indigenous land-based practices, including those glossed as spiritual, is both urgent from an ethnological point of view, as well as in violation of specific relational ecologies of practice vis-à-vis non-humans. In short, what we document here is nothing less than the future of a natural, cultural, and moral catastrophe—one that is based on a speculative, magical, fantastic, and highly questionable set of projections.

## Notes

1 This situation was brought to our attention by Alberta media sources, most notably a series of articles by Sheila Pratt in the *Edmonton Journal*. We are also grateful to Keepers of the Athabasca for information about this example.

2 Project proponents are exploring the de-watering of tailings as an approach to minimizing their volume. This approach is not to be confused with the use of de-watering in wetlands contexts, which is an emergent industrial process in northern Alberta as well.

3 Established in 2000, the Cumulative Environmental Management Association was a leading multi-stakeholder group in the Regional Municipality of Wood Buffalo, advising governments and regulators through consensus-based decisions. After CEMA's funding was cut in 2016, its operations were suspended.

## References

Alberta Energy Regulator (AER). 2009. *Directive 074: Tailings Performance Criteria and Requirements for Oil Sands Mining Schemes*. Edmonton, AB: Alberta Energy Regulator.

———. 2016. *Directive 085: Fluid Tailings Management for Oil Sands Mining Projects*. Edmonton, AB: Alberta Energy Regulator. https://www.aer.ca/documents/directives/Directive085.pdf.

———. March 17, 2017. "Decision on Application Nos. 1857270, 1857274, and 075-094." Alberta Energy Regulator. https://www.aer.ca/documents/decisions/2017/20170317A.pdf.

Barker, Neil. December 21, 2005. "Alberta Sustainable Resource Development Position Statement." Letter to Clearwater Environmental Consultants.

Basso, Keith. 1996. *Wisdom Sits in Places: Landscape and Language among the Western Apache*. Albuquerque, NM: University of New Mexico Press.

Brinker, Curtis J., Marc D. Symbaluk, and J.G. Boorman. 2011. "Constructing Habitat for a Sustainable Native Fisheries in the Sphinx Lake End Pit Lake System."

In *Proceedings of the Sixth International Conference on Mine Closure*, Lake Louise, Alberta, Canada, September 18–21, 2011, 525–34. Perth: Australian Centre for Geomatics.

Buffalo, Karla, Carol E. Jones, John C. Errington, and M.I.A. MacLean. 2012. "Fort McKay First Nation's Involvement in Reclamation of Alberta's Oil Sands Development." Paper presented at the *35th Annual B.C. Mine Reclamation Symposium*, Lake Louise, AB.

Canadian Oil Sands Innovation Alliance (COSIA). 2018. "Tailings Reduction Technologies." http://www.cosia.ca/initiatives/tailings/tailings-reduction-technology (accessed August 17, 2018).

Canadian Press. August 27, 2012. "Federal Scientists Still Wary of Shell's Jackpine Oilsands Expansion." *CBC News*. https://www.cbc.ca/news/technology/federal-scientists-still-wary-of-shell-s-jackpine-oilsands-expansion-1.1182544.

———. March 18, 2017a. "Alberta Energy Regulator Rejects Suncor Oilsands Tailing Pond Strategy." *CBC News*. http://www.cbc.ca/news/canada/calgary/suncor-tailing-pond-alberta-energy-regulator-rejection-1.4031251.

———. October 26, 2017b. "Suncor Plan for Managing Tailings Ponds Approved by Alberta Energy Regulator." *CBC News*. http://www.cbc.ca/news/canada/calgary/energy-regulator-alberta-suncor-tailings-1.4373317.

Candler, Craig, Rachel Olson, Steven DeRoy, and the Firelight Group Research Cooperative, with the Athabasca Chipewyan First Nation and the Mikisew Cree First Nation. 2010. *As Long as the Rivers Flow: Athabasca River Knowledge, Use and Change*. Edmonton, AB: Parkland Institute.

Castree, Noel. 2014. *Making Sense of Nature*. New York: Routledge.

Commissioner of the Environment and Sustainable Development. 2014. *Fall Report of the Commissioner of the Environment and Sustainable Development*. Ottawa: Office of the Auditor General. http://www.oag-bvg.gc.ca/internet/English/parl_cesd_201410_e_39845.html.

Cronon, William. 1991. *Nature's Metropolis: Chicago and the Great West*. New York: W.W. Norton.

Cruikshank, Julie. 2005. *Do Glaciers Listen? Local Knowledge, Colonial Encounters, and Social Imagination*. Vancouver: University of British Columbia Press.

Cumulative Environmental Management Association (CEMA). 2012. *End Pit Lakes Guidance Document*. Fort McMurray, AB: Cumulative Environmental Management Association.

End Pit Lake Working Group. 2003. *End Pit Lake Working Group Guidelines for Lake Development at Coal Mining Operations in the Mountains and Foothills of the Northern East Slopes*. Report #ESD/LM/00-1. Edmonton: Alberta Environment, Environmental Service.

Environmental Defence Canada. 2017. *One Trillion Litres of Toxic Waste and Growing: Alberta's Tailings Ponds*. Canada: Environmental Defence Canada and the Natural Resources Defense Council. PDF File.

Environmental Protection and Enhancement Act. 2000. R.S.A. 2000 Chapter E-12. Revised version. http://www.qp.alberta.ca/documents/acts/e12.pdf (accessed August 30, 2018).

Ervin, Alexander M. 2012. "The Vulnerabilities of Native People in the Mackenzie and Athabasca Drainage Systems: Tar Sands, Gas, Uranium." In *Water, Cultural Diversity, and Global Environmental Change*, edited by Barbara Rose Johnson, Lisa Hiwasaki, Irene J. Klaver, Ameyali Ramos Castillo, and Veronica Strang, 277–91. Dordrecht, NL: UNESCO and Springer Publishing.

Gerbrandt, Jennifer L. 2015. "Energy Uncertainty: The Effects of Oil Extraction on the Woodland Cree First Nation." MA thesis, University of Saskatchewan.

Gosselin, Pierre, Steve E. Hrudey, M. Anne Naeth, André Plourde, René Therrien, Glen Van Der Kraak, and Zhenghe Xu. 2010. *The Royal Society of Canada Expert Panel: Environmental and Health Impacts of Canada's Oil Sands Industry*. Ottawa: The Royal Society of Canada.

Haraway, Donna. 1991. *Simians, Cyborgs, and Women: The Reinvention of Nature*. New York: Routledge.

Hopke, Philip K., Jenkins Alan, Douglas H. Johnson, Klánová Jana, Le Chris, and Gerald J. Niemi. 2016. *Assessing the Scientific Integrity of the Canada-Alberta Joint Oil Sands Monitoring (2012–2015): Expert Panel Review*. Canada: Joint Oil Sands Monitoring, AEMERA, and Environment and Climate Change Canada. http://aemera.org/wp-content/uploads/2016/02/JOSM-3-Yr-Review-Full-Report-Feb-19-2016.pdf.

Hutchins, Aaron. December 9, 2013. "What Lies Beneath Alberta's Man-Made Lakes?" *Maclean's*. http://www.macleans.ca/economy/business/what-lies-beneath-albertas-man-made-lakes/.

Ingold, Tim. 2000. *The Perception of the Environment: Essays on Livelihood, Dwelling, and Skill*. New York: Routledge.

Joly, Tara. 2017. "Making Productive Land: Utility, Encounter, and Oil Sands Reclamation in Northeastern Alberta, Canada." PhD diss., University of Aberdeen.

Kelly, Erin N., Jeffrey W. Short, David W. Schindler, Peter V. Hodson, Mingsheng Ma, Alvin K. Kwan, and Barbra L. Fortin. 2009. "Oil Sands Development Contributes Polycyclic Aromatic Compounds to the Athabasca River and Its Tributaries." *Proceedings of the National Academy of Sciences* 106 (52): 22346–51.

Li, Fabiana. 2015. *Unearthing Conflict: Corporate Mining, Activism, and Expertise in Peru*. Durham, NC: Duke University Press.

Little, Peter. 2014. *Toxic Town: IBM, Pollution, and Industrial Risks*. New York: NYU Press.

McLeod, Neil. 2007. *Cree Narrative Memory: From Treaties to Contemporary Times*. Saskatoon, SK: Purich.

McNeill, Jodi and Nina Lothian. March 13, 2017. "Review of Directive 085 Tailings Management Plans." Backgrounder paper, Pembina Institute. http://www.pembina.org/reports/tailings-whitepaper-d85.pdf.

Mertz, Emily. July 14, 2016. "New Rules State Alberta Tailings Ponds Must Be Reclaimed after 10 Years." *Global News*. https://globalnews.ca/news/2825108/new-rules-state-alberta-tailings-ponds-must-be-reclaimed-after-10-years/.

Miller, Glenn C. November 6, 2012. "End Pit Lakes: Unresolved Issues." Hearing exhibit submitted by Oil Sands Environmental Coalition [OSEC], Reno: Oil Sands Environmental Coalition. http://www.ceaa.gc.ca/050/documents/p59540/83373E.pdf.

National Energy Board. 2004. *Canada's Oil Sands: Opportunities and Challenges to 2015*. Calgary, AB: National Energy Board. https://www.neb-one.gc.ca/nrg/sttstc/.../rprt/.../pprtntsndchllngs20152006-eng.pdf.

Natural Resources Canada. May 2015. "Oil Sands: A Strategic Resource for Canada, North America and the Global Market." https://www.nrcan.gc.ca/sites/www.nrcan.gc.ca/files/energy/pdf/oilsands-sablesbitumineux/14-0704%20Oil%20Sands%20-%20Water%20Management_e.pdf.

Petticrew, Ellen L., Sam J. Albers, Susan A. Baldwin, Eddy C. Carmack, Stephen J. Déry, Nikolaus Gantner, Kelly E. Graves, Bernard Laval, John Morrison, Philip N. Owens, Daniel T. Selbie, and Svein Vagle. 2015. "The Impact of a Catastrophic Mine Tailings Impoundment Spill Into One of North America's Largest Fjord Lakes: Quesnel Lake, British Columbia, Canada." *Geophysical Resources Letters* 42: 3347–55. doi: 10.1002/2015GL063345.

Piper, Liza. 2009. *The Industrial Transformation of Subarctic Canada*. Vancouver: University of British Columbia Press.

Price, Matt. 2008. *11 Million Litres a Day: The Tar Sands' Leaking Legacy*. Canada: Environmental Defence Canada. http://environmentaldefence.ca/report/report-11-million-litres-a-day-the-tar-sands-leaking-legacy/.

Rooney, Rebecca C., Suzanne E. Bayley, and David Schindler. 2012. "Oil Sands Mining and Reclamation Cause Massive Loss of Peatland and Stored Carbon." *Proceedings of the National Academy of Science* 109 (13): 4933–37. doi: 10.1073/pnas.1117693108.

Schindler, David. 2010. "Tar Sands Need Solid Science." *Nature* 468 (7323): 499–501.

Strang, Veronica. 1997. *Uncommon Ground: Cultural Landscapes and Environmental Values*. Oxford: Berg.

———. 2014. "Fluid Consistencies: Material Relationalities in Human Engagements with Water." *Archaeological Dialogues* 21 (2): 133–50.

Timoney, Kevin P. 2015. *Impaired Wetlands in a Damaged Landscape: The Legacy of Bitumen Exploitation in Canada*. London: Springer International Publishing.

Vanderklippe, Nathan. October 3, 2012. "Ambitious Plans for Oil Sands Would Create Lakes from Waste." *Globe and Mail*. http://www.theglobeandmail.com/news/national/ambitious-plans-for-oil-sands-would-create-lakes-from-waste/article4583817.

Westman, Clinton N. 2012. "A Critical Review of Traditional Land Use Components for Environmental Impact Assessment Studies in the Oilsands Region." Unpublished report prepared for Mikisew Cree First Nation.

———. 2013a. "Cautionary Tales: Making and Breaking Community in the Oil Sands Region." *Canadian Journal of Sociology* 38 (2): 211–32.

———. 2013b. "Social Impact Assessment and the Anthropology of the Future in Canada's Tar Sands." *Human Organization* 72 (2): 111–20.

———. 2015. "The *Wihkohtowin*: Ritual Feasting among Cree and Métis Peoples in Northern Alberta." *Anthropologica* 57 (2): 299–14.

———. 2017. "Cultural Politics of Land and Animals in Treaty Eight Territory (Northern Alberta, Canada)." In *Entangled Territorialities: Negotiating Indigenous Lands in Australia and Canada*, edited by Françoise Dussart and Sylvie Poirier, 117–39. Toronto: University of Toronto Press.

Westman, Clinton N., and Tara Joly. 2017. "Visions of the Great Mystery: Grounding the Algonquian *Manitow* Concept." *Social Compass* 64 (3): 1–16.

Wheatley, Katherine. 2018. "Oil Sands Energy Governance: An Ethnography on Negotiating Development and Indigenous Rights in Northern Alberta." MA thesis, University of Saskatchewan.

Wilton, Mike J., and Gregory A. Lawrence 1998. "The Evolution of the Island Copper Mine Pit Lake." *Proceedings of the 22nd Annual British Columbia Mine Reclamation Symposium*, Penticton, BC. http://www.trcr.bc.ca/wp-content/uploads/2011/11/1999-wilton-lawrence.pdf (accessed September 24, 2018).

# 9 Conclusion

## Studying the Social and Cultural Impacts of "Extreme Extraction" in Northern Alberta

*Patricia A. McCormack*

In the spring of 2018 several of the people represented in this volume gathered together at an anthropology conference in a session titled "New Ethnographic Research on 'Extreme Extraction' in the Boreal Forest." The session was the third such concerted effort by social scientists to share a range of research findings about the impacts of energy industries on people in northern Alberta.[1] A few are affiliated with the University of Saskatchewan, where Clinton Westman directs a major project called the Cultural Politics of Energy in Northern Alberta. The session and this book are two outcomes of that project (see Westman, Joly, and Gross, this volume; also see Joly and Westman 2017). In short, the Cultural Politics of Energy project is gaining momentum, and affiliated researchers are becoming more productive. Unfortunately, judging from the citations in the Environmental Impact Assessments (EIAs) and related reports I have reviewed, it seems unlikely that consultants and decision makers in industry, government, or Indigenous organizations make much effort to read such professional literature. There is still a substantial disconnect between critical scholarship and the work involved in developing formal policy and evaluating oil sands projects. This conclusion addresses some issues critical to such decision making, including the evidence that is available, the nature of social and cultural impact assessment, and relationships between people and place.

Dedicated social and cultural research related to the impacts of energy industries in northern Alberta has been marked largely by its absence, despite over half a century of oil sands projects, both open-pit mining and in situ operations.[2] Since 1973, when the federal government introduced its Environmental Assessment and Review Process (Government of Canada 1978; Noble 2013) and the Government of Alberta passed its Land Surface Conservation and Reclamation Act (Bott et al. 2016, 31), all new major energy projects must go through an EIA process.[3]

Serious work to develop the oil sands—then usually known as the tar sands—began in the 1950s with exploration leases and pilot plants (e.g., Canadian Resourcecon 1974, 5, 37–41; see Longley, this volume). These projects have expanded steadily both in number and in the extent of their land-altering activities since the oil sands industry began in earnest with the plant built by the Great Canadian Oil Sands Consortium (now Suncor Energy) near Fort McMurray in the Treaty 8 region. This plant began production in 1967 (Suncor Energy 2018; Alberta Culture and Tourism 2018a; Canadian Resourcecon 1974, 5, 42–43). It was followed by proposals by Syncrude Canada Ltd. to build the Mildred Lake Oil Sands Mine and Upgrader in the same region.[4] The Syncrude project was finally approved on September 12, 1969, by the Alberta Oil and Gas Conservation Board, and on September 4, 1973, it submitted an EIA statement to then Alberta Minister of the Environment William (Bill) Yurko (Syncrude Canada 1973, 1:n.p., 2:10). It was the first oil sands mining proponent required to prepare an EIA and the first EIA done in the province.[5] The first in situ project in Alberta was Esso Resources Canada Ltd.'s Cold Lake Heavy Oil Extraction and Upgrading proposal, whose EIA was submitted October 1, 1979 (Government of Alberta 2017).[6]

Syncrude's forty-five-year-old EIA today seems naive and incomplete. Its basic premise was the "conviction that human use of the environment need not be destructive. With careful planning, based upon good information, man-altered and natural ecosystems can exist in harmony" (Syncrude Canada 1973, 1:n.p.). The EIA raised a fundamental philosophical question: "The question of the moment is…how much of the quality of our environment are we entitled to trade away, to develop our natural resources, and to sustain the standard of living which we feel we should be enjoying?" (1:3). It declared, "Blasting ahead with resource exploitation without concern for the ecological consequences is no longer acceptable. Neither is calling for unlimited amounts of money to restore the environment to its exact original condition in a relatively short period of time.…It is unrealistic to assume that industry will do the job at no cost to the environment or to the resource consumer" (1:8). The EIA pointed frankly to some differing positions about this issue (none from northern residents): "We don't need to be told that this question is complex, and is often emotional. Industry tends to take the position which will produce the best profit and loss margins. Government tends to follow the current popular lines of thought in order to gain support at election time. Environmentalists have helped to confuse the issue by creating a new set of terms. We now have the 'ecology,' for example, for what we used to call the 'balance of nature'" (1:3).

The Syncrude EIA spoke of undertaking "a comprehensive program of surveillance of the effects of our technology" to prevent "accidental damage to the environment" (1:n.p.).[7] Monitoring was envisioned only for the biophysical environment, not for the human environment, although the federal guidelines referred to "areas of potential social impact" and recommended that proponents should "consult with experts in the social field to identify areas of potential social impact" (Government of Canada 1978, 5). The Syncrude EIA itself advised that "all technological, economic and *sociological* constraints and opportunities" should be considered, as well as "all costs and revenues, including *social* costs and reclamation" (Syncrude Canada 1973,

1:10, emphasis added). While it concluded that "assessment of the ecological effects of human use by indigenous people and their dependence upon the ecosystem itself should be part of the analysis," it failed to do so (1:94). The "preliminary study of the demographic characteristics" in Volume 4 did not provide a profile of any northern residents, acknowledge the complexity of the regional population, or refer to Treaty Rights. The section that discussed the "Economic and Social Impact of the Syncrude Project," which appeared in Volume 4, was based on a study of the potential regional economic impact, deemed to be a benefit, and a study of the impact of the project on Fort McMurray.[8] The EIA's overall conclusion was that the Syncrude project would contribute to the growth of the Alberta economy, which the company believed was in the public interest.

At about the same time that Syncrude Canada Ltd. submitted its EIA, the Science Council of Canada commissioned Canadian Resourcecon Limited (1974) to prepare a report called *Decision Making in the North*, using development of the oil sands as a case study. The report noted the low priority placed on the northern environment by Alberta regulators: "Protection of the environment is perceived to be an important but not critical issue governing the rate of oil sands exploitation. This is largely due to the fact that because much of the deposit is covered by muskeg and scrubby forest growth, alternative human uses for the area are small…Environmental concerns are of secondary importance in Alberta to the objective of developing the oil sand resource" (Canadian Resourcecon 1974, 14). Canadian Resourcecon Limited pointed to the lack of "basic ecological information about the oil sands areas, which makes identification of the possible impacts difficult" and the lack of "a forward looking planning process which considers the environmental impacts of multi-plant operations"—that is, cumulative impacts (19). The report noted, "The province does not appear to have any well defined growth philosophy; at the moment it is encouraging growth within the constraints of available labour, equipment and capital; implicit is the belief that fast growth is to be preferred to slow" (22).

That position has not changed nearly a half century later. Economic growth is still one of the standards for what constitutes the "public interest," which in Alberta seems to be primarily about the capacity of a project to generate revenue and jobs (McCormack 2016, 151). The "public interest" is simply invoked, never defined or debated. Westman claims that "oil is conflated with the public interest, resulting in a distorted, imbalanced, political economy, in which other visions of community are devalued" (2013a, 213).

Forty-five years after the first EIA was completed, oil sands EIAs have mushroomed to thousands of pages of complex information relating to both the biophysical and human environments and speaking to the decommissioning of projects. Public hearings are long, complex, and contentious, involving multiple reports and the testimony and cross-examination of witnesses that both support and challenge industrial plans and their impacts. Lawyers are deeply involved, and the review panels are tribunals that operate in a highly legalistic manner. As such, review panels can fail to admit critical information for their consideration.[9]

Nevertheless, the social and cultural impact assessments commissioned by industry proponents are little more than window dressing (see Baker and Westman 2018). They fail to provide either social and cultural baselines or evidence-based assessments of social and cultural impacts, *even when they are required to do so*. In short, modern EIAs are little improved in this dimension from the original Syncrude EIA, despite the fact that proponents are given clear direction for the content of their EIAs (see also McCormack 2016; Westman 2012, 2013a). Review panels allow proponents to proceed to hearings without having adequate social and cultural assessments in place, and their final recommendations and subsequent government approvals still fail to call for any study or monitoring of social and cultural project impacts. The consultants who provide these assessments—sometimes even those working for Indigenous groups—seem unfamiliar with current literature on the subject, not even the principles and guidelines or "best practices" provided by international experts such as Frank Vanclay under the aegis of the International Association for Impact Assessment (e.g., Vanclay 2003; Vanclay et al. 2015). In fact, even with these guidelines in mind, it may not be possible at this time for EIAs to provide good social or cultural impact assessments due to the lack of evidence about social and cultural impacts of the expansion of energy projects on local people, whether they are Indigenous or non-Indigenous, over the past fifty years. An extensive database could have been generated from a half century of study, but it was not. Little is known other than anecdotal accounts and some information about changes in land uses based on Traditional Land Use studies.

First Nations and Métis Locals (the term for community-based Métis organizations) have conducted numerous Traditional Land Use studies, which point to the extensive and intensive uses of the land by their members in the past and persisting into the present (but see Baker and Westman 2018; also Wanvik, this volume). To outsiders, the extent of contemporary land use seems to be scant and replaceable. A modest compensation program exists for holders of Registered Fur Management Areas (traplines), although not for other people using those lands. Some information is available about changes in animal populations, and local people speak about their unwillingness to drink water or harvest resources that they believe may be contaminated (see Baker, this volume). Strong fears exist about the health impacts of pollution, especially cancer (see Lee-Jones, this volume). People who testify at EIA hearings frequently talk about their close identification with the land and their dismay at being displaced. Traditional Land Use studies are not comprehensive, which contributes to difficulties in identifying cumulative impacts. They focus on individual sites, not broad landscapes. They emphasize uses by adult men, not by women or youth. They ignore important spiritual dimensions. They are not designed to study other forms of social and cultural impacts.

In light of the above, one can safely say that the predictions found in social and cultural impact assessments, and the conclusions drawn by review panels, are based on nothing more than guesswork, hope, and assumptions that are flawed and untested (McCormack 2016, 152, 157–59). Little has changed since 1982, when Roger Justus and JoAnne Simonetta did a review of the impacts of oil sands projects. They concluded:

> In the preparation of environmental impact statements, and particularly in the assessment of socio-cultural and community impacts of industrial projects on or near Indian reserve lands, it is often assumed that the regional economic and participation benefits of such projects accrue more or less 'automatically' and far outweigh any localized social, cultural, political or economic burdens and costs. This assumption often underlies the focus of the design of such studies, their implementation and subsequent decision-making relating to the project(s) in question (1982, 238).

It is a shortcoming that would not be tolerated for the biophysical domain (although even ecological information is still incomplete and often contested), yet strangely, it persists in the social and cultural domains, due to assumptions by government regulators and industry executives that local people need jobs and thus will benefit by being integrated more fully into the wage economy. Another factor may be that the proponents and decision makers tend to be familiar with biophysical aspects but not with the extensive literature on either social and cultural dimensions and histories of northern Indigenous Peoples or social and cultural impact assessment. That means that they are guided by their "common sense," not by scholarly evidence.

The philosophical issues boldly raised by Syncrude in 1973 have never become a matter for public debate. Instead, it appears that the Government of Alberta and Alberta's largely southern population are willing to sacrifice most of the lands of northern Alberta for industrial activities to generate provincial revenues that are critical for yearly budgets and are mostly siphoned off to serve other parts of Alberta. That suggests the persistence of the old belief in the North as a largely unpopulated wilderness, a *terra nullius*. Although the revenue is generated on traditional lands of Indigenous people, there is little or no reinvestment of provincial revenues in any substantial way into Indigenous communities.

It is difficult indeed to imagine that the massive land-altering activities engaged in by energy companies in northern Alberta would ever be allowed on the outskirts of Edmonton or Calgary, the population centres of the province.[10] They also demonstrate the relative powerlessness of Indigenous residents, who have unsuccessfully opposed the unrestrained expansion of oil sands industries in their homelands and are deeply worried about the resulting devastation to the immediate industrial landscape and to the broader ecosystem from air and water pollutants. In the eyes of government regulators, industry executives, and the general public, Indigenous "alternative uses" are considered to be inconsequential compared to the benefits flowing from the oil sands industry. Yet no evidence exists that local Indigenous people benefit *equitably* from the industrial presence and revenues generated, despite some job and business creation and Impact and Benefit Agreements with some First Nations.[11] Nor has there ever been even a modest attempt to perform a forensic audit to weigh the local social, cultural, health, and environmental costs against the local benefits or even broader provincial benefits.

Indigenous fears for the well-being of their lands and their ongoing displacement from those lands, both caused by oil sands industries, are at the heart of Indigenous resistance to the "extreme extraction" of these northern energy industries. Both in community meetings and in their testimony at hearings, people talk over and over again about how their cultures, societies, and even their very identities are endangered by the environmental havoc caused by oil sands projects, which makes it difficult and even unsafe for them to engage in harvesting and other activities on their traditional lands. Those activities also include the transmission of knowledge, much of it place-based, that is integral to their self-definitions as Indigenous Peoples.

Oil sands projects have very long timelines, extending over multiple generations into the far future, and prospects for eventual reclamation of disturbed lands and toxic tailings remain uncertain (see Wheatley and Westman, this volume; and Joly, this volume). During the 1990s, "the preferred goal for oil sands reclamation was upland forests" (Powter et al. 2012, 47), consistent with Alberta's support for commercial boreal forestry operations. Today, the focus has shifted—in theory—to "the re-establishment of wetlands and biodiversity consistent with natural boreal forests," based on a concept of "equivalent land capability" and "ecosystem functionality" (Powter et al. 2012, 47, 48). However, reclamation plans submitted by proponents still emphasize uplands over wetlands, most of which probably cannot be restored to their original conditions. Indigenous people want restoration of the original ecosystems, which are culturally and economically meaningful to them. Instead, oil sands companies propose reclamation strategies that may or may not work. As John Sandlos and Arn Keeling have argued, "remediation" is "a poorly understood aspect of extractive development" that is commonly seen as "an engineering and technical problem" governed by low standards and uninformed by the cultural values of Indigenous people about what constitutes "productive lands" (2016, 279, 280, 283; see Joly 2017).

The fate of orphan wells and pipelines in Alberta does not bode well for the eventual reclamation of oil sands operations. These are wells and pipelines from the conventional energy sector on rural lands whose owners have simply walked away without securing the safety of these installations or doing surface restoration. While this problem has been known since the late 1980s, the Government of Alberta, now represented by the Alberta Energy Regulator, has not required the responsible companies to provide enough money up front to guarantee that the companies will also look after remediation (e.g., Kienlen 2018; Orphan Well Association 2017; Southwick 2016). Provincial taxpayers are already paying for much of the cleanup. No one knows exactly how many wells, pipelines, and other facilities will be "orphaned" in the final tally or how much money it will cost taxpayers in the end.

The final technologies and costs required to remediate oil sands industrial lands are also unknown, especially for the enormous tailings ponds, which contain toxic wastes. From 1967 to 2009, the province allowed the oil sands corporations to self-regulate their handling of tailings, and none of them met their original commitments for reclamation. No companies met the new requirements of Directive 074 in 2009, which required companies to capture and dry up to 50 percent of all new fluid tailings by 2013 (McNeill and Lothian 2017, 4). By 2015 the volume of fluid tailings was estimated at 1.18 trillion litres covering 220 square kilometres. In 2016 Alberta issued Directive 085, which provides for a more flexible reclamation and management strategy than previously (e.g., AER 2018; Healing 2018; McNeill and Lothian 2017, 5). Meanwhile, the Alberta Energy Regulator continues to approve unproven technologies for tailings pond remediation, especially the creation of end pit lakes, which would store toxic tailings permanently at the bottom of engineered water bodies. If the end pit lakes fail to become healthy and sustainable landscape features, Alberta will have to manage these toxic wastes into an indefinite future, probably at taxpayer expense. The Alberta Energy Regulator has allowed oil sands companies considerable leeway, even when their reclamation plans violate formal requirements (e.g., Healing 2018). Under the government's Mine Financial Security Program, administered by the Alberta Energy Regulator, the estimated reclamation liabilities are C$20.8 billion, while only $1.57 billion are held as assets (Auditor General of Alberta 2015b, 25; McNeill and Lothian 2017, 9). That suggests that in the future, an association parallel to today's Orphan Well Association may be needed to manage the ongoing problems of oil sands reclamation, funded by "substantial amounts of public money" (Auditor General of Alberta 2015b, 5).

Eventual oil sands reclamation could be comparable in scale and difficulty to management proposed for the Giant Mine in Yellowknife, which extracted gold for over fifty years and produced an astonishing amount of arsenic. After the last owner went bankrupt, the federal Department of Indian Affairs and Northern Development became responsible for cleaning up the mine site. The current remediation plan provides for stabilization and "long-term management" of the arsenic, not for its removal and restoration of the land, which was what local Dene people wanted. Disputes exist over what standards should be applied, whether the current plan itself will ensure safety, what new risks will result, and whether the federal government can even be trusted with the oversight of the project (Government of Canada 2018; Sandlos and Keeling 2013, 2016, 280–84). The reclamation of uranium mines in northern Saskatchewan pose a similar, long-term challenge (e.g., Canadian Nuclear Safety Commission 2018; Canadian Nuclear Laboratories 2018; Saskatchewan Environmental Society 2015; but also see Cameco Corporation 2018). Sandlos and Keeling call these "zombie mines," because they "continue to exert some sort of malevolent effect during their afterlife"

(2013, 81). They are tragic examples that provide strong parallels to proposals for toxic wastes from the oil sands.

Related to this issue is the fact that proposals for remediation ignore or marginalize Indigenous knowledge and values, an issue discussed extensively in Tara Joly's 2017 dissertation. Instead, Sandlos and Keeling claim that company officials and regulatory agencies consider their plans for remediation "as improvements or rehabilitation of the local environment, and thus above criticism or controversy" (2016, 280). Some EIAs claim that land and access will improve at the end, what Westman calls "fantastic predictions" (2013b, 115). Proponents and government regulators fail to consider Indigenous values about the land in any meaningful way and seem to disregard Indigenous criticisms of reclaimed lands as being without foundation. Yet in the discourse of many Indigenous land users in northern Alberta, reclamation to date has been a failure for their purposes, reclaimed land has lost its meanings, and it may not be safe to eat animals and plants harvested from reclaimed areas. They have good reason to fear that the modern wastelands of tailings ponds and site installations may persist and require ongoing management into an even farther future. Even if those lands can be reclaimed successfully—according to Indigenous understandings of success—they worry that so much time will have passed that their descendants will have lost the skills required for knowledgeable land use and travel.

Many First Nations and Métis people continue to contest the lack of balance between their visions for the land and their futures with those held by governments and energy industries. These conflicts are about what constitutes the public interest. By 1973, at about the same time as oil sands industries were beginning, First Nations and Métis people in northern Alberta were also beginning new lives in centralized settlements at the locations of former fur trade posts (e.g., McCormack 1984, 513–33).[12] That did not mean that they gave up using the land and its wildlife. First Nations people continued to hunt, fish, trap, gather, and conduct associated activities, all guaranteed by Treaty 8. Métis also enjoy new rights for bush-based activities, won through litigation. Even today, many Indigenous people strive to maintain some measure of their former mixed economy, one in which land-based pursuits remain an integral element in their lives, even if they also have paid employment, and which depends on maintaining the health and resources of their traditional lands. One has only to listen to public testimony by Indigenous people at oil sands hearings to realize that that is still where their hearts and identities lie. The testimony by First Nations people and their challenges to proposals for new oil sands projects typically raise the assurances made to them by the treaty commissioners in 1899 when Treaty 8 was negotiated, which promised them protection for their lands and wildlife resources and protection against harm caused by outsiders (see Table 9.1). These powerful promises reassured First Nations that they would be able to continue to determine their own way of life, although the commissioners never wrote them into the text of the treaty.

*Table 9.1* Promises Made by the Treaty Commissioners in 1899 about Lands and Resources

**Commissioner David Laird** (circular letter sent to northern trading posts, February 3, 1899, RG 18, vol. 1435, no. 76, pt. 1, Library and Archives Canada [LAC])

"The Indians will be allowed to hunt and fish all over the country as they do now, subject to such laws as may be made for the protection of game and fish in the breeding season."

"White men, Halfbreeds and Indians who do not take Treaty, will not be allowed by the Great Mother [the Queen] to disturb or hurt any of her children whatever their colour."

**Commissioner David Laird, at the treaty negotiations at Lesser Slave Lake** (transcript by Charles Mair 1908)

"Indians have been told that if they make a treaty they will not be allowed to hunt and fish as they do now. This is not true. Indians who take treaty will be just as free to hunt and fish all over as they now are" (56).

"Your forest and river life will not be changed by the Treaty" (63).

**Commissioner James Ross, at the treaty negotiations at Lesser Slave Lake** (transcript by Charles Mair 1908)

"As all the rights you now have will not be interfered with, therefore anything you get in addition must be a clear gain" (61).

"We are glad you understand the treaty is forever. If the Indians do as they are asked we shall certainly keep all our promises" (62).

**Commissioners' report, Treaty No. 8** (Government of Canada [1899] 1966, 5–7)

"We pointed out that the Government could not undertake to maintain Indians in idleness; that the same means of earning a livelihood would continue after the treaty as existed before it, and that the Indians would be expected to make use of them" (5).

"The provision in the treaty under which ammunition and twine is to be furnished went far in the direction of quieting the fears of the Indians, for they admitted that it would be unreasonable to furnish the means of hunting and fishing if laws were to be enacted which would make hunting and fishing so restricted as to render it impossible to make a livelihood by such pursuits. But over and above the provision, we had to solemnly assure them that only such laws *as were in the interest of the Indians* and were found necessary in order to protect the fish and fur-bearing animals would be made, and that they would be as free to hunt and fish after the treaty as they would be if they never entered into it" (6, emphasis added).

"We assured them that the treaty would not lead to any forced interference with their mode of life" (6).

"It does not appear likely that the conditions of the country on either side of the Athabasca and Slave Rivers or about Athabasca Lake will be so changed as to affect hunting or trapping, and it is safe to say that so long as the fur-bearing animals remain, the great bulk of the Indians will continue to hunt and trap" (7).

"[T]he Indians were generally adverse to being placed on reserves. It would have been impossible to have made a treaty if we had not assured them that there was no intention of confining them to reserves" (7).

These promises have never been repudiated, and they resonate with the articles of the modern United Nations Declaration on the Rights of Indigenous Peoples (2007). However, the provincial government has historically overlooked these promises in favour of a strict interpretation of the treaty's written text, and it continues to do so today (e.g., McCormack 2013; 2010, 208–11, 216–21). The federal government has historically been unwilling to push for Indigenous and Treaty Rights when challenged by provincial policies and governance, despite its fiduciary relationship with Indigenous people, especially First Nations (in Alberta, Treaty "Indians"). Indigenous testimony about their persistent Treaty and Indigenous Rights means that the definition of the "public interest" by the province is not the same definition of the "public interest" by Indigenous citizens.

The written treaty contains a "taking up" clause, which means that the lands "ceded" as part of the treaty process can from time to time be used for other purposes by newcomers, presumed to be non-Indigenous people.[13] It is clear from the accounts of the treaty negotiations that the treaty commissioners themselves envisioned only small amounts of land being removed from First Nations uses, and they felt comfortable making sweeping promises about how entering into the treaty "would not lead to any forced interference with their [Indian] mode of life" (Government of Canada [1899] 1966, 6) and that "'your forest and river life will not be changed by the Treaty'" (Mair 1908, 63). When the federal government used the "taking up" clause of Treaty 8 in 1914 to justify creating a large park, J.D. McLean, the assistant deputy minister and secretary for the Department of Indian Affairs had opined, "I think that the setting apart of as large a tract as proposed for a game preserve *was scarcely contemplated in the Treaty*."[14] Nevertheless, neither the federal nor the provincial governments tried then or later to reconcile the powers they believed they could exercise under the written terms with the verbal promises about unimpeded access to land and resources by First Nations and protection from harm by newcomers. The recommendations of oil sands review panels and the Alberta Energy Regulator never consider the detailed promises of the treaty commissioners shown in Table 9.1.

The Government of Alberta's Policy on Consultation with First Nations on Land and Natural Resource Management, 2013, defines consultation as "a process intended to understand and consider the potential adverse impacts of anticipated Crown decisions on First Nations' Treaty rights, with a view to substantially address them" (Government of Alberta 2013).[15] Yet this policy fails to acknowledge the breadth of Treaty Rights that should bind both the provincial and federal governments and inform the accommodation that is required by court decisions. Accommodation itself is barely addressed in this policy document. It is not surprising that First Nations have considered the provincial consultation policy to be inadequate.

The ever-expanding industrial footprint of energy industries in northern Alberta has displaced both First Nations and Métis from their traditional land bases in multiple ways that are more than simply direct displacement due to removal of land for oil sands operations or fear of polluted lands and waters. On the one hand, Indigenous people of the region are engaged in what Gerado Castillo and David Brereton (2018) call "mobility dynamics," which remain unstudied and are little understood but are clearly important for understanding the social and cultural impacts of industrialization. They involve both push (negative) and pull (positive) factors. Many people within the region have moved to locations where they can find jobs, thereby disrupting their home communities in unknown ways. For example, in the 1970s Syncrude initiated an innovative fly-in, fly-out program for Fort Chipewyan residents to work in the oil sands. Although the program was largely seen as positive, it still involved fathers and mothers, husbands and wives being away from their families and communities for long stretches of time. Some people move permanently, while others travel back and forth between home and other communities or maintain more than one residence. Many outsiders have moved to the region, some permanently, with families, and some only for shift work (see Spady, this volume). Thus, as Castillo and Brereton have proposed, "it makes little sense to think of rural spaces as autonomous physical, social, productive and conceptual entities separated from the cities" (2018, 310). Instead, they may be better understood as components of a regional plural society, though one whose structures and dynamics are widely felt but poorly understood (see Westman 2013a).

At the same time, some individuals may become displaced without ever leaving home. Hedda Askland has raised "symbolic and political, encapsulating questions of the meaning of land and landscapes, notions of continuity, temporality and power" among Indigenous people in a heavily mined region in Australia (2018, 230). She points to experiences of loss and displacement among people who live in a context dominated by mining and speaks of "an ethnography of loss," in which people feel frozen in a place that has no future for them (230). In this vein, Westman has compared "extreme extraction" to the frightening predatory behaviour of the *wîhtikow*, which in Cree traditions can be either a cannibal spirit or a person who becomes crazed for human flesh (2013a, 221–24). As with mobility dynamics, displacement "in place" is unstudied, so its impacts are unknown, but it resonates with testimony by Indigenous people about their fears for the losses of their cultures and identities if they no longer can use their lands in the bush. They believe that in regions affected by oil sands pollution, the animals, plants, and water that used to give them life may now make them ill. It is a profound disturbance in a millennia-old social contract.

Feelings that their lands may not be part of their futures may have been enhanced by the failure of federal and provincial governing institutions to help Indigenous people build their capacities, especially by failing to provide high-quality schooling that will keep students in school through Grade 12 and continue on to postsecondary education (Auditor General of Alberta 2015a; see Kunkel 2017, 8). One consequence is that for many Indigenous people, good jobs in oil sands-related industries seem mostly out of reach, with First Nations and Métis confined mainly to lower-end, unfulfilling occupations.[16] Yet as former Mikisew Cree chief Steve Courtoreille explained, "We have no choice but to seek work because our way of life has been destroyed" (quoted in Westman 2006, 32). Given the extent to which Indigenous people are being turned into full-time wage labourers due to the lack of other options, it can be interpreted as a new form of forced assimilation, which has long roots as a government strategy for Indigenous people in Canada.

Both First Nations and Métis Locals have been developing their own governance structures to respond to the challenges of the burgeoning oil sands industry. The provincial government provides funding to First Nations to build their capacity "to participate in the consultation process" (Alberta Indigenous Affairs 2018). A similar funding program should also be available to Métis once a consultation policy for them is in place. Oil sands proponents have also provided project-specific funding to support Indigenous participation in EIA hearings. Many First Nations have created departments or quasi-independent arms that allow them to respond to industry. For example, the Athabasca Chipewyan First Nation registered its Industry Relations Corporation in 2002 (email, Lisa Tssessaze, July 20, 2018). Mikisew Cree First Nation (MCFN Government and Industry Relations) and Fort McKay First Nation (Fort McKay Sustainability Department) created their own organizations to work with industry and government at about the same time. Métis Locals, with fewer financial resources and less political clout than First Nations, have recently been developing similar arms so that they, too, can engage with oil sands processes (see Wanvik, this volume). Resident non-Indigenous people are not organized into territorial entities and tend to represent their concerns as individuals, so they are less visible (see Lee-Jones and Spady, this volume). They are also presumed to be represented by the municipalities.

Indigenous people in oil sands regions are today turning to the United Nations Declaration on the Rights of Indigenous Peoples (UNDRIP), especially clause 19 and its wording about "free, prior and informed consent," to support their treaties in their ongoing negotiations with government officials. Both Canada and Alberta have adopted this human rights document, although they claim that it does not give Indigenous people a veto over new industrial activity on their lands. The result may be heightened conflicts and new complications for how the public interest is defined. Canada is actively trying to incorporate the UNDRIP into its own legislation through Bill-C262. Table 9.2 shows some of the most relevant clauses for Indigenous issues in areas of oil sands projects.

Given the vested interests of governments and industries historically and today in removing Indigenous people from their lands in order to generate revenues, it is easy to understand their facile definition of Indigenous involvement in industry as desirable and their lack of research into real impacts. It is encouraging to see more academic study of Indigenous and

*Table 9.2* Excerpts from the United Nations Declaration on the Rights of Indigenous Peoples (2007)

| *Article* | *Text* |
| --- | --- |
| 8 (1) | Indigenous peoples and individuals have the right not to be subjected to forced assimilation or destruction of their culture. |
| 11 | Indigenous peoples have the right to practise and revitalize their cultural traditions and customs. This includes the right to maintain, protect and develop the past, present and future manifestations of their cultures, such as archaeological and historical sites, artefacts, designs, ceremonies, technologies and visual and performing arts and literature. |
| 12 | Indigenous peoples have the right to manifest, practise, develop and teach their spiritual and religious traditions, customs and ceremonies; the right to maintain, protect, and have access in privacy to their religious and cultural sites; the right to the use and control of their ceremonial objects; and the right to the repatriation of their human remains. |
| 18 | Indigenous peoples have the right to participate in decision making in matters which would affect their rights, through representatives chosen by themselves in accordance with their own procedures, as well as to maintain and develop their own decision-making institutions. |
| 19 | States shall consult and cooperate in good faith with the indigenous peoples concerned through their own representative institutions in order to obtain their free, prior and informed consent before adopted and implementing legislative or administrative measures that may affect them. |
| 25 | Indigenous peoples have the right to maintain and strengthen their distinctive spiritual relationship with their traditionally owned or otherwise occupied and used lands, territories, waters and coastal seas and other resources and to uphold their responsibilities to future generations in this regard. |
| 31 | Indigenous peoples have the right to maintain, control, protect and develop their cultural heritage, traditional knowledge and traditional cultural expressions, as well as the manifestations of their sciences, technologies and cultures, including human and genetic resources, seeds, medicines, knowledge of the properties of fauna and flora, oral traditions, literatures, designs, sports and traditional games and visual and performing arts. They also have the right to maintain, control, protect and develop their intellectual property over such cultural heritage, traditional knowledge, and traditional cultural expressions. |

non-Indigenous communities and people at a time when they are heavily affected by the oil sands industrial presence, although defining genuine social and cultural impacts of industry, and distinguishing those from impacts of other assimilative factors, will require considerable analytical finesse. The fact that such studies are academic means that research must adhere to accepted scholarly standards, including engagement with theory. Today, it is common for studies to be community-based, which presumes close engagement with community members. Most importantly, researchers seek to publish, which pushes these mostly young scholars to disseminate their findings. Publication in peer-reviewed sources, such as this volume, is the gold standard for scholarly competence and credibility (McCormack 2016, 150, 158–59).

## Notes

1 The session was part of the annual meeting of the Canadian Anthropology Society, in Santiago de Cuba, May 16–20, 2018. The two earlier sessions occurred in 2016, also at anthropology conferences (see Preface, this volume).

2 Similarly, there has been little research into the social and cultural impacts of the extensive forestry industry in northern Alberta (but see McCormack 1984, chp. 7). Curiously, neither logging operations nor sawmills have been required to do EIAs, even though the modern forestry industry, involving large blocks of forestry reserves, began in 1993, by which date EIAs were being done for other major projects in Alberta (e.g., Powter et al. 2012, 40).

3 Projects that do not meet the threshold for "major" will not trigger an EIA; it is beyond the scope of this chapter to expand on this issue. The EIA process has evolved over time at both federal and provincial levels of jurisdiction, heavily influenced by environmental and legislative developments in the United States dating back into the 1960s. The US National Environmental Policy Act (NEPA) was passed in 1970. In Canada environmental protection initiatives began with a federal cabinet decision of June 8, 1972, to screen proposed projects for potential pollution effects (Government of Canada 1978, 3). In Alberta regulations and policy for conservation and reclamation of industrial operations have a long and complex history that began in 1963, when the province passed legislation for land reclamation. The province created a Department of the Environment in 1971 (Bott et al. 2016; Powter et al. 2012). Shortly after, Peter Lougheed and the Progressive Conservative Party took power. The new Minister of Environment, William (Bill) Yurko, was responsible for passing the proactive Land Surface Conservation and Reclamation Act, 1973, which required EIAs in Alberta (Bott et al. 2016, 18). It is remarkably difficult to uncover details of the early years of impact assessment in Alberta, although completed EIAs can be found on a Government of Alberta website (2017). Impact assessment in Alberta has only recently become a focus of scholarly study (e.g., McCormack 2016, 2017; Westman 2006, 2012, 2013a, 2013b).

4 Syncrude Canada Ltd. made its first application for a licence on May 9, 1962, after having spent seven years and over C$15 million in costs of various kinds. It seems odd today that it took so long for the Syncrude project to be approved, especially at a time when neither impact assessments nor public hearings were required, and the Great Canadian Oil Sands plant had just been approved, but in the early 1960s the provincial government wanted to ensure that its conventional oil industry was not jeopardized by a new source of oil (Bott et al. 2016, 119; Canadian Resourcecon 1974, 6, 43–47; Syncrude Canada 1973, 2:1–4).

5 Other projects required to have EIAs completed are coal mines, petrochemical plants, oil sands upgraders, power plants, gas plants, agricultural products plants, water management projects, waste management projects, recreational projects, and unspecified "others" (Government of Alberta 2017). The province did not develop guidelines for EIAs until 1976 (Bott et al. 2016, 33).

6 Oil sands underlie lands in three treaty areas, those covered by Treaties 6, 8, and 10. The Cold Lake operation is situated in Treaty 6 lands. In this volume, Gross and Wheatley and Westman focus to some extent outside of the Treaty 8 region, and Lee-Jones is working in the Peace River country, a portion of the Treaty 8

region with a different history and extractive model from the Fort McMurray area. Shell began an in situ pilot project in the Peace River region in 1977, which was approved in 1985 for substantial production (Alberta Culture and Tourism 2018b). However, it is the Athabasca oil sands of northeast Alberta that receive the most scholarly and public attention.

7 Harm to humans was not envisioned at this stage. See Gross's chapter in this volume for a more contemporary take on this issue.

8 The influx of such a large number of outsiders, many of whom have become permanent residents, was never contemplated at this time. Spady's chapter in this volume considers the perspectives of some of these newcomers.

9 For example, in a recent oil sands hearing I attended a First Nation was not allowed to prepare a rebuttal report to a report prepared by a proponent on procedural grounds, and the review panel also refused to allow rebuttal testimony during the hearing. As a result, it seems unlikely that the panel, not one of whom was a social scientist, understood the problems with the original report and thus would not know how to give it proper weight.

10 For example, in 2008, over 800 people from Edmonton and the immediate vicinity turned out to a meeting to oppose a gravel mining operation proposed for the southwest edge of Edmonton, which would have been a modest operation compared to those in oil sands country (e.g., CBC News 2008). In the end, Edmonton refused to approve the gravel mine.

11 Impact and Benefit Agreements (IBAs) are formal contracts between a company and a specific Indigenous group that are intended to build community support for the company's project and provide specified benefits to the Indigenous community (e.g., Wright 2013). First Nations residents in Fort Chipewyan have spoken about signing IBAs with oil sands companies because they are unhappily resigned to the reality that they cannot stop the proposed projects and believe that an IBA may be the only way to realize any benefits. Because IBAs are typically confidential, it is impossible to assess their impacts (see Caine and Krogman 2010).

12 The inability of Indigenous people to continue their former bush-based lives can be attributed mainly to the expansion of provincial governance regimes and the violation of treaty promises by federal and provincial governments for most of the twentieth century and especially since the First World War (see McCormack 1984, 2010). Most people were forced out of the full-time bush life after the Second World War and did not leave it voluntarily.

13 Indigenous people who entered into Treaty 8 probably did not understand the full meanings of either "taking up" or "ceding." Even today, it is common discourse in First Nations communities that they did not give up the land and that the goal of the treaty was for peace and friendship.

14 J.D. McLean to J.B. Harkin, July 23, 1914, RG 85, vol. 664, file 3910, pt. 2, Library and Archives Canada (LAC), emphasis added.

15 Mixed ancestry people who applied for Half-breed Scrip rather than entering into treaty were presumed thereafter to be legally identical to non-Indigenous Canadians and expected to continue to become more like Euro-Canadians in their way of life. In 1899 it was never envisioned that distinctive northern Métis populations would still exist today; government officials believed that they would eventually be fully assimilated into the broader Canadian society. Their contemporary legal situation vis-à-vis land and wildlife is changing rapidly due to recent court cases. The Government of Alberta is currently developing a Métis consultation policy for Métis who do not live on the Metis Settlements.

16 The 1974 report *Decision Making in the North* talked about how most northern Indigenous people were "unemployed or under employed" (Canadian Resourcecon 1974, 11), and how trained Indigenous labour could meet the high

demands of oil sands industries. In 1972 representatives of the Indian Association of Alberta, the Métis Association of Alberta, Syncrude executives, and the Alberta trade unions put forward a proposal to the Department of Advanced Education that would have supported adult training. The government failed to act on this proposal (Canadian Resourcecon 1974, 25, 98–99).

## References

Alberta Culture and Tourism. 2018a. "Oil Sands, Industry Landmark: The Great Canadian Oil Sands Plant." Alberta Culture and Tourism. Accessed August 2, 2018. http://history.alberta.ca/energyheritage/sands/mega-projects/experimentation-and-commercial-development/industry-landmark-the-great-canadian-oil-sands-plant.aspx.

———. 2018b. "Oil Sands, Peace River." Accessed September 23, 2018. http://history.alberta.ca/energyheritage/sands/underground-developments/in-situ-development-peace-river.aspx.

Alberta Energy Regulator (AER). 2018. "Tailings." Accessed August 4, 2018. https://www.aer.ca/providing-information/by-topic/tailings.

Alberta Indigenous Affairs. 2018. "First Nations Consultation Capacity Investment Program." Accessed August 9, 2018. http://indigenous.alberta.ca/cc-training-outreach.cfm.

Askland, Hedda Haugen. 2018. "A Dying Village: Mining and the Experiential Condition of Displacement." *The Extractive Industries and Society* 5 (2): 230–36. https://doi.org/10.1016/j.exis.2018.02.007.

Auditor General of Alberta (Merwan N. Saher). 2015a. *Report of the Auditor General of Alberta, March 2015*. March 6, 2015. https://www.oag.ab.ca/webfiles/reports/OAG%20March%202015%20Report.pdf.

———. 2015b. *Report of the Auditor General of Alberta, July 2015*. June 26, 2015. https://www.oag.ab.ca/webfiles/reports/OAG%20Report%20July%202015.pdf.

Baker, Janelle Marie, and Clinton N. Westman. 2018. "Extracting Knowledge: Social Science, Environmental Impact Assessment, and Indigenous Consultation in the Oil Sands of Alberta, Canada." *The Extractive Industries and Society* 5 (1): 144–53. https://doi.org/10.1016/j.exis.2017.12.008.

Bott, Robert, Graham Chandler, and Peter McKenzie-Brown. 2016. *Footprints: The Evolution of Land Conservation and Reclamation in Alberta*. Cochrane, AB: Kingsley Knowledge Publishing. https://era.library.ualberta.ca/downloads/5d86p322r.

Caine, Ken J., and Naomi Krogman. 2010. "Powerful or Just Plain Power-Full? A Power Analysis of Impact and Benefit Agreements in Canada's North." *Organization & Environment* 23 (1): 76–98. doi: 10.1177/1086026609358969.

Canadian Nuclear Safety Commission. 2018. "Uranium Mines and Mills Waste." Last modified September 5, 2018. www.nuclearsafety.gc.ca/eng/waste/uranium-mines-and-millswaste/index.cfm.

Canadian Resourcecon Limited. 1974. *Final Report. Decision Making in the North: Oil Sands Case Study*. Prepared for Science Council of Canada, Ottawa. Vancouver: Canadian Resourcecon Limited.

Cameco Corporation. 2018. "Dispelling Falsehoods." Accessed August 4, 2018. https://www.cameconorth.com/about/dispelling-falsehoods.

Canadian Nuclear Laboratories. 2018. "National Programs." Accessed August 4, 2018. www.cnl.ca/en/home/environmental-stewardship/national-programs.aspx.

Castillo, Gerardo, and David Brereton. 2018. "The Country and the City: Mobility Dynamics in Mining Regions." *The Extractive Industries and Society* 5 (2): 307–16. https://doi.org/10.1016/j.exis.2018.02.009.

CBC News. 2008. "Gravel Pit Meeting Draws Hundreds in Opposition." April 29, 2008. https://www.cbc.ca/news/canada/edmonton/gravel-pit-meeting-draws-hundreds-in-opposition-1.746526.

Government of Alberta. 2013. "The Government of Alberta's Policy on Consultation with First Nations on Land and Natural Resource Management, 2013." Accessed August 5, 2018. http://indigenous.alberta.ca/documents/GoAPolicy-FNConsultation-2013.pdf?0.18486296174452366.

———. 2017. "Completed EIAs by Date." Accessed July 19, 2018. aep.alberta.ca/land/programs-and-services/environmental-assessment-EIAs/documents/CompletedEIAsByDate-Mar08-2017.pdf.

Government of Canada. [1899] 1966. *Treaty No. 8*. Facsimile ed. Ottawa: Queen's Printer.

Government of Canada, Federal Activities Branch. 1978. *Federal Environmental Assessment and Review Process: Guide for Environmental Screening*. Federal Activities Branch, Environmental Protection Service, and Federal Environmental Assessment Review Office. Accessed July 18, 2018. http://publications.gc.ca/collections/collection_2017/eccc/En21-26-1978-eng.pdf.

Government of Canada, Indigenous and Northern Affairs Canada. 2018. "Giant Mine Remediation Project." Last modified April 13, 2018. https://www.aadnc-aandc.gc.ca/eng/1100100027364/1100100027365.

Healing, Dan. 2018. "Oilsands Tailings Pond Approval Terms Shortened for Former Shell Facilities." *CBC News*, May 24, 2018. https://www.cbc.ca/news/canada/edmonton/oilsands-tailings-Alberta-shell-1.4675691.

Joly, Tara. 2017. "Making Productive Land: Utility, Encounter, and Oil Sands Reclamation in Northeastern Alberta, Canada." PhD diss., University of Aberdeen.

Joly, Tara, and Clinton N. Westman. 2017. *Taking Research Off the Shelf: Synthesizing Existing Sources of Knowledge about Impacts, Benefits, and Participatory or Consultative Processes around Extractive Industry in Northern Alberta*. Final Report for the Social Sciences and Humanities Research Council of Canada Imagining Canada's Future Initiative, Knowledge Synthesis Grants: Aboriginal Peoples. September 11, 2017. https://artsandscience.usask.ca/profile/CWestman#/profile.

Justus, Roger, and JoAnne Simonetta. 1982. "Oil Sands, Indians and SIA in Northern Alberta." In *Indian SIA: The Social Impact Assessment of Rapid Resource Development on Native Peoples*, edited by Charles C. Geisler, 238–57. Ann Arbor: University of Michigan, Natural Resources Sociology Research Lab.

Kienlen, Alexis. 2018. "Orphan Wells a Growing Problem for Alberta Farmers." *Alberta Farm Express*, April 11, 2018. https://www.albertafarmexpress.ca/2018/04/11/orphan-wells-a-growing-problem-for-alberta-farmers-2/.

Kunkel, Titi. 2017. "Aboriginal Values and Resource Development in Native Space: Lessons from British Columbia." *The Extractive Industries and Society* 4 (1): 6–14. http://dx.doi.org/10.1016/j.exis.2017.01.001.

Mair, Charles. 1908. *Through the Mackenzie Basin*. Toronto: William Briggs.

McCormack, Patricia A. 1984. "How the (North) West Was Won: Development and Underdevelopment in the Fort Chipewyan Region." PhD diss., University of Alberta.

———. 2010. *Fort Chipewyan and the Shaping of Canadian History, 1788–1920s*. Vancouver: University of British Columbia Press.

———. 2013. "Treaty No. 8 and the Aboriginal Signatories of Northern Alberta." Expert report prepared for Janes Freedman Kyle Law Corporation on behalf of Athabasca Chipewyan First Nation, Dene Tha' First Nation, Driftpile First Nation, Duncan's First Nation, Fort McKay First Nation, Horse Lake First Nation, Loon River First Nation, Mikisew Cree First Nation, and Swan River First Nation (Notice of Application for Judicial Review 1203-01106) and MacPherson Leslie & Tyerman LLP on behalf of Bigstone Cree First Nation and Sucker Creek First Nation (Notice of Application for Judicial Review 1203-01520). October 29, 2013.

———. 2016. "Doing Credible Cultural Assessment: Applied Social Science." *Environmental Practice* 18: 1–18. http://dx.doi.org.10.1017/s146604 6616000259.

———. 2017. "Walking the Land: Aboriginal Trails, Cultural Landscapes, and Archaeological Studies for Impact Assessment." *Archaeologies.: Journal of the World Archaeological Congress* 13 (1): 110–35. doi: 10.1007/s11759-017-9309-7.

McNeill, Jodi, and Nina Lothian. 2017. "Review of Directive 085 Tailings Management Plans." Pembina Institute, March 22, 2017. http://www.pembina.org/reports/tailings-whitepaper-d85.pdf.

Noble, Bram F. 2013. "Environmental Impact Assessment." In *Canadian Encyclopedia*. Last modified December 6, 2013. https://www.thecanadianencyclopedia.ca/en/article/environmental-impact-assessment.

Orphan Well Association. 2017. *Orphan Well Association 2016/17 Annual Report*. June 2017. http://www.orphanwell.ca/OWA%202016-17%20Ann%20Rpt%20Final.pdf.

Powter, Chris, Neil Chymko, Gordon Dinwoodie, Darlene Howat, Arnold Janz, Ryan Puhlmann, Tanya Richens, Don Watson, Heather Sinton, Kevin Ball, Andy Etmanski, Bruce Patterson, Larry Brocke, and Ralph Dyer. 2012. "Regulatory History of Alberta's Industrial Land Conservation and Reclamation Program." *Canadian Journal of Soil Science* 92: 39–51. doi: 10.4141/CJSS2010-033.

Sandlos, John, and Arn Keeling. 2013. "Zombie Mines and the (Over)burden of History." *Solutions* 4 (3): 80–83.

———. 2016. "Aboriginal Communities, Traditional Knowledge, and the Environmental Legacies of Extractive Development in Canada." *The Extractive Industries and Society* 3 (2): 278–87. http://dx.doi.org/10.1016/j.exis.2015.06.005.

Saskatchewan Environmental Society. 2015. "The Legacy of Uranium Mining in Saskatchewan: The Unacceptable Environmental Impacts of Uranium Mining." March 2015. http://environmentalsociety.ca/wp-content/uploads/2015/08/The-Legacy-of-Uranium-Mining-in-Saskatchewan-FINAL.pdf.

Southwick, Reid. 2016. "Number of Orphan Wells in Alberta Spikes as Companies Struggle to Survive in Downturn." *Calgary Herald*, July 27, 2016. https://calgaryherald.com/business/energy/alberta-posts-spike-in-orphan-well-count/.

Suncor Energy Inc. 2018. "The Oil Sands Story (1960s, 1970s & 1980s)." Suncor Energy Inc. Accessed August 2, 2018. https://www.suncor.com/en-CA/about-us/history/the-oil-sands-story.

Syncrude Canada Ltd. 1973. *Syncrude Canada Ltd. Environmental Impact Assessment*. 4 vols. Edmonton: The Company. Accessed July 19, 2018. ftp://ftp.gov.ab.ca/env/fs/EIA/1973-09-SuncrudeMildredLake/.

United Nations. 2007. "United Nations Declaration on the Rights of Indigenous Peoples." Accessed September 13, 2007. www.un.org/esa/socdev/unpfii/documents/DRIPS_en.pdf.

Vanclay, Frank. 2003. "International Principles for Social Impact Assessment." *Impact Assessment and Project Appraisal* 21 (1): 5–11.

Vanclay, Frank, Ana Maria Esteves, Ilse Aucamp, and Daniel M. Franks. 2015. *Social Impact Assessment: Guidance for Assessing and Managing the Social Impacts of Projects*. Fargo, ND: International Association for Impact Assessment. https://www.iaia.org/uploads/pdf/SIA_Guidance_Document_IAIA.pdf.

Westman, Clinton N. 2006. "Assessing the Impacts of Oilsands Development on Indigenous Peoples in Alberta, Canada." *Indigenous Affairs* 2–3 (6): 30–39.

———. 2012. *A Critical Review of Traditional Land Use Components for Environmental Impact Assessment Studies in the Oilsands Region*. Report prepared for Mikisew Cree First Nation and JFK Law, January 2012.

———. 2013a. "Cautionary Tales: Making and Breaking Community in the Oil Sands Region." *Canadian Journal of Sociology* 38(2): 211–31.

———. 2013b. "Social Impact Assessment and the Anthropology of the Future in Canada's Tar Sands." *Human Organization* 72 (2): 111–20.

Wright, Adam J. 2013. "Impact and Benefit Agreements: The Role of Negotiated Agreements in the Creation of Collaborative Planning in Resource Development." MSc thesis, University of Guelph.

# Index

Note: Page numbers in italics indicate a figure, page numbers in bold indicate a table, and page numbers followed by "n" denote note numbers on the corresponding page.

For Product Safety Concerns and Information please contact our EU representative GPSR@taylorandfrancis.com
Taylor & Francis Verlag GmbH, Kaufingerstraße 24, 80331 München, Germany

www.ingramcontent.com/pod-product-compliance
Ingram Content Group UK Ltd.
Pitfield, Milton Keynes, MK11 3LW, UK
UKHW021302190926
475701UK00009B/614

* 9 7 8 1 0 3 2 0 8 3 0 6 3 *